LET THE COMMUNION COMMENCE

*Lighthearted Reflections on the
Heart of God for Humanity*

KEVIN DEAN SMITH

WESTBOW
PRESS®
A DIVISION OF THOMAS NELSON
& ZONDERVAN

WestBow Press books may be ordered through booksellers or by contacting:

WestBow Press
A Division of Thomas Nelson & Zondervan
1663 Liberty Drive
Bloomington, IN 47403
www.westbowpress.com
844-714-3454

ISBN: 978-1-6642-2720-0 (sc)
ISBN: 978-1-6642-2721-7 (hc)
ISBN: 978-1-6642-2719-4 (e)

Library of Congress Control Number: 2021905099

Printed in the United States of America.

WestBow Press rev. date: 08/26/2021

TO: _____

FROM: _____

DATE: _____

NOW THAT'S
DEDICATION

This book is dedicated to all my Rising Sun Shiner students—past, present, and future. It is a tremendous honor and privilege to help prepare you for the commencement of all that God has yet in store for your life.

To produce a mighty book, you must choose a mighty theme. No great and enduring volume can ever be written on the flea, though many there be who have tried it. ~ Herman Melville, *Moby-Dick or, the Whale*

CONTENTS

ACKNOWLEDGEMENTS

A Writer's Block of Support

As I have turned the pages of my life, many have contributed to making this book possible. Most of all, I am eternally grateful to God for providing the inspiration and sense of purpose that carried me through the fifteen plus years of compiling the thoughts herein, including over three years of assembling the book as time allowed around other efforts to pursue my Christian calling. Anything worth reading here is a gift from God, and I apologize in advance for everything else.

Secondly, I am extremely grateful to my parents, Jay and Amy Smith, who helped to make me possible and thus this book. They diligently and sacrificially tended to my physical and spiritual sustenance, sticking together through good times and bad. I am so blessed that God placed me in their care and has allowed us to consolidate households so that I can help look after them in their golden years (although thus far they do more looking after me). My father has always been a conscientious worker and a great provider who has exemplified for me the ability to become a better person throughout the stages of one's life. I will never be able to know or fully appreciate in this life how much my mother's daily prayers contributed to any success that I have achieved in my life while protecting me from innumerable harms. Furthermore, she was the first to review this manuscript, offering helpful suggestions and, even more supportively, doing much more than her share in maintaining the household as I was writing this book and investing countless hours in my teaching career. As I write these words, I can see through the picture window my mother on her hands and knees working to make the yard presentable. I am deeply appreciative, even if I think she tends to make mountains out of molehills. The alternative origin story of this book project

1

is that I told my mother that I was writing a book just so that she would give me peace while I spent long hours on the computer. Then, when she proudly told people that I was writing a book, I figured I better actually write one.

Indeed, I have been blessed with many wonderful formative influences in my life, including an extended family of grandparents awaiting me in Heaven, as well as aunts and uncles and cousins who are very talented in their own "write." My extended family members serve as surrogate brothers and sisters for this only child. I have also been blessed through the encouragement and thoughtfulness of good friends such as Rhoda Joy Long and Whitney and Delores Long.

The founding pastors of Community Fellowship Church in Union City, Indiana—David Carpenter and George and Marie Hughes—as well as youth leaders including Marlene Nicely and David Key were especially insightful and inspirational in seeking opportunities to involve and encourage young people in ministry. They, along with many other members of the congregation, helped immensely to prepare me for a career of public service to God and man. At the tender age of twelve, I was tapped to deliver the sermon on the first of several occasions of allowing the youth to conduct the entire church service. I later heard a recording of this message, and it sounded like the Gospel presented by Mickey Mouse. Due to nerves and a touch of flu, I proceeded to throw up all over the church to conclude the service. The fact that such an experience did not end my public speaking forever is certainly a testament to the support that I enjoyed from family and friends.

I also fondly remember the informative and formative influences of many great teachers at Union City Community High School, including my high school English instructor, Ted Leahey, who corrected, nurtured, and reinforced my writing. Teachers such as Phil DeHaven, John Schmidt, Greg Black, and Paul Brumley not only provided effective instruction but also modeled a sense of humor in the classroom. The person and educator that I am today is also in part a legacy of many other teachers, including Beverly Chenoweth, Jani Glenn, Ann Butler, Darlene Austin, Monte Nash, Linda Nash, Rick Lacy and Jane Fulton among many others.

Oral Roberts University in Tulsa, Oklahoma offered me an incredible opportunity to build and reinforce my Christian faith in preparation for my teaching career, or as they say at ORU, to get my learning and keep my burning for God. Ball State University in Muncie, Indiana provided a very welcome graduate assistantship and opportunity to earn a master's degree while I searched for my first teaching position. Oakland City University, also in Indiana, offered me many hours of graduate coursework to maintain dual credit certifications. Encouraging feedback from my OCU professors on the first papers that I had written for evaluation in twenty-five years was instrumental in encouraging me to tackle this book project.

I am also incredibly grateful to the Rising Sun-Ohio County School Corporation and community that offered me my first teaching job. I came to town expecting to move elsewhere within a few years, but I came to enjoy the students, parents, colleagues, administrators, and community so much that I could not escape the gravitational pull of Rising Sun. Some may recognize themselves when reading between the lines of what follows, although names have been omitted to protect "the guilty."

Last but certainly not least, I must acknowledge my appreciation for Pastors Peter and Monica Bryk and give a shout out to the congregation of Hosanna Assembly of God in Aurora, Indiana, where I have attended church for most of my adult life. Certainly, this book would not exist without Pastor Pete's efforts to involve the congregation in the ministry of the church. Such opportunities serve to continue the formative influences of the pastors of my youth. Much of the content within this manuscript was initially presented to the congregation of Hosanna, and their encouragement was instrumental in bringing this book to fruition.

Even as much of the content of this book originally came together through years of oral presentations, I sought to distinguish my thoughts from those of others. However, I may not have recorded the details for every source of inspiration that informed my remarks as they were prepared piecemeal over the past fifteen years. In compiling these presentations into a book, I have diligently sought to footnote sources where possible, but I sincerely apologize for any failure to give credit where credit is due.

The Holy Bible, which I believe to be the inspired and infallible Word of God, has been my primary source. Many Scriptures are paraphrases from the SSV (Smith Substandard Version) to avoid any infringements on copyrighted versions and to keep a certain flow in the writing. Although I have done my very best to mind the jots and tittles, and to be consistent with well-established interpretations of any Scriptures paraphrased

3

herein—please, please, please check the Scripture citations in a credible version of the Bible before building any spiritual life doctrine around my portrayals of the Holy Word of God (see Matthew 5:18–19 in the King James Version and Revelation 22:18–19 for the inspiration for this fateful disclaimer).

I realize that these acknowledgments are on the verge of becoming a book in themselves, but amateur writers require a lot of support. Many things have come together under the auspices of my Creator to make communion and commencement themes in my life and to bring them together in what may be a once in a lifetime opportunity to write a book. Yet, what good is a book if it is not read. So finally, I am most humbly grateful to those who invest the time to read and reflect on what is written here. Let the communion commence!

PREFACE

What Was I Thinking?

At last, I sit down to put pen to paper, or finger to keyboard as it were, to begin an effort to fulfill a desire that has been building within me for a few years. Where this will lead, if anywhere, I know not. Will I have the discipline and drive to finish one of the most ambitious tasks of my lifetime? Or will I come across this computer file years from now on my "too hard" drive and remember that time when I actually thought that I would write a book?

One paragraph down and I am still going. So far so good. If you are reading these words, then you know something that I do not as I write this; my musings have apparently materialized into a book. Perhaps you are wondering if reading on is worth your time, just as I am currently wondering if it is worth my time to write on. Although I have often been intrigued by the thought of joining the ever-growing club of people writing books, so I have also contemplated learning to play the piano, developing a killer app, or starting a business. I do not have any realistic expectations of fulfilling any of those latter ambitions, and yet here I am attempting to author a book that maybe, just maybe, someone will actually read. This raises the question: if a tree falls in the woods to create the pages on which I write my message, will anyone hear it? This question presently has me stumped, but I will go out on a limb by pressing on with my writing in faith that these words are not for my eyes only and will leave an impression on someone (and that bad puns will not prevent my prospective audience from seeing the forest for the trees).

Perhaps a little backstory is warranted to explain why my endeavor to write a book has evidently been elevated on my bucket list to the point of becoming reality while displacing many daily pursuits that I find more immediately gratifying. I was incredibly fortunate to be born into a devoted

5

Christian family with a mother who considered her most important life's work to be raising her only child "in the nurture and admonition of the Lord" (Ephesians 6:4), or in other words, inspiring me to live according to the teachings of Jesus Christ and for the purpose of fulfilling His will for my life. My life's pursuit since I was old enough to contemplate such things has been to make my life count for the highest possible purpose. Sharing with others the Christian faith that has brought so much satisfaction and fulfillment to my life has informed both the means and the end of my existence (my actions and my purpose).

When I entered high school, I intensified my efforts to prepare for a meaningful career. Like all students of that age, I was presented ad nauseum with the question, "so what do you want to do after you graduate." My frustration with the question stemmed from there being so many intriguing possibilities. Perhaps the one thing that I was most sure that I would not do was to spend the next several decades of my life getting up every morning and going to school—been there, done that, have the cap and gown.

I took most of the more rigorous classes in my high school, which were science courses, so I fully expected that God was preparing me for a career in the natural sciences, perhaps medicine. I entered college as a premed major for lack of a more obvious choice. Although I did well academically that first semester, I began to seriously question my commitment to years of long, early morning or late afternoon labs and late nights learning arcane biology terminology.

Although my interest in the life sciences was waning, my passion for politics and other social sciences was taking on a life of its own. I developed a fascination with what we can learn from studying the rough-and-tumble of human behavior; consequently, I switched to a political science major for my second semester of college. The subject matter did not disappoint, but I was still uncertain as to what career this would prepare me for that would match my abilities, my interests, and most importantly, my purpose.

Gradually, I came to the realization that, for me, there was probably no more exciting career prospect than sharing my passion with others. Thus, within about a year of graduating high school, I was a Social Studies Education major committing to a lifetime of service in a setting from which I thought I had recently escaped. Perhaps I should have anticipated a future in front of a classroom of students after my eleventh grade speech teacher commented that I had a voice that put her to sleep. She meant that as a compliment—I think.

This book is not intended to be about me, or about my profession, or about how the two became connected. Bear with me just a little bit longer, and I will connect my backstory to the existence of this book. Nowadays, when I meet new people, I often get the same question that everyone else does under similar circumstances, "So what do you do for a living?" When I reply that I am a social studies teacher, the typical responses are either: "I loved those subjects," or "I hated those subjects when I was in school."

Alas, I have not found the magic bullet to make all my students fall in love with the subjects that I teach, and the Lord knows that I have tried a lot of bullets in my PowerPoint presentations. Suffice it to say that my passion for the social studies, or the social sciences, stems from their common pursuit of a better understanding of human behavior and all that flows from it. Government, economics, history, psychology, sociology, and even geography—that half-breed between the natural and social sciences—I love and teach them all. As much as any human endeavor, I find that they speak to the very nature of human existence. Perhaps it is my professional bias speaking, but I find that the social sciences provide context and meaning for the practical application of math, language arts, natural sciences, and all other intellectual pursuits. A career as a teacher of these love-them-or-hate-them subjects provides a unique opportunity for the pursuit of my passion and purpose, not to mention inspiration for much of what follows in this book. If you were one of those who hated history and the like, please do not dropout on me yet.

Most importantly, teaching the social sciences allows me to provoke students to think about things that truly matter, including where their lives fit into the ultimate scheme of things. As a public school teacher, I cannot, and should not, try to use my position to push my conclusions about such matters on my students inside the classroom. Between the beginning and ending bells, I will settle for trying to get them to think about something deeper than what's for lunch or their weekend plans, and then I will trust that they will respond to the ring of truth when it peels between their ears.

I am always gratified when my graduating seniors extend to me an invitation to their graduation at the culmination of my time teaching them, and for many years now I have seen this as an opportunity to gift them with a book written by someone else who took the time to encourage reflection on the deeper meaning of life. I would inscribe the book with a reminiscence of my time teaching them, along with a little personal message and testimony from yours truly. Over the years I have found some wonderful books that fit the bill, but none that said exactly the parting words that I wanted to share with the young people whom God had granted me the privilege of teaching. So, at last we have arrived at one reason for the existence of this book: to share with any of my graduating students who would welcome it (and anyone else willing to read along) reflections on some of the learning objectives of the curriculum designed for us by our Creator. Perhaps I could subtitle this book: "What I wish I could have taught you."

I am struck by how presumptive it is to write a book that you hope will be worthwhile for other people to read. Sharing my wit and wisdom, especially that which has not been published by others many times before, could make for a rather short book. Not that there is anything wrong with being a person of few words—student reactions to my lectures often remind me that there is beauty in brevity. The most original thinking that I can offer involves connecting another component of my adult life with my passion for sharing with people what I believe to be eternal truths—presentations on the theme of Communion that I prepared for my church congregation over several years. As I write on, I hope and pray that I am right on.

Since the church that I attend began incorporating the sacrament of Communion[1] into our weekly services many years ago, our Pastor has rotated the opportunity for laypersons to share some thoughts before presenting the elements symbolizing the body and blood of Jesus Christ to the congregation. For the several dozen times that this responsibility has fallen to me, I have prayerfully sought some insight to share with the congregation regarding this holy ceremony. In each of my deep dives into exploring the meaning of the Communion sacrament, an understanding that surfaced to my attention is that consuming the elements of bread and juice, or wine, serves as a symbolic reminder of the very crux of Christianity and of our existence on earth, the death of Jesus Christ to pay the penalty for our sins. Only this sacrificial death allows for the fulfillment of God's

---

[1] The sacrament of Communion is also known as the Lord's Supper, Lord's Table, or Eucharist.

consuming desire to experience a relationship of spiritual intimacy with us that is so close that it is like He is living inside of us while we are living inside of Him, which means that we can "be 'two' close for comfort." There is no deeper truth than this that I can seek to convey to my graduates, friends, family, or anyone else willing to offer their time and attention to this book: the Creator God desires to be in communion with humanity, His most special creation. However, this is only possible for those who take affirmative steps to lay down their own lives and take up the life of Jesus Christ.

So, there you have it. What follows is my humble effort to combine my earnest desire to leave an eternal mark on my students with a presentation of my Communion contemplations to a larger audience. The balance of this book is based upon oral Communion presentations that are modified, supplemented, and arranged hopefully into a somewhat coherent message for a reading audience. There is necessarily some overlap and repetition since the book is largely a compilation of vignettes originally prepared to introduce the sacrament of Communion in church services over the course of fifteen years, but I also hope that the book successfully integrates these reflections into the Gospel message that calls all of humanity to communion with our Creator for all of eternity. Furthermore, I am hopeful that this endeavor will serve to introduce the Gospel message of Jesus Christ to those unfamiliar with His most incredible offer of adoption into the family of God for anyone who accepts His forgiveness and Lordship, while also reinforcing the faith of "all in the family" of God already.[2]

Let the Communion Commence is comprised of my personal reflections on a message that is likely the most written about theme in the history of humanity, and rightly so. I am writing under the presumption that, if God is truly impressing upon me a desire to contribute to the mix, then He will provide me with a unique voice to speak to His timeless truths without messing with His message. As someone whose profession as a social studies teacher involves communicating information about subjects

---

[2] This message is not one of my own making and is unabashedly fundamentalist and evangelical in that it proclaims what I earnestly believe to be certain universal and timeless truths that are to be shared with everyone. Each person is then free to decide how to respond to this message and is responsible for that decision.

that many find boring to an age group that is easily bored, the challenge of maintaining the attention of my adolescent audience has led me to strive to develop an unusual communication style that some may occasionally find to be amusing, and that many, no doubt, may often find to be annoying. Nonetheless, I suspect that all word and no play would make for a very dull book indeed, especially one written by me.

My students can attest to my senseless humor and affirm that it is always "opun season" to bag a laugh in my classroom. So, if you are reading along and stumble upon some unconventional phrasing, it could just be poor editing on my part, or it could be an attempt to add some layers of entendre, or "I see what you did there." On such occasions, there may in fact be "nothing to see here," or there may be an effort at a little word play or poetic license to say with a slightly different spin what has already been said by so many people more eminently qualified than I am to write about such things. I sincerely hope that my efforts to be "clever" offer all due respect and do not distract from the clarity of the Creator's call for you, His special creation, to be in communion with Him forevermore.

I know that I have learned much and grown spiritually as God made connections between mundane topics that I researched and my preparation for Communion messages over these many years. If you are still with me and willing to continue reading, I am incredibly grateful for your willingness to give your time and attention to my humble efforts to share these reflections with you to inspire and encourage you in your relationship with the Author and Creator of the Universe, who also aspires to be your personal friend. For my former students, and for anyone else who is venturing to read *Let the Communion Commence*, the answer to the question, "What was I thinking?" in writing this book is that I was thinking about you; more importantly, God is thinking about you.

INTRODUCTION

A Fitting Conclusion

Perhaps the point that I would most like to impress upon young people, or people of any age for that matter, is to make your life about something. The older I get, the more I recognize that each day that we live is a precious gift of increasing scarcity, and that each spin of the earth on its axis that includes us presents many unique opportunities, not only to enjoy life, but also to make an enduring statement that we were here.

Although I truly love my job, perhaps my least favorite chore as a teacher is grading student writing, primarily because it is so difficult to get many students to take pride in and proofread their work before turning it in. Now, the occasional well-written student paper I can enjoy grading, and even a good effort that requires some improvement provides me with the satisfaction of helping a student to become a better writer. As a teacher, I feel obligated for instructive purposes to mark every mistake that I find, and I most seriously contemplate retirement while I am tediously trying to decipher student writing with so many mistakes that it might as well be written in code. The most disillusioning aspect of all is the realization that many, dare I say most, students do not even bother to review my corrections to avoid similar mistakes in the future.

Originally, my strategy for maintaining my sanity while grading slipshod student papers was to keep writing assignments short and encourage students to quest for quality over quantity. When I needed the students to write longer papers for college credit courses, I figured that I should try to coach them through the writing process in hopes of generating a more polished finished product.

One of the challenges in motivating students to demonstrate the "write stuff" is to convince them to invest time in selecting a topic or a research question that interests them. I try to persuade them that such an effort is a worthwhile endeavor that will increase their inspiration and minimize the misery of the writing process, both for them and for me. I have classes of students with mixed motivations, from those wanting the highest grade possible and college credit to those just wanting to pass and graduate with a high school diploma and minimal hassle for the tassel. So, I started differentiating my expectations, telling students the standards for an A or a B grade on a research paper as well as the requirements just to earn a passing grade.

The minimum standard for all students is to have at least a topic sentence and to stick to the topic. If you want an A or a B, however, you must have a thesis statement that you develop throughout the paper. A thesis makes a claim about a topic and then supports that assertion with specific evidence. The essay not only needs to be about something; it also needs to make a point. A mere report about a topic might get you a passing grade, but an original argument is required to earn the highest mark.

I offer students something I call the "thesisometer," which offers descriptions and samples by which to measure the quality of their thesis, from a "cold start" with no indication as to what the paper is about, to a "smokin' hot" assertion of an interesting and novel argument. I must warn students upfront, however, that crafting a clever thesis sets them up for a much more challenging task than writing a mere report about a topic. Identifying a thesis is only the beginning of a writing process in which they must then find credible sources that contribute specific information that advances their argument while anticipating and addressing contrary points of view.

I suspect that at this point, alumni of my classes are having unpleasant flashbacks to traumatic past experiences, so I will try to connect to a larger point. Perhaps living our lives is somewhat like the process of writing a term paper. Many people are rambling aimlessly through their lives, just trying to fill up space without making a meaningful or memorable statement. Their lives may be about living for the moment, but they do not manifest any sense of enduring purpose. They lack a focus, let alone a guiding thesis statement, and their lives are just passing at best. Others may have some themes that

PART ONE
WHAT WAS ~ NEW START

When someone becomes a Christian, he becomes a brand new person inside. He is not the same anymore. A new life has begun! ~ Second Corinthians 5:17 (TLB)

CHAPTER 1

END OF THE BEGINNING: BEGINNING OF THE END: END OF ENDS

Perhaps as you are reading this book, you are anticipating graduating or have recently done so, or perhaps your formal school graduations are in your distant past. Because graduations tend to occur at the end of a schooling experience, there is a tendency to think of them as finales, but graduation ceremonies are called "commencements" for a reason. They mark the beginning of or a transition to something new and likely bigger and better. I suppose you could say that graduations are just the end of the beginning of the rest of your life.

I have observed differences in traditions in the commencement exercises that I have attended. My high school graduation was a few hours long one evening in late May. I gave a speech during which people were stuck to their seats, but that was just because it was so hot and sticky in that high school gym. Sweltering heat does seem to be a common denominator for commencement exercises. Where I teach, graduation ceremonies are expected to be short and sweet. Administrator heads may roll if they make people swelter in the Sunday afternoon heat for more than an hour.

One year while attending our school's graduation ceremony, my mind wandered to an observation that if we just knocked out a wall in the gym, from where they were seated, our graduates would be staring directly at the town cemetery. With just a few more steps and a slight turn in their walk across the stage to receive their diplomas, their pomp and circumstance would be among the graves of some of our long ago, dearly departed graduates. Those of us who have been out of school for a few years, or a few decades, likely have similar contemplations of just how quickly we cross off the stages of our lives. In a sense, graduation is also the beginning of the end of the rest of our lives. Morbid observations such as these are among the reasons I will probably never be in demand as a commencement speaker.

I have collected a few interesting quotes offered as inspiration in various commencement speeches of the past. Bette Reese advised graduates that if you think you are too small to be noticed, then you have never tried to sleep in a room with a mosquito buzzing around. Robert Orben observed that "a graduation ceremony is an event where the commencement speaker tells thousands of students dressed in identical caps and gowns that 'individuality' is the key to success." Gary Bolding proclaimed, "Your families are extremely proud of you. You can't imagine the sense of relief they are experiencing. This would be a most opportune time to ask for money." Someone described graduation as a ritual in which they award you a diploma in the hopes that you have learned enough to be able to read it. Russell Baker said, "The best advice I can give anybody about going out into the world is this: Don't do it. I have been out there. It is a mess."

Robert M. Hutchins stated that "the college graduate is presented with a sheepskin to cover his intellectual nakedness." I will use that comment to connect back to my thesis. All commencement exercises likely have at least one thing in common: marking the culmination of a learning process and the transition to a new experience. Genesis 3:7 tells us that the father and mother of us all, Adam and Eve, learned that they were naked after they sinned or disobeyed God's instructions for them to live by, and thus commenced the depravity of human nature that separates each of us from God as we traverse through our lives on the way to the graveyard.

The school graduations that we celebrate mark the end of something good for the beginning of something even better, and fortunately, for most of us, there will be a lot of life in the years between our graduation and funeral processions. This book is about transitioning from a life of learning rules, limitations, and consequences during the few dozen revolutions around the sun that we are allotted in a world that has fallen from God's grace to a life of purpose and prospects for eternity. Ellen DeGeneres offered this commencement advice: "Follow your passion, stay true to yourself, never follow someone else's path, unless you're in the woods, and you're lost, and you see a path, then by all means you should follow that."[3] I propose to you that we are all lost when trying to make our own way in this world, and that the way forward is to follow the path blazed by Jesus Christ. He is knocking on the door of your heart, inviting you to open up for a relationship with Him (Revelation 3:20). If you have not already done so, today provides an occasion to end your time in the school of hard knocks and to begin following Jesus Christ in a new life that need never end. May you graduate into ever-increasing levels of knowledge in pursuit of your Creator's plan for your life.

---

[3] Ellen DeGeneres, (speech, Tulane University, 2009).

CHAPTER 2

FATHERS FIGURE

Commencements are often correlated with moving away from our parents and establishing our independence and identity in the world. The commencement that I am describing, however, is the beginning of a process of drawing ever closer to our Creator, who presents Himself to us as a Father in Heaven. He seeks to adopt us into His family, and He is looking forward to welcoming us home.

I am sure that there are many different experiences with earthly fathers represented among my readers. Some may have never known their fathers. Some may have had many unpleasant experiences, while others may have mostly cherished memories. For most of us, there is probably a mixed bag of good and bad experiences with our imperfect, earthly fathers.

Jonathan Edwards was a renowned Puritan preacher in the 1700s. I remember first learning about him in a high school American literature course when we read his famous sermon "Sinners in the Hands of an Angry God," which was delivered in 1741 in the midst of a revival of interest in and conversions to Christianity called the Great Awakening. Here is an excerpt to give you an idea as to why I found it so memorable:

> The God that holds you over the pit of hell, much as one holds a spider, or some loathsome insect over the fire, abhors you, and is dreadfully provoked; his wrath towards you burns like fire; he looks upon you as worthy of nothing else, but to be cast into the fire; he is of purer eyes than to bear

to have you in his sight; you are ten thousand times more abominable in his eyes, than the most hateful venomous serpent is in ours. You have offended him infinitely more than ever a stubborn rebel did his prince; and yet it is nothing but his hand that holds you from falling into the fire every moment. It is to be ascribed to nothing else, that you did not go to hell the last night; that you were suffered to awake again in this world, after you closed your eyes to sleep. And there is no other reason to be given, why you have not dropped into hell since you arose in the morning, but that God's hand has held you up. There is no other reason to be given why you have not gone to hell, since you have sat here in the house of God, provoking his pure eyes by your sinful wicked manner of attending his solemn worship. Yea, there is nothing else that is to be given as a reason why you do not this very moment drop down into hell.

Perhaps this was the first fireside chat in American history. Maybe Edwards's style and substance worked for that particular time, place, and people; reportedly, the sermon was interrupted many times by those calling out in anguish, "What must I do to be saved?" However, you do not hear too many people preach this way today, and frankly, I would not recommend it. Although I share the desire to get people fired up for God so that they do not fall down into the fires of Hell, I do not believe that God is merely calling Christians into the business of selling people on eternal "fire insurance."

Another quote of Jonathan Edwards, in a much different context, may offer a better illustration of how God prefers for us to perceive Him, as a Father in Heaven who desires relationship with us as His children and even as His friends. Shortly before he died, Edwards wrote to his daughter Lucy the following about being a child of God, "And as to my children you are now to be left fatherless, which I hope will be an inducement to you all to seek a father who will never fail you."[4] I do not think that Reverend Edwards's change in tone was necessarily because his image of God mellowed as he got older, but because he distinguished between those who pursue God and those who run away from Him.

I believe that we are currently living in an age of mercy and grace whereby God is welcoming people into His family and even pursuing His wayward children. God loathes sin but loves the sinner. However, this is not to say that God is a permissive parent who neglects to set appropriate boundaries. Every meaningful relationship has rules. Although we may not currently be living under God's judgment, we are fortunate indeed that He is an authoritative Father who is wise enough, and loving enough, to discipline us when we do things contrary to what He knows is best for us.

The Bible tells the story of Adonijah, a son of perhaps the most famous leader of ancient Israel, King David. First Kings 1:6 (TLB) says about Adonijah, "Now his father, King David, had never disciplined him at any time—not so much as by a single scolding!" Adonijah tried to overthrow the rightful heir to the throne and met an untimely demise in an extreme example of sibling rivalry. I am sure that David loved his children; it seems that he loved some of them to death.

Do not take for granted that great men and women of God will successfully pass their faith along to their children. Interestingly, Jonathan Edwards had a grandson named Aaron Burr, who was a scandalous Vice-President of the United States notorious for many bad behaviors in addition to his infamous killing of Alexander Hamilton in a duel. Our Heavenly Father is of course the role model for effective discipline; we as His children decide how we will respond to it. Hebrews 12:5–11 (MSG) says:

> So don't feel sorry for yourselves. Or have you forgotten how good parents treat children, and that God regards you as his children? My dear child, don't shrug off God's discipline, but don't be crushed by it either. It's the child he loves that he disciplines; the child he embraces, he also corrects.

---

[4] Heidi L. Nichols, "Those Exceptional Edwards Women," *Christianity Today*, last modified 2003, https://www.christianitytoday.com/history/issues/issue-77/those-exceptional-edwards-women.html.

God is educating you; that's why you must never drop out. He's treating you as dear children. This trouble you're in isn't punishment; it's training, the normal experience of children. Only irresponsible parents leave children to fend for themselves. Would you prefer an irresponsible God? We respect our own parents for training and not spoiling us, so why not embrace God's training so we can truly live? While we were children, our parents did what seemed best to them. But God is doing what is best for us, training us to live God's holy best. At the time, discipline isn't much fun. It always feels like it's going against the grain. Later, of course, it pays off handsomely, for it's the well-trained who find themselves mature in their relationship with God.

Our earthly parents do not always get it right. No doubt there are many reasons for transmission failures when it comes to passing the Faith to the next generation. Perhaps there is a lack of discipline, or maybe an abuse of discipline. Have you ever heard a father say, "No son of mine is going to do that," or "no daughter of mine is going to go out looking like that?" I am sure that no rejection is usually intended, but I cannot help but think that the role model of perfect discipline, our Heavenly Father, would say it better. Perhaps just a simple "No, son of mine," or "No, daughter of mine." What a difference a comma can make to give us pause in how we speak to others. God embraces His children with discipline and corrects them without the threat of disownment.

The Holy Bible indicates that there will come a day when we will undergo a paternity test to determine whether we are blood brothers with Jesus Christ, the Son of God, who offers to transfuse His blood into ours to allow adoption into the family of God (Galatians 4:4-5). If we lack the proper identifying DNA (Divine Nature by Adoption), then Jonathan Edwards's vision of our fate, described in "Sinners in the Hands of an Angry God," may not be far off the mark. The alternate reality, however, is described in James 1:17–18 (MSG), which assures us that, "Every desirable and beneficial gift comes out of heaven. The gifts are rivers of light cascading down from the Father of Light. There is nothing deceitful in God, nothing two-faced, nothing fickle. He brought us to life using the true Word, showing us off as the crown of all his creatures."

There is an abundance of evidence from social science research that a lack of responsible fatherhood contributes to many personal and societal problems. Communion with our perfect Heavenly Father can fill in the inevitable deficiencies in our relationships with our earthly fathers. God presents Himself to us as a father figure because fathers figure into our lives. Our great awakening is to understand that our destiny is our choice: sinners in the hands of an angry God or saints in the lap of a loving Father.[5]

---

[5] For musical reinforcement of this theme and encouragement from someone who was raised by an abusive father, who sought to be a better father, and who eagerly anticipates communion with his Heavenly Father, listen to: David Meece, "My Father's Chair," track 7 on *Once in a Lifetime*, Star Song, 1993, compact disc.

CHAPTER 3

A LONG TIME AGO IN A
GARDEN FAR, FAR AWAY

As a teacher of history and related subjects, my job is to teach about the past, in the present, to influence the future. Such a timeline could also provide an outline for the message that I am seeking to present in this book. According to my thesis, God's quest for communion, or relationship, with people like you and me is the central element of human history, the driving force in the present day, and the culmination of our existence for all of eternity to come. Most of my readers are probably familiar with the backstory that set the stage for us to be part of the family of God, but just to make sure, please allow me to return briefly to the commencement of all commencements—the events that set in motion the entire unfolding of human history up to the present moment of you reading this sentence in this book at this stage of your life.

In the beginning, God created everything out of nothing but His own existence, including Adam and Eve, whom He created in His own image from the dust of the ground. After breathing life into them, He placed these two ancestors of us all in a perfect environment, the Garden of Eden, where He could commune with them on a regular basis because they were innocent of any wrongdoing. Adam and Eve were given only one job, to tend to the Garden, and only one rule to obey, to stay away from the Tree of the Knowledge of Good and Evil. Alas, they exercised the free will God had given them to break this rule, and all their posterity (read you and me), were introduced to every bad thing that comes from sin, or willful disobedience to God's expectations and instructions for our lives.

Worse yet, death entered the world. In God's dictionary, death is not so much a physical event when our heart stops beating as it is a spiritual condition where we are separated from the heartbeat of God that is required to sustain us for eternal life. When I was a kid, a source of amusement among my friends was to try to get someone to believe a tall tale, and if they fell for it, then to rub it in by telling them, "you know if you look up the word 'gullible' in the dictionary you will see your picture as an illustration." Well, your picture, or mine, could have illustrated the definition of death in the Lord of all Creation's lexicon. What follows in this book are illustrations of how a perfectly righteous God seeks to restore relationship with each and every person that He has created, after which our picture can grace the very definition of life.

Consider the mother of us all, Eve. Eve was the first casualty in the war between good and evil that began in the Garden of Eden and that continues to rage among us today. In fact, all of us who are born of Eve, born of woman, have been casualties of that war. The battle between evil and good can be described as a war between flesh and blood. Flesh, in this context, represents our inborn tendency to fulfill our physical desires and to obtain immediate gratification. Such desires inevitably result in our death and separation from God. Blood, in contrast, represents life, the Spirit of God coursing through our being. God created us to be both flesh and blood, intending for us to immensely enjoy our temporal lives on this earth in spiritually responsible ways.

The Bible says that Adam and Eve were created to exist in a perfect environment where they could commune with, or have a relationship with, their Creator. Because God did not seek to fellowship with creatures who had no choice but to worship Him, He uniquely created humans with a free will to choose between good and evil, or obedience and disobedience. As the story goes in Genesis, Chapter 3, first Eve and then Adam yielded to temptation to fulfill fleshly desires, and thus they disobeyed God by eating the forbidden fruit. As a result of this disobedience, Adam and Eve and every one of us who descended from them would be unworthy of communion with a perfectly righteous God.

Yet in this biblical account that sets the stage for every bad thing that has since happened to every man, woman, and child who has ever existed, there is a glimmer of hope—a glimpse of God's plan to restore communion with people. Speaking to the serpent that represented the force of evil in the Garden of Eden, God declared that, although evil might bruise the heel of all who descend from Eve, her seed would bruise the head of the force of darkness—a promise that one day there would be born to a woman Someone who would make right all that is wrong with the human condition (Genesis 3:15). That sounds to me like the mother of all promises.

A bruise is formed when a trauma to the body causes an unsightly and abnormal mingling of our literal flesh and blood. Adam and Eve's traumatic fall in the Garden of Eden marked them, and all their posterity, with a blemish of sinfulness that a perfectly righteous God could not even look upon, let alone tolerate in His presence. Life for all of us continues as a struggle between flesh, what we want to do, and blood, what we should do. God has created our bodies so that a bruise will heal with the passage of time, and He has also set in motion a healing process whereby, through Jesus Christ, He took on a human form of flesh and blood that could take upon Himself the consequences of our disobedience and thereby restore His fellowship with us forevermore (Galatians 4:3–5).

Perhaps you, like me, would occasionally hear a parent say, "you're cruisin' for a bruisin'" when you were misbehavin'. That seems to me to be a rather apt description of where our lives are headed B.C. (Before Christ) when we are on the eve of a new life. Please read on for more reflection on our need for an intervention by which Jesus Christ made possible a new birth that restores us into the communion with God our Father that was lost to us a long time ago in a garden far, far away.

CHAPTER 4

LIVING IN THE FREE "WILL-DERNESS"

Once again, I call your attention to my assertion that God created each and every human being to live in a personal relationship with Him in a perfect environment reminiscent of the Garden of Eden. However, the sinfulness that we inherit and perpetuate keeps us out of His presence—lost in the woods or the wilderness on the way to the Promised Land, so to speak. The history of the Hebrews, or Jews of ancient times, may provide a useful comparison. According to the Bible (Deuteronomy 14:2), God chose the Hebrews to model for the rest of humanity the benefits of relationship with the Creator in whose image all people are created.

I will pick up their story after God delivered the Hebrews, or Israelites, from a few hundred years of slavery in Egypt. After a series of miraculous plagues that really messed with their Egyptian taskmasters, the Israelites were free at last to begin their journey from the only home any of them had ever known, horrible as it might have been, to a promised land that their ancestors had been forced to leave generations before. They had a straight shot of a few days journey, but despite the assurances from God Almighty that He would equip them for the task afoot, most of them were too intimidated to take on the effort and the risk that would be required to reestablish their claim to their homeland. Many even wanted to return to slavery in Egypt. They desired to "dance like an Egyptian," or like nobody was watching over them, rather than to dance with the one who brung 'em out of bondage in Egypt. So, God charged them to roam around in the wilderness for forty years until a new generation answered the call to lay claim to the Promised Land that would eventually become the nation of Israel.

Two of my life's ambitions have been to visit all fifty states and to step foot on all the inhabited continents before becoming incontinent. God blessed me with opportunities to fulfill both life goals, and to live to tell about doing so. On my continental quest, I decided to combine a visit to Asia and Africa on a single trip. Israel was my choice destination in Asia, and a visit there would be very compatible with a side trip to see the Great Pyramids in Egypt and thus establish my claim to visiting the African continent. My trip coincided with an even higher than usual level of hostilities in the region as Israel was under daily rocket attacks from Palestinian controlled areas. In fact, the nation of Israel was mobilized on a war footing.

My research about excursions from Israel to Egypt found an itinerary for a day or so trip to visit Cairo and the Pyramids by tracing a route that would have roughly coincided with the most direct path for the Israelites to follow from Egypt. However, this avenue had been closed for quite a while since it required traversing a hotbed of terrorist activity. Like the Israelites, I had to follow a more circuitous and time-consuming route around the Sinai Peninsula to make it down to Egypt and then back to Israel.

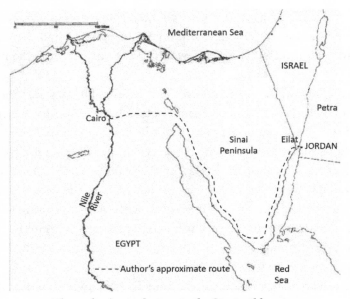

The author's wanderings in the Sinai wilderness.

Apparently, I was one of very few Americans interested in making such an excursion to Egypt at this time given the regional unrest, so I had the full attention of some of the best tour guides that the country had to offer. The van trip from the Israel border to Cairo was about thirteen hours, although at times it seemed more like 40 years. The Israelites would often have to stop and wait for God's approval to move on. I was reminded of this during the long delays at checkpoints waiting for police vehicles to form a convoy to escort a lone American and his entourage of Egyptian tour guides and government officials through the unsecured stretches of the Sinai.

I was finally able to get to the point of my side trip, spending a day visiting the Great Pyramids and some other fascinating sites around Cairo, followed by an early morning pick up the next day for the return trip to the Israel border. My driver was anxious to complete the journey and to get back home to his family, so he did not want to wait at the police checkpoints for armed escorts. He told me to lay down in the back of the van as he smuggled me around the Sinai Peninsula in about six or seven hours. Given my nonexistent understanding of Arabic, I can only assume that his conversations at checkpoints involved assuring the police that he was not transporting anything of consequence.

It may not have been as ceremonious as my arrival, but my personal exodus from Egypt was largely uneventful. I had only slight apprehension that the driver might expect a better tip from terrorists for turning me over to them than what a humble schoolteacher could offer him in appreciation for a safe return to the border, but he took good care of me. As it turned out, the only sticky situation on the return trip resulted from my driver stopping at a roadside stand to buy some fresh mangoes, which he insisted that I eat without the assistance of any utensils, plate, or means to wash before or after I mangled the mangoes. He watched with great amusement my fruitless efforts to avoid making a mess.

Assuming that the most perilous part of my adventure was over, I transited the border back to Israel to meet an escort who would transport me to my hotel in the city of Eilat on the shore of the Red Sea. After an exchange of greetings, my Israeli driver stated that, although he did not wish to alarm me, I should know that just a few hours earlier a Palestinian rocket had hit and exploded a couple hundred yards from my accommodations for the next night. He advised that I should locate the hotel's bomb shelter in case the air raid sirens sounded during my stay. This was quite a wake-up call given that the extent of my hotel check-in precautions in the United States amounts to checking for bedbugs.

I had a few hours before nightfall to part the Red Sea (not a major feat, just wading in on my feet), visit the site of the rocket explosion, and wash the mango out of my shirt. Fortunately, there were no outside disturbances during the night since microbes from the unwashed mangoes launched their own attacks on my insides—leaving me in no condition to leave the room, come what may. I now have a theory as to how the mango got its name. The only explosions and evacuations that night were in the bathroom, but fortunately I was well enough the next morning for a day trip to Petra in the nation of Jordan.

Damage from rocket attack in Eilat, Israel. (Photo by author)

By the grace of God, my one and only vacation to a war zone was without any serious disruptions. While I was awaiting a domestic flight, I had to make my only visit to a bomb shelter during the trip when incoming rockets were detected near the airport. Since I was soon airborne, I presume that the rockets either landed harmlessly or were intercepted by Israel's Iron Dome missile defense system. In what I earnestly believe to be an answer to prayers for God to order my steps (Psalm 37:23), my regularly scheduled flight for home was close to, if not the very last one, before international flights were suspended for several days due to the soaring number of rocket attacks.[6]

Perhaps my writing has wandered into a wilderness of vacation stories, so I shall try to return home and to the point. The Promised Land for the Israelites was a place where they could be free to be whom God wanted them to be. The Promised Land for followers of Jesus Christ is a time and place where they, and indeed everything, will be set right with God. This is the birthright that God intended for all people. Alas, we were born wrong to a lass who could offer us nothing better than her own enslaved condition. Once we recognize that we were born into bondage with an inborn tendency

---

[6] Adding to tensions and precautions during my trip was the coincident shootdown of a Malaysia Airlines flight over Eastern Ukraine. This tragedy occurred not too far from my Finnair flight path from Tel Aviv to the U.S. via Helsinki, Finland.

to do wrong, then we can use the free will that got humans into such a pickle in the first place to instead choose to proceed posthaste toward the Promised Land where we will enjoy communion with our Creator forever. However, the path to the Promised Land requires a sojourn in the wilderness for our remaining days on this earth. The wilderness experience is a time of God's remarkable provision and preparation. It is also a time of testing and humbling that will determine our character and whether we will exercise our free will to do things God's way or our own way (Deuteronomy 8:1–5).

One of the fundamental concepts of Christianity is that it is our human nature, or natural tendency, to disobey God and to make self-destructive decisions, usually without perceiving them as such. This concept, that we are fatally flawed from birth in both our actions and perceptions, is also called original sin. We are instinctively inclined to serve ourselves rather than to serve our Creator.

One of the most enduring philosophical debates of human existence rages around the different belief systems regarding the forces that shape people into who they are or who they become. What we as individuals and as a society believe about the default programming of human beings is basic to how we run, or ruin, our lives. Whether we are aware of it or not, our view of human nature shapes our personal decisions and even our political perspectives. In the subjects that I teach, the sum total of who we are is often reduced to nature or nurture—the extent to which we are a product of our genes or of our environment. For any given component of our humanness, whether it be our intelligence, aptitudes, personality, or pretty much anything else, the nature-nurture debate drives social scientists to seek to determine the exact proportion derived from our DNA. The remaining influence is generally presumed to be a product of our environmental exposures or interactions with others. For those who attempt to explain how the universe and everything in it works without positing a Creator God, all human behavior is likely assumed to be just a sequence of cause-and-effect reactions. This concept is called biological determinism, which, when taken to its logical conclusion, allows no room for right or wrong let alone for a free will for individuals to make decisions that will control their destiny.

A flawed view of human nature would no doubt lead to flawed personal decisions and a flawed society. American history offers examples of failed efforts to reduce human behavior either primarily to the environment or primarily to genetics. The utopian movements of the 1800s proposed the perfectibility of people through control of their environments, and the eugenics movement of the 1900s consigned people to the scrapheap based upon deficient genetics.

Although both our genetics and our environment are no doubt critical influences in our lives, I suspect that the reduction of humanity merely to nature or to nurture misses a key element of fully understanding who we are. The Bible proposes that God created each of us with the free will to choose whether or not to live according to the purpose for which we were created (John 7:17), but sinfulness corrupted both our genetics and our environment. Those who choose to believe and follow the teachings of Jesus Christ overcome both born and bred detrimental influences to become children of God (John 1:12–13).

I have taught thousands of students over the course of my career, and I could probably count on one hand the number of students that I could not like or find some good in at some level. If you happen to be one of my former students reading this, chances are you are not on my short list of infamous pupils. Even most of the students who were on that list seem to have matured into more respectful and respectable human beings. Add in the additional thousands of colleagues and acquaintances who have responded favorably to my give respect and get respect approach to people, and one might question the presumption that human nature is fundamentally and universally flawed.

Most of the people with whom I have rubbed shoulders during my lifetime have not proven to be murderers or thieves or scandalous sinners as the world is wont to categorize such people, and I generally do not give a cold shoulder even to those who seem to be such since I can usually find some disarming and redeeming value in them. However, each of us perpetually wrestles with inherent tendencies to do or say things that work against the well-being of ourselves or others. Who among us has not said hurtful things, or pursued immediate gratification over long term interests, or blamed others for our deficiencies, or expected others to bear the cost of our failings rather than us taking personal responsibility for them?

One needs to look no farther than the tens of trillions of dollars of U.S.

national debt and unfunded liabilities[7] along with the finger pointing as to who is responsible for all the red ink to see our own fingerprints on this tendency to live beyond our means and to let future generations bear the burden. Oh, we may call for cutting the spending that seems personally wasteful to us, but perish the politician who messes with our pet government programs (college funding, Social Security, etc.). Our flawed human nature is evident not just in our tendency to do deliberate wrong, but also in our inclination to follow the path of least resistance regardless of later consequences for ourselves or for others. In other words, we all fall short of what we should be—what we need to be for everyone to live happily ever after (Romans 3:23).

I remember a student once taking issue with my assertion that we are born instinctively to act selfishly. She countered with an appeal to the innocence of sweet, little babies. Indeed, infants may be the most innocent among us due to sheer lack of opportunity to mess up (other than their diapers of course). But consider a young child who just did something that she knows from experience displeases her parents. When asked if she did the misdeed, she is likely to say "no" to avoid punishment. A child does not need to learn to lie to try to save her skin.

We do not have to learn to be bad, but we do have to learn to be good. Psychologists and sociologists have advanced all kinds of theories as to how moral development can or should happen. Even some biological determinists have concluded that people behave better, and society works better, when people believe that they have some control over their destiny through the choices that they make, even if the concept of free will turns out to be an illusion.[8] The hard truth is that we will never be good enough for relationship with our Creator unless we choose to live for a purpose and to seek a power higher than ourselves so that we can rise above our natural limitations.

Some of our mistakes are a product of nature, some of nurture, and some of neither. We are born into a "free will-derness" in which we must navigate

---

[7] I originally incorporated the latest estimate of national indebtedness, but the number was increasing so quickly with each subsequent draft that I elected to use a more generic number.

[8] Morton M. Hunt, *The Story of Psychology* (New York: Anchor, 1994), 160.

through the consequences of the bad decisions of ourselves and others. Nonetheless, amid all our failings, following Jesus Christ will allow us to rise above both the internal and external forces seeking to destroy us, and it will make us eager to do good on our path to the Promised Land where we can enjoy communion with our Creator forever (Titus 2:14).

CHAPTER 5

CHARTER MEMBERS OF
THE DISHONOR SOCIETY

An e-mail from a former student of many years ago inspired me to contemplate what we remember and what we forget—and to reflect on the importance of second chances.[9] I thought of this student a few times in the years after she graced my classroom. I particularly remembered that in class discussion she expressed some different perspectives than mine. I also vaguely remembered that she demonstrated some troubled behavior, but I did not retain much in the way of details.

Many years later, this former student, a teacher now herself, decided to write some thank you letters to people from her past who had touched her life. I was blessed to receive one of those letters, although I had forgotten the encounter that meant the most to her. Here is part of what she wrote to me:

> I would like to say, 'you probably don't remember me'...but I may have made that a bit hard to do ☺ If you don't … I was the one who ran away for 2 weeks, then proceeded to buzz my hair pretty short. I'm sure I was a joy to have in class, since I felt the need to argue on a daily basis, lol. …
>
> Anyway, I felt like I should let you know that you did something very wonderful for me, but probably don't

---

[9] I am incredibly grateful to this student, both for her thoughtfulness in initiating the e-mail exchange and for allowing me to include it in this book.

remember it. My senior year I decided to actually get my act together thanks to a school system that gave me a second chance & some absolutely amazing parents. I remembered that I wanted to try to get into the National Honor Society. Being able to wear one of the "blue things" with my cap & gown was something I felt would make all this hard work worthwhile. I was offered a place my [sophomore] year, but felt it was more important to crumple the letter up & laugh about how lame it was in front of my friends.

Now that graduation was approaching, it seemed all I wanted was to get in…to prove all of the people wrong who thought I was a lost cause [and prove] that I was capable. Honestly, I thought you were one of those people who hated me & believed I was a lost cause. I didn't make it easy on my teachers. I remember how shocked I was on conference night when you gave my parents a positive report. Then there was the meeting after the first quarter of my senior year. My GPA had been brought up soooo close to the mark of being accepted into the honor society. I remember showing you and the guidance counselor my grades & GPA, begging for a way to make it. I had worked so hard & just wanted it to finally be enough.

I ended up being about a 10th of a point away. I didn't make the cut, but that wasn't the point. What made such an impact on me was I remember watching you look over my transcripts, going over numbers in your head, & looking for any way to get me into the honor society. I saw you recognize my hard work & really pull for me. I hadn't done anything to make my teachers want to pull for me …. That is something that will always stick with me and helps me hang in there when I come across a student who is trying everything, it seems, to make me give up on them.

Somehow I think, if you could find a way to pull for me, I can find a way to pull for my students & find something I haven't tried. It didn't seem to matter that I didn't make

it [into the honor society] after that. I remember that
someone who should have given up on me, had faith in me.

... My principal usually places the students with
emotional disabilities in my class. Somehow I feel all of the
problems I caused in high school gave me a knack for this.
I had so much anger about trying so hard all throughout
grade school & never being accepted, I think I just gave
up. I was quite a people pleaser & perfectionist before high
school, I think I just got tired of trying to be perfect. In
some strange way that has prepared me for this job. I love
the challenge of trying to be that person that reaches a
child & makes them feel so smart, like they are capable of
anything.

You made me feel that way. You could have just said,
no, you didn't make it. Shouldn't have [messed around] for
3 years then try to clean up the mess, but you didn't. By just
taking a look at the paper, you taught me a valuable lesson
about what teaching means.

What I could not tell from her correspondence was if this young lady
had accepted God's forgiveness for her mistakes. I wrote back sharing with
her that my passion for teaching, and for all my pursuits, flows from the
opportunities they present to share the compassion and second chance that
I have experienced through Jesus Christ. My ultimate purpose is to plant or
water seeds of faith that will one day sprout into salvation. I was thrilled by
her response that she had in fact rededicated herself to a relationship with
Jesus Christ. Here is an excerpt from the wonderful description that she
provided recounting how that renewed relationship came to pass while she
was listening to Christian music:

My tears of sorrow turned to tears of joy. I knew he [Jesus]
was with me, right there with me & always had been. I've
tried to show others through my actions that the person I
used to be has been able to find peace knowing there was
a plan now. I still have my struggles, but that day being
a Christian became more than just a set of rules I had to

follow & always fell short. I know he loves us, no matter
what & just wants us to share that with others as he did.

Perhaps I seem like the villain in this story since I did not let the poor
girl into the honor society after she worked so hard and came so close,
but my position as adviser did not authorize me to make exceptions to the
minimum grade point average requirement. The thresholds for membership
were established before my time, and only students who achieve them can
be recognized as members of our honor society. Failure to maintain the
scholarship and character ideals is grounds for permanent expulsion.

We are all born as card-carrying members of the dishonor society.
Fortunately, there is an Adviser, Jesus Christ, who is not only compassionate,
but who is also authorized through His sacrifice to induct us into relationship
with our Creator. Our demerits are overcome by His merits (Hebrews
2:9–10).

When I reflect on my exchange with this former student, I am struck
by what she remembered, and by what I forgot. She remembered receiving
a second chance; I forgot the problems that she presented. I remember
the sacrifice of Jesus Christ, which makes it possible for God to forget my
sinfulness and for me to earn His unmerited favor (Ephesians 1:6). Because
God did not judge us on the demerits of our cases, this former student and
I have both been expelled from the Devil's dishonor society, of which we
were charter members, and we have both been inducted as cross-carrying
members of Heaven's Honor Society.

CHAPTER 6

EXPERIENCES, SHMEXPERIENCES

Decisions, decisions. Life is chock-full of them—little ones, big ones, and destiny-defining ones, such as determining our purpose and how we will proceed through the "free will-derness." If you accept my proposition that you have control over many decisions that you make and that some choices are better than others, then consider the possible factors that inform your decisions, especially the most fateful ones. Some people seem to fly by the seat of their pants much of the time, which means deciding "a course of action as you go along, using your own initiative and perceptions rather than a predetermined plan or mechanical aids."[10] This would seem to involve thinking with the wrong part of your anatomy.

Consciously or subconsciously, we probably have some basis for most decisions that we make—gut feeling, personal opinion, advice from others, individual experiences, and so on. The reality is that we must base our decisions on something. Most people naturally make decisions informed and influenced by what happens to them. Personal experiences can be instructive when viewed as both outcomes of previous decisions as well

---

[10] I did not want to fly by the seat of my pants in creating a definition here, so I relied upon:

Gary Martin, "The meaning and origin of the expression: Fly by the seat of your pants," The Phrase Finder, accessed 2020, https://www.phrases.org.uk/meanings/fly-by-the-seat-of-your-pants.html.

as inputs for future ones. However, for many, subjective perceptions of experiences seem to be the primary basis for their assumptions and behaviors, with apparently limited reflection or objective analysis of other factors at work in determining their fate.

I occasionally encounter people who have different belief systems than mine, but who are willing to engage in thoughtful and respectful philosophical discussions of our differences. Rather than challenging their beliefs derived from interpretations of their personal experiences, I tend to lead the presentation of my perspective with an acknowledgement of my own limitations. For instance, I am not capable of even understanding, much less fully explaining, how such a complex and marvelous universe came into existence. Truth be told, I do not think any honest person, no matter how educated or brilliant, can do so either. Consequently, I propose that we must not put too much stock in our limited perceptions of reality lest we be morally bankrupt.

Christians may sometimes tend to be so defensive of their beliefs that they become offensive, seeming to judge or to condemn those with whom they disagree—or at least that is what some nonbelievers have told me as to why previous experiences lead them to shy away from conversations with Christians. Perhaps it is better to pursue existential conversations with humility, acknowledging that we all tend to be wrong about too many things too often to trust our interpretation of our own experiences. I doubt that you would have to much more than scratch the surface of the lives of even the most intelligent among us to find major snafus resulting from lapses in judgment.

I often contemplate why people make the decisions that they do. What are they thinking? Or are they thinking? Christians are often thought of as rather arrogant when they dare to suggest that there are absolute standards that everyone should live by; however, I suggest that there is an inherent humility in accepting that there is right and wrong that exists outside of our independent judgment—in acknowledging that we may not get to decide what is right or wrong, even for ourselves.

The whole notion that anyone's beliefs and behaviors should be labeled as right or wrong is troubling to many. After all, who are we to judge lest we also be judged? There is an element of wisdom in this reflexive reluctance to pass judgment on others (Matthew 7:1–3), but it also provokes the question,

"So who is to judge? (James 4:11–12). I doubt that most people are prepared to accept the notion that every decision is as good as any other. I propose that there is a distinction to be made between condemning a person and pointing out that some choices or behaviors are likely to yield negative consequences for that person or for others and thus should be avoided. We can respect that each person has the same rights and responsibilities to make personal decisions as we do, but we do not get to determine for ourselves or for others what is the "good and acceptable and perfect" will of God (Romans 12:2).

If we are not authorized to judge the behavior of others as wrong, then we also cannot decree that their behavior is acceptable, at least not by our own authority. We do not get to exempt ourselves or others from the consequences of bad decisions, so giving people a pass for everything that they do may not be the most thoughtful or compassionate approach to those whose lives intersect with ours and whose lifestyle decisions diverge from ours. Perhaps our most constructive and compassionate contribution to the lives of others is to humbly offer them our informed and prayerfully considered perspective while respecting their humanity and their responsibility for their own decisions. To embrace every decision that others make may not do them any favors, and to dare to disagree with their personal choices need not be hateful.[11]

I have heard students, and even their parents, embrace risky choices on the grounds that mistakes are an inevitable part of learning in life. Indeed, if you make a mistake, learning from it is certainly advisable; however, making mistakes for the sake of learning from mistakes seems mistaken to me. Do you know what sounds better to me than learning from mistakes—how about learning to avoid mistakes? Of course, no one will avoid all misfortunate decisions, but the psychological concept of social learning proposes that observing the positive and negative consequences resulting from other people's actions can help us to make better decisions for a more successful life. Throw in a pinch of personal reflection and a heaping helping

---

[11] If you are still uncomfortable with labeling certain beliefs or behaviors as wrong, then would you say that it is wrong to do so? Do you see the logical inconsistency? If nothing we do is wrong, then nothing we do can be right. If nothing is false, then nothing is true. Logic dictates that the belief that there is no wrong cannot be right. If you think that I am wrong, then you have proven my point. Does that deep fry your brain?

of sound spiritual guidance, and it sounds like you have a recipe for avoiding disaster.

Although my life decisions fall far short of perfection, I credit spiritual and social learning with allowing me to avoid many mistakes that have wreaked havoc in the lives of others. Consequently, I tend to have strong opinions that some beliefs and behaviors are right, and others are wrong. Nonetheless, the older that I get, the humbler I become in taking credit for the good decisions in my life. After observing a couple generations of students growing up in many different environments, I now more fully realize how much different my choices might have been under less favorable circumstances. As the saying goes, "There but for the grace of God go I." Without strong, positive family and spiritual influences in my most formative years, my capacity for success might have been greatly diminished.

No doubt all of us have some challenging circumstances that we must rise above in our lives. I have identified two aspirations to be among the most uplifting forces in my life, and I offer them for your consideration. First, cut other people some slack when they make mistakes because you do not know all the challenges that they face. Secondly, do not cut yourself any slack for bad decisions. I do not mean that you should beat yourself up for inevitable misjudgments, but rather that you should take some responsibility for them instead of making excuses, laying blame, or assuming a victim status—even when doing so might be somewhat warranted. Self-reflection and divine instruction can allow you to rise above any influences, circumstances, or experiences that might weigh you down.

Experience is often not the best teacher. The Israelites wondering around in the wilderness after escaping bondage in Egypt experienced God's miraculous provision time after time, and yet they could not seem to avoid being discouraged by the next hardship or falling for the next temptation. Often, the better things are for us, the less we are tuned in to the source of our blessings. Proverbs 3:5–8 (NLT 1996) says, "Trust in the LORD with all your heart; do not depend on your own understanding. Seek his will in all you do, and he will direct your paths. Don't be impressed with your own wisdom. Instead, fear the LORD and turn your back on evil. Then you will gain renewed health and vitality."

The sum of all our personal experiences still gives us an extremely limited perspective that is influenced by our perceptions, preconceived notions, and assumptions. Psychology has documented a human tendency to be very selective in learning from our experiences. We tend to latch on to anything that reinforces our established beliefs while disregarding anything that contradicts them. And if our personal limitations are not enough reason to distrust our experiences, then consider the possibility that there is a Deceiver who constantly moves among us, looking for every opportunity to distort our earthly experiences to distract us from the true and unchanging principles established by our Creator (1 Peter 5:8). Proverbs 14:12 (NLT) says, "There is a path before each person that seems right, but it ends in death." The words experience and experiment come from the same root, so do not be surprised if relying on experience results in a lot of trials and errors.

There is one person whose experience can shape the destiny of each one of us, Jesus Christ. Our sinful experiences led Him to die on the cross in our place; His experience leads us to eternal life. Although the Jews finally regained their Promised Land after their wilderness sojourn, they were eventually forced to leave their homeland again and to scatter around the globe. The formal language of the Jews, from ancient Israel to the present day, is Hebrew; however, over centuries of hardships without a homeland, during which time they were forced to make their way among other cultures, the Jews developed Yiddish as a more informal means of communication that blends Hebrew with the languages of the lands to which they dispersed in exile. Among the many Yiddish means of expression is adding "shm" in front of a word to indicate blatant mockery—so, experiences, shmexperiences.[12] I for one am so glad that a fallible human being such as myself does not have the responsibility to determine what is right or wrong. I just need to follow the One who does.

---

[12] Straight Dope Staff, "Yiddish, shmiddish—why do we repeat a word but start it with 'shm-'?," The Straight Dope, accessed 2020, https://www.straightdope.com/columns/read/1997/yiddish-shmiddish-why-do-we-repeat-a-word-but-start-it-with-shm/.

CHAPTER 7

KNOW GOD IN THE BIBLICAL SENSE

Who am I? Why am I here? How did I get here? I am not just describing the apparent cluelessness of some students entering my classroom for the first time. I suggest that your attention to and answers to these questions will shape the story of your life and determine its conclusion. As I mentioned in the introduction, I realize that not everyone who reads this book will be prepared to accept my assumptions about the existence of God and His plan for humanity through Jesus Christ. Since my thesis is based on these assumptions, please allow me to try my hand at a little apologetics, or defense of what I believe, and if you are a skeptic, please give me a thorough hearing. You can also check out the Appendix, which offers a list of additional resources that present a more comprehensive argument.

Let us start with what would seem to be an incontrovertible and self-evident assertion; there are things that no one can know for sure, at least not in the conventional way of knowing through our senses and perceptions. Even the most brilliant among us must reach conclusions based on logical and rational arguments that rest on certain assumptions and inferences that cannot be proven with absolute certainty. Everything that we believe will stand the test of time, or fall in hard times, depending on whether it is built on a foundation of truth.

I assert that the most foundational tenet for the entire nature of our existence must be based upon one of only two possible realities: either there is a Creator who brought everything into existence, or there is no Creator, in which case everything exists solely as a product of random chance and natural forces. Although neither of these assumptions can be factually established given human constraints, logically one of them must be true, and the other must be false. It strikes me that the significance and meaning of every aspect of our lives is reducible to which one of these two mutually exclusive possibilities is true. I certainly know which one I want to be true, for if all matter came from nothing, then it would seem to me that nothing matters.

I once had a discussion with a student who seemed to have thought very deeply about such things yet was skeptical about the existence of God. He acknowledged that sure, there could be a Creator God. There could be a lot of things, like a flying spaghetti monster outside the classroom wall, but he would bet almost anything that there was not. My assertion was that either there was or there was not a flying spaghetti monster outside my classroom, and I for one would want to know! I believe them to exist only in grainy images, although I could swear that they have made appearances in my classroom during stomach flu season.

Anyway, I get the point that many things are possible that are not necessarily probable. Even a flat earther can argue around in circles that we cannot rule out every possibility that the shape of the earth is less curvaceous than the almost universally accepted model.[13] Nonetheless, if we accept the proposition that there must either be or not be a Creator God, and if we accept that proving one position or the other scientifically is impossible, then that would leave us with logically examining the probabilities of each possibility in order to develop our assumptions into at least presumptions.[14] Again, I would refer you to the more professional attempts to address such matters listed in the back of this book, but I will share just a few logical arguments that have provoked my thinking.

One classroom exercise that I have used to generate discussion involves

---

[13] My approach to arguing with flat earthers is to tell them to start walking away from me. If I never see them again, then I will consider the possibility that the earth is flat, but if they come around again, then they must admit that the earth is round.

[14] While neither presumptions nor assumptions can be considered proven, the distinction is that a presumption relies on at least some logic and evidence, whereas an assumption rests more on the "seat of your pants" thinking as described earlier.

laying out several apparently random-shaped stones and one arrowhead. I ask the class which one is different from the others, and most students seem to think that the arrowhead really sticks out. I then ask why they think so. They will usually note that the sharper stone seems to have been shaped for a specific purpose. They usually agree that it is conceivable that random forces shaped the relatively simple stone into the appearance of an arrowhead, but it does not seem probable.

Which one of these is not like the others? (Photo by author)

Based on my extensive criminalistics expertise as an avid watcher of dramas where the good guys investigate crimes to catch the bad guys, I understand that one of the primary tasks presented to investigators upon discovery of a dead body is to determine the manner of death, whether it be natural causes, accident, suicide, or homicide. It would not take a Columbo to rule out natural causes when finding a person killed by a bullet through the heart. The chance of random metal atoms bonding into the form of a bullet and spontaneously hurtling through space to impact a person in the heart would no doubt be impossible for anyone to accept as probable, or even as remotely possible. Now, consider a human being, perhaps the most complex phenomenon of all. If we perceive even an arrowhead, let alone a bullet and a gun, as too complicated to likely exist without a purposeful designer, then how much more does it defy credulity to presume that the human beings that we know to be essential elements in creating such things are themselves a product of happenstance.

Another example of purposeful complexity that gives legs to believing in the existence of a Creator is the lowly, creepy spider. There are so many amazing arachnid features, but I will focus on just the eight legs that they creep around on. Each leg has seven segments. Now I am not a math teacher, but by my calculation, that equals fifty-six separate body parts that must coordinate every time the spider takes a step. Humans no doubt have a leg up in the complexity factor, which they often use to step on spiders. Anyway, most of the joints between a spider's leg segments are operated by muscles, but for some reason, two of the joints in each leg do not have the same muscles and instead operate with a hydraulic system. The design of spiders that allows them to fit through the smallest of inner spaces is inspiring engineers to develop hydraulic tools that work in outer space.[15] Oh what a tangled web must be woven to seek to explain such an intricate design by impersonal forces of random mutations in simpler life forms that created advantages that allowed for the development of more complex organisms that were naturally selected to survive and reproduce. Each of us must use our spider-sense to determine the most probable explanation for the existence of such things that creep upon the earth (Genesis 1:24–26).

Some have offered evidence of allegedly flawed or inefficient components of the natural world to argue against the likelihood of an omniscient, or all-knowing, Creator. For instance, I have heard the claim that the laryngeal nerve that connects the brain of a giraffe to its larynx takes such a circuitous, pointless route through the giraffe's entire body that it would be a poor design indeed by Someone who knew what they were doing.[16] If only giraffes

---

[15] Helen Czerski, "Spiders' Legs Are Hydraulic Masterpieces," *The Wall Street Journal*, August 29, 2019, https://www.wsj.com/articles/spiders-legs-are-hydraulic-masterpieces-11567088612.

[16] Casey Luskin, "The Recurrent Laryngeal Nerve Does Not Refute Intelligent Design," Intelligent Design and Evolution Awareness Center, accessed 2020, https://www.ideacenter.org/contentmgr/showdetails.php/id/1507.

could speak, perhaps they would respond to this assertion with a challenge to stick your neck out and create your own living, functioning giraffe from scratch. Until critics can do this, their assumption that they could do better than the fully functional design of a creature actually standing tall before us gets on my last nerve, which happens to be a short one.

In my personal assessment of the prospective realities before us, presuming the existence of an Intelligent Designer, a Creator God, who transcends both time and space, stretches credulity far less than the notion that everything came from nothing, or that everything came from some inanimate matter that always existed. One thing that I fully understand is the limits of my own understanding, and I assert that no person is beyond such limits. It is true that throughout human history, there has been a tendency to attribute phenomena that we do not understand to supernatural causes, only to later find perfectly natural explanations through application of the scientific method. Many assume that, given enough time, this progression will eventually lead to human understanding encompassing everything. This is where I become a skeptic. It seems to me that every new discovery merely opens the door to more questions and a deeper awareness of how much more infinitely complex existence is than we ever before imagined.

For instance, there are many different levels of understanding electricity. I know that if I flip the light switch on, there is light. Others understand how electricity is generated and flows through wires to the lightbulb. Some understand electricity at the atomic and subatomic levels, but no doubt there are shocking new discoveries awaiting everyone that will generate even more questions in the quest for ever deeper levels of understanding of what lights up and powers our lives. I propose that any typical two-year old could eventually stump the world's foremost expert on anything merely by asking "Why?" at each deeper level of explanation. At some point the best answer to our ever-expanding ignorance would seem to be, "Because God."

I have often heard people question the existence of God on the grounds that they could not grasp the concept of a being with no beginning, yet we must either assume the existence of something that always was from which everything else came, or posit that something, indeed everything, came out of nothing. Both believers and disbelievers in God are in the same boat in this regard, and any other proposition is all wet. Concepts of nothingness, eternity, and infinity defy the intellectual limits of all of us. May I suggest that a Creator God fills this void quite nicely.[17]

There are many people far more brilliant than I am who have come to different conclusions regarding the existence of God. One well-respected historical figure to offer perspective on this issue was the French philosopher, mathematician and physicist, Blaise Pascal (1623-1662). Pascal recognized that life was fraught with uncertainty—uncertainty as to what if any purpose life held, uncertainty in the ability to reason, uncertainty in science, and uncertainty as to what if any religion presented truth. He was even uncertain if everything was uncertain.

Pascal proposed that all human beings bet with their lives whether there is a God with a purpose and plan for them. If you choose to live as if there is accountability to God, you gain a sense of purpose and source of guidance. If you are right, you will reap the rewards of a life well-lived. If you are wrong, your conscious awareness will end when your heart stops beating, and there will be no realization of or consequences for being wrong. If you choose to live your life according to the assumption that there is no God, and you are right, then you gain nothing. If you are wrong, well the sudden enlightenment could be from the fires of Hell. Sure, you can choose not to think about such a weighty matter, but the default selection would be assuming that there is no accountability to a Higher Power who demands a decision. I am not a betting man, but since this is an unavoidable gamble, I will wager that the surest bet is to be all in on looking for a Creator willing to deal me in to a purpose and a plan for my life. I have certainly found great comfort in doing so when the chips are down.

It is not trendy today to advocate for absolute truth upon which to base someone's life decisions—concepts of right and wrong that exist independently of our personal beliefs. Atheism, or the presumption that no god or gods or supernatural forces exist, seems increasingly popular in the modern Western mindset. My alternative definition of atheism would

---

[17] Here are some questions so deep that I will bury them in a footnote. Why is there not nothing? What is nothing? How can a thing come into being from no thing? What is it to be or not to be?—that is the question. If nothing is God, then the concept of "nothing" becomes God, merely a term for that which we cannot know and must assume to be true. Nothing doing! I believe that God is really something! See: Nicholas Frankovich, "Do Atheists Exist?," *National Review*, December 31, 2013, 36-38.

be the belief that oneself is god, for to declare that there is no God is to presuppose that you are the highest authority to make such a determination. By assuming that we can determine for ourselves what is right or wrong, we become our own god. Most atheists that I have spoken with will default to agnosticism, acknowledging that it is impossible to disprove the existence of a Higher Power. Since it is impossible to know if there is a God, why bother contemplating the possibility? My question is, how do we know that we cannot know, at least at some level?

Remember the logical sequence that I introduced earlier. If we decide that there most likely is a Creator God, would it follow that He created with purpose? And if God created with purpose, would it be rational to presume that He would make Himself and that purpose discoverable? Sure, He could make Himself detectable by sight and sound, and perhaps on occasion He does; however, our senses can be deceived. Magicians make a living at this, so even what we perceive to see and hear can be illusions. Thus, we cannot assume that our eyes and ears offer rock solid evidence of reality. Perhaps therefore God wants us to rely on a different type of detector, faith (Hebrews 11:1).

Only a small portion of the electromagnetic spectrum of energy is detectable to our eyes and ears, but with the right detector, we can tune in to otherwise imperceptible wavelengths of energy in the form of television images and radio sounds. Indirectly, we can see the evidence of X-rays at work revealing our bones and of microwaves cooking our food. Similarly, there may be direct and indirect evidence of God if we only know where and how to look. Faith and reason can both inform us about the fundamental nature of reality; they just operate on different wavelengths. Whether pursuing a natural or a supernatural explanation for the universe, there is a point at which facts are not in evidence, and that is when we must all fall back on faith—in our own judgment, in the expertise of others, or in an omnipotent God.

Of course, determining whether to believe in a Creator God is not the end of discussion. Most people throughout human history have professed belief in supernatural beings. Many religions with seemingly infinite variations have formed, and many of these make conflicting claims. Christianity, for instance, is based on the assertion of Jesus Christ that following Him is the only path to right relationship with God. As C.S. Lewis observed, this would make Jesus Christ either a liar or lunatic unworthy of our devotion and trust, or the Lord of All that He claims to be. The fact that people disagree as to what is true does not negate the possibility that absolute truth exists.[18]

Like Blaise Pascal, I cannot claim to have eliminated all uncertainty in my thinking. I am constantly seeking to tune both my faith and reason detectors to ultimate truth. Of all belief systems, I have personally found Christianity as described in the Holy Bible to resonate by far the best with logic and experience, and it is the inspiration for this book. I have determined that, even if I am wrong, living according to the teachings of the Bible interpreted in proper context is serving me well, and I have found no reason to trade places with anyone who has made different decisions.

I have had the opportunity to travel to many places in the United States and throughout the world, and some of what I have learned from those experiences is included in this book. I have always loved maps and relied on them extensively in my travels. I have generally found them to be remarkably accurate in providing the lay of the land wherever I go. Most missteps in my travels have been the result of my mistaken reading of a map rather than due to its inaccuracy. There are still far more places in the world that I have not seen than that I have seen, but I have great confidence in maps when using them to explore new corners of creation due to their previous reliability in getting me where I was going and then back home again in Indiana.

Experience can be a great teacher, but only when we know our final destination and can recognize the signs that we are on the right route. We need a source of moral authority to evaluate whether the outcomes of our decisions are the best for us in the long run or are leading us down a "beaten path." I have tried and tested the Holy Bible in many life situations and decisions, and it has never steered me wrong. I confess that I am not always patient enough to read the instruction manual for the latest gadget or gizmo that I acquire, but I try to give due diligence to the Holy Bible as God's instruction manual for a priceless, fragile, and complex being. I rely on it to

---

[18] To say that there is no truth is to proclaim something to be true. To say that you cannot know what is true is to assert something that you must believe to be true. To appropriate a term from computer programming, I will label both ideas as logic bombs that explode the notion that the pursuit of discernible truth is a fool's errand that can be avoided.

tell me what to believe, what I am getting wrong, how to make things right, and how to live a life in right standing with God (2 Timothy 3:16).

Remember my thesis, which asserts that the ultimate purpose of our existence is to establish relationship with our Creator, a connection that can be more intimate and fulfilling than any carnal relationship that can exist between human beings. However, we cannot rely alone on our own experiences or judgments, or even on those of others, to find the one true love of our lives. Let me draw you a map. I propose that the Holy Bible is the key for finding the treasure of a legendary relationship with God that will unfold into eternity.

I encourage you to know God in the biblical sense as you seek to discover the reason for human existence, for your existence, with all the diligence that it is due. Sometimes people tend to short-circuit deep discussions of such existential matters with a statement like, "Oh, I believe in God, next topic please." The follow up question would be: is believing in Him all that God asks, or does He have greater demands and expectations for us to realize the purpose for which He created us? That notion will be explored throughout this book in which I humbly offer, as input for your truth detector, some of the life experiences and reflections that have thus far guided me as I seek to come to terms with God and His plan for my life. My life is His story, and I am sticking to it—hand to the Bible.

CHAPTER 8
FINAL JEOPARDY
ANSWER: WHAT IS SIN?

Free will implies that we have choices to make, and that these choices can be either right or wrong and can result in either good or bad consequences. One Good Friday, an article by Cathy Grossman in *USA Today* caught my attention.[19] The headline was "Is sin dead?" The answer according to Grossman was, "No, not by a long shot." The subheading asked a more complex question however, "How can Christians celebrate Jesus' atonement for their sins and the promise of eternal life in his resurrection if they don't recognize themselves as sinners?" In other words, why seek a Savior if you do not need saving?

Grossman contrasts the traditional, biblical view of sin with what is, according to opinion polls, the modern conception of sin in a society that is often described as post-Christian. She quotes several conservative, evangelical theologians who seek to share the fundamentals of Christianity with nonbelievers. Perhaps the good news for those who proclaim the need for salvation from sins is that 87% of U.S. adults still believe in the existence of sin, which was defined in the survey as "something that is almost always considered wrong, particularly from a religious or moral perspective."

Americans apparently have a rather non-biblical view of what is sin,

---

[19] Perspectives presented in this chapter that are not original to the author are a summary of:
Cathy L. Grossman, "Is Sin Dead?," *USA Today*, March 20, 2008, 1D.

however. Most seem to be comfortable defining it according to their personal judgment in a given situation. Grossman reports the results of a survey of Americans as to what they consider to be sin.[20] We could make this a game show, like *Family Feud*. Name something that Americans consider to be sin. Surveys said:

- 81% of Americans consider adultery to be a sin. I guess that is relatively good news; however, only 45% consider premarital sex to be wrong, just narrowly beating the 41% who consider doing something to harm the environment as sinful.
- 50% consider reading or watching pornography to be a sin.
- 47% consider gossip to be a sin.
- 46% consider swearing to be a sin.

This is just a sampling from the survey, but as Grossman goes on to describe, overall, it seems that most Americans make their assessments of sin based on what feels right in the moment rather than on absolute truth, especially if the latter would require some inconvenience or self-denial. For many Americans, life choices are more about etiquette—the appearance of doing what is right depending on the situation rather than acting according to core principles of what is right or wrong. Happiness rather than holiness is the motivation, and the goal is to avoid punishment in this world, not the next. The objective is not to escape burning in the fires of Hell, but rather to avoid burning in the court of popular opinion.[21]

Another issue identified by Grossman is the standard by which Americans evaluate themselves. Sixty-five percent of Americans believe that they are going to Heaven, while just a tiny fraction of one percent believe that they are going to Hell. I would like to believe that such optimism is warranted, but what if it is not? It seems that most Americans not only consider what sin is to be relative, but they also evaluate their goodness based on how noble their intentions are or how hard they try. They want their conduct to be evaluated on a curve or perhaps as a batting average.

---

[20] Conducted by Ellison Research in August 2007 and summarized by Cathy Grossman in "Is Sin Dead?".

[21] This perspective is attributed to sociologist Barry Kosmin in "Is Sin Dead?" by Cathy Grossman.

An awareness of the need for transformation of our fundamentally sinful human nature seems to be lost in the present psyche of Western culture. Americans seem to believe that what comes naturally is normal, and they just need to be concerned about doing the best they can to improve themselves to obtain God's favor. Religion is not for transformation, but rather for therapy.

Now we are back to the original question posed in the article: if we can solve our own problems, "what difference does it make that Jesus Christ was crucified?"[22] Pope Benedict is quoted as saying, "people who trust in themselves and in their own merits are, as it were, blinded by their own 'I,' and their hearts harden in sin. On the other hand, those who recognize themselves as weak and sinful entrust themselves to God, and from him obtain grace and forgiveness."

Two evangelical ministers are described in the article as avoiding the use of the word "sin" in presenting the gospel to Americans today, although for two different reasons. One prominent minister and best-selling author said he did not throw the word sin around because he assumed that most of his audience knew what they were doing was wrong, and he wanted to help them change. Hopefully, this approach does not neglect to emphasize the fact that we cannot save ourselves through all the good intentions, positive thinking, and self-help in the world unless we allow a divine intervention to make right all our wrongs.

Tim Keller ministered to several thousand predominantly young people in New York City every week. He believes that sharing the concept of sin is critical to evangelism, but that the word "sin" has lost its biblical meaning to many in the younger generation. He wants to "rebrand" the word by teaching its core meaning as living in a self-centered way rather than living to bring glory to God. He emphasizes not only doing the right thing, but doing it for the right reasons, and he teaches that many of our social problems are the inevitable consequences of living contrary to God's will.

Sharing the front page of the "Life" section of this particular *USA Today* was a review of a book by David Hajdu entitled *Ten-Cent Plague*, which describes how, in the 1950's, many people were expressing concern to the

---

[22] This question is posed in this form by Reverend Michael Horton in "Is Sin Dead?" by Cathy Grossman.

point that Congress was holding televised hearings about the link between juvenile delinquency and a trend toward depicting more graphic violence, vice, lust, and disrespect for authority in—gasp!—comic books.[23] How times change, and yet stay the same. The reviewer describes the book as "a cautionary tale about censorship" of content that will eventually be accepted by society. I am not asserting that government censorship is an effective way to restrain bad taste in entertainment, whether it is the comic books of yesteryear or the graphic movies, music, and video games of today. I do propose that we tend to become increasingly conditioned to accept sinful behavior and its consequences as just a normal part of living.

Pollution can be defined as unclean or impure substances in the environment. Our society has become obsessed with the consequences of such contamination in our land, air, and water while turning a blind eye to the possibility that our hearts, minds, and souls can be polluted as well. We may be rightly reluctant to judge and condemn people because of their behavior, but we may also often be averse to subscribing to a standard of absolute right and wrong. We appropriately ask ourselves, "who am I to judge?" but we seem reluctant to ask, "who is to judge?"

Our society is often described as post-Christian, as if the relevance of God's message to us has come and gone; however, the United States has actually experienced a few cycles of spiritual slumbering and awakening. There is nothing new under the sun, or in the relationship between God and people. Every day, we as individuals, and as a society, face the same choices that every human being has faced since the events that unfolded in the Garden of Eden:

- Is life about happiness or holiness?
- Is our concern what other people think or what God thinks?
- Should our moral compass be our feelings and desires of the moment, or the absolute truth of God's Word?
- Do we just need moral therapy, or do we need complete transformation?

---

[23] Bob Minzesheimer, "In 'Ten-Cent Plague,' comic books and censorship are drawn in detail," *USA Today*, March 20, 2008, 1D.

- Are we basically good creatures who just need a little fine tuning, or are we fundamentally flawed by a sinful human nature?
- Can we effect change from within ourselves, or must we rely on a Higher Power?
- Do the inevitable lingering sins in our lives consist of merely mistakes that we repent of and move on from, or do they reflect continuing rebelliousness and willful disobedience of God?
- Will we do things our way, or God's way?

Life is not a game show—the jeopardy is real! The category is "Relationship with God," and the wager required is our eternal destiny. We need a clue as to what separates us from God. The correct response is asking, "what is sin?" so that we can avoid obstructions to living according to God's best plan for our lives. Jesus Christ, the reigning champion over sin and death, is waiting in the wings to offer a share of His winnings, eternal life in relationship with our Heavenly Father.

CHAPTER 9
STUFF MATTERS

I cannot claim to understand everything about God's original plan for humanity, or exactly what the nature of the relationship is between God and Jesus Christ, who is presented to us as the Son of God. I cannot explain exactly how the death and resurrection of Jesus Christ works to restore us into relationship with our Creator and Heavenly Father. I also cannot explain infinity or eternity or what exists beyond the borders of the universe. I believe that I am in good company since I have yet to meet anyone who can fully explain any of these phenomena. The world's foremost scientific experts cannot even explain for sure why a moving bicycle with sufficient momentum tends to stay upright even without a rider, let alone explain mysteries of the universe with much more gravity. Physicists are still peddling different theories about the gravity-defying bicycle phenomenon,[24] but having ridden my bicycle more than 25,000 miles and counting over the contours of my corner of the universe, what is important to me is that it keeps me upright, except for those occasional, misfortunate instances of rider error. Similarly, what is important to me about God's plan is not that I fully understand it, but that it works for me.

I also do not understand perfection, despite my oftentimes counterproductive and fruitless pursuit of perfection in my personal and

---

[24] Charlie Sorrel, "The Bicycle Is Still A Scientific Mystery: Here's Why," *Fast Company*, accessed 2020, https://www.fastcompany.com/3062239/the-bicycle-is-still-a-scientific-mystery-heres-why.

professional life. What I do understand is that a perfectly righteous God could have made us mindless, soulless automatons that obey Him reflexively, but instead He made us creatures with a free will to choose whether or not to be in fellowship with Him. As a teacher, I can attest to how much more endearing it is to have students who want to be in my classes compared to students who are just doing desk duty until they are released upon the world. Similarly, God wants us to choose His instruction in righteousness.

Of course, having choices also presents an opportunity to do self-serving, neglectful, or harmful actions, and our choices between good or bad conduct must result in different consequences to be meaningful. Remember my earlier assertion that making exceptions to the academic standards of the honor society would necessarily diminish the significance of membership for everyone who made better decisions.

In a legal system, judges and juries face a binary choice of "guilty" or "not guilty." A ruling of "whatever" offers no resolution whatsoever. Imagine someone who brutally killed one of your family members being brought before a judge, only to have the case dismissed without consequence for the offender because the judge did not want to be judgmental. Maybe the judge would like to be perceived as a compassionate, loving person, but passing no judgment would necessarily, even if unintentionally, convey that the harm and loss to you and your family is inconsequential.

Justice demands accountability for behavior or there will be no distinction between heroes and Hitlers. We may tend to think of our wrongdoings as relatively tame compared to the atrocities committed by the dregs of humanity, but God's perfection cannot tolerate even the slightest imperfection. If the bad stuff that we do does not matter, then neither does the good stuff that we do. For a life to have consequence, there must be consequences for how that life is lived. The stuff that we do matters. We need the righteous stuff.

CHAPTER 10

I'LL SEE YOUR HEAVEN
AND RAZE HELL

One of the hang ups that many people have with Christianity is the notion that a loving God could allow people to go to a horrible place like Hell. According to a survey, 71% of Americans believe in Heaven as a place of eternal reward, while 64% believe in Hell as a place of eternal punishment,[25] although as reported previously, only a fraction of a percent of the population believe that Hell is where they are headed.

Once again, I return to my assertion of the logical sequence flowing from the presumption that there is a Creator God: that God created human beings for the purpose of relationship with Him, that He makes that purpose knowable through the Bible and the presence of His Spirit within His creation, and that He allows for the free will to choose whether or not to pursue such a relationship with Him. Finally, it would follow that there would be negative consequences for rejecting God's plan, not because God is mean, but because He wants our choices to have meaning. As explained earlier, for a choice to be meaningful, it must be consequential. If everybody receives the same result regardless of the decisions made, then there is no justice in this world or in the one to come.

A loving God provides the opportunity for everyone to be in relationship

---

[25] Statista Research Department, "Belief of Americans in God, heaven and hell, 2016," Statista, published June 29, 2016, https://www.statista.com/statistics/245496/belief-of-americans-in-god-heaven-and-hell/.

with Him for all of eternity. A purposeful and desirous, yet respectful, God does not force people to fulfill His plan for their lives. A just God holds people accountable for the decisions that they make. God does not send people to Hell, but the consistency of His character makes the existence of Hell a necessity to separate those who make different consequential choices.

I try to avoid passing judgment as to the eternal destiny of any individual. I am not qualified to be the operator of the elevator to eternity, deciding whether to push the up or down button when someone's existence must be taken to another level. Nonetheless, the Holy Bible identifies Hell as a place of punishment for people who have rejected salvation for their sins, or their disobedience to God. Sin, whether in the form of committing acts that we should not do or of omitting what we should do, will inevitably do harm that will cry out for justice, and such cries cannot be ignored by a righteous God.

The Bible describes Hell in ways to get our attention—as an eternal existence of unimaginably horrible sights, sounds, smells, and other physical sensations. I have no reason to doubt that these descriptions of Hell are intended to be literal, but perhaps the most certain and terrifying aspects of Hell are the spiritual sensations of eternal hopelessness and anguish over what might have been. One might wonder why a loving and compassionate God would not just leave those who reject Him alone forever rather than consigning them to a condition of perpetual torment, but I suggest that such eternal separation from God is the most abysmal condition of all.

I remember a segment from a *Twilight Zone* series revival called "Take My Life…Please!" that aired around the time that I was a senior in high school. As the story goes, a comedian dies and ends up in a comedy club where he must audition for the afterlife. All his best material merely gets him booed, and hecklers in the audience goad him into telling about the bad things that he did during his life. The more he confesses, the more laughs he gets, and the more miserable he feels. At the end of his performance, he comes to the realization that he lived a lousy life, and that his fate is to tell about the rotten things that he did in life over and over again forever.[26]

I return to the blessing and the curse of being created with free will. There is an unimaginably unlimited upside for choosing wisely, but for those

---

[26] "Take My Life…Please!" *The Twilight Zone*, written by Gordon Mitchell, aired March 28, 1986.

who chose otherwise, well perhaps the horrors of Hell are best measured in degrees of separation from God. My fondest hope is that my life service, and yours, will contribute to populating Heaven and plundering Hell. May we all one day hear God say, "well done my good and faithful servant, enter into the joys of the Lord" (Matthew 25:21), and may none of us end up well done in the fires of Hell.

CHAPTER 11

HANG TIME

There is a story told that I have heard several times. It may or may not be true, but I certainly find it instructive. As the story goes, during some of the horrendous travails of the early 20th century, a newspaper put out a call to the religious leaders, philosophers, and great thinkers of the time to answer this question: "What is wrong with the world today?" Many prominent persons reportedly responded, pontificating at length with their analysis of all the world's woes. G.K. Chesterton—the English writer, philosopher, playwright, journalist, orator, lay theologian, literary critic, and all around good guy—is said to have sent a reply stating something like this: "Dear Sirs, You ask what is wrong with the world today. I am. Yours truly, G.K. Chesterton."

This story illustrates a couple points. First, every generation bemoans how messed up the world is, and second, Chesterton's response stands out because it does not attribute the blame to someone else. When mass shootings and other despicable events happen, you see much finger pointing, but not much in the way of accepting responsibility. I doubt that anyone reading this has gone on any killing sprees, or probably done much else that would shock the average conscience. How can we be on the same moral plane as those who commit blatant atrocities?

Imagine that there was a challenge to jump between two tall buildings. The span between them exceeds the distance that any human has ever long jumped before. One individual takes up the challenge, runs to the edge of the roof, trips over his own feet, and plunges hundreds of feet to his death—barely clearing the side of the building from which he was jumping.

A second individual, who is one of the world's most accomplished athletes, decides that he is up for the challenge. Unlike the first jumper, however, he takes some time to prepare himself physically and mentally. He warms up with some stretches and takes a few practice runs to the side of the building to determine the best stride. He gauges the wind conditions and visualizes himself on the roof of the other building. When he at last thinks that he has done everything that he can do to prepare, he goes to the far edge of the building and assumes the starter position. He makes a great start out of the blocks, and after his fastest sprint ever, he launches himself perfectly into the vast void between the two buildings. He flies through the air, farther than any human has ever propelled himself before. Alas, his fingertips just miss the edge of the adjacent roof, and he plummets to his death below—landing just a few feet from the previous jumper. An audience on the same rooftop plane as the jumpers might have been extremely impressed by the far better performance of the last jumper, but from the ground level, both just made an equally spectacular splat.

Romans 3:23 says that everyone has sinned and fallen short of God's righteous standards. The qualities of the last jumper that I described remind me somewhat of the Reverend Billy Graham, certainly an accomplished man of God if there ever was one—a man whose public ministry is often described as being without a hint of any personal or professional scandal. He quite possibly ministered the Gospel of Jesus Christ directly to more people than anyone who has ever lived in the history of the world. I remember observing that when he passed away, a couple political cartoonists paid their respects by portraying Reverend Graham's welcome at the gates of Heaven, where he is told how much Heaven had to be expanded because of his decades of evangelistic service. My mother came to salvation through his ministry, and I through hers.

Even though Billy Graham is very much responsible for me writing this book, a spiritual grandfather of sorts, I firmly believe that he would have been the very first person to acknowledge how far he fell short of the glory of God through his own accomplishments. One of the only substantiated criticisms that I ever heard about Reverend Graham was regarding some anti-Semitic remarks that he made to President Richard Nixon after a prayer breakfast in the early 1970s. When allegations of the remarks surfaced years later, Graham denied making them, almost certainly because he truly did not remember them. When audiotapes surfaced of the comments, Graham was mortified, acknowledged his failing, and pled for forgiveness of the Jewish people and anyone else that he had offended. He said that he truly did not remember ever having such feelings toward anyone.

My point is this: no matter how good of a life we have lived, it is not good enough to allow us to bridge the span of sin that separates us from our perfectly righteous Creator. How many of our bad feelings and failings have we forgotten? How many times have we compromised our principles for the sake of expediency or rationalized our mistakes? Hopefully, our imperfections caused no great physical harm to anyone, but what about the bad examples set for those watching us who no doubt noticed our shortcomings? Fortunately, our Creator is more interested in catching us when we fall than punishing us when we fail.

A second, equally important point is that no matter how bad of a life we have lived, we are not beyond the mercy and grace of God. When we take the leap of faith in Jesus Christ, His sacrificial death is more than adequate to elevate us out of whatever moral quagmire we may have fallen into. We are bound up with Jesus as we leap tall buildings, or anything else standing between us and our Heavenly Father. When we make a spectacle of ourselves by falling into sin while "movin' on up . . . to a deluxe apartment in the sky,"[27] His forgiveness provides a safety net that catches us and allows us to soar through the air again. The "I am" who is what is wrong with the world today becomes a part of the great I Am, Jesus Christ, who provides the ultimate meaning and purpose for existence (John 8:24; John 8:58). May your hang time be long, and your hang ups—and your bang ups—be few. And may the Lord put a spring in your step to Heaven.

---

[27] A reference to John 14:1–4, with an assist from:
Ja'Net DuBois and Jeff Barry, "Movin' on Up," 1975, *The Jeffersons* television show theme song.

CHAPTER 12

LAY DOWN THE LAW

A couple times each year, public school teachers in our State must be evaluated by administrators. One year, the "educrats" in our State government bureaucracy decided to create an evaluation that all schools would be "strongly encouraged" to use to assess teachers, at least if the school corporation valued its State funding. It was called RISE, which apparently was not some clever acronym since the letters did not stand for anything that I could find—just one of many let downs. I suppose the intent was to set high standards in the never-ending quest to improve education, but the evaluation matrix served mostly just to get an emotional rise out of teachers. In this humble educator's estimation, it was a ridiculously complex evaluation system that diverted time and attention from becoming a better teacher to instead checking a bunch of boxes. I never could muster the ability to read through all the expectations, let alone try to master them; I just decided to teach the best that I could and let the checkmarks fall where they may on my evaluation. Any teacher worth his chalk dust[28] would know better than to use such a complicated assessment system with students. Apparently, I was not the only one with such a low opinion of RISE as most school systems soon replaced it with simpler evaluation instruments with the blessing of the State government.

Nonetheless, I am still humbled by the many standards by which I am

---

[28] I chalk this reference up to being so "old school." I could say any teacher brighter than a dry erase marker, but that would be a low mark indeed.

evaluated. I find it impossible to give my full attention to each one, and my efforts to improve in one area often distract from my efforts in others. I certainly leave plenty of room for nitpicking if my bosses were so inclined. I am often reminded of my unlimited potential for improvement, and I rely on the mercy of my evaluators to recognize my effort and heart for the profession. I am always gratified when the box at the bottom of the evaluation form is checked recommending renewal of my teaching contract.[29]

I am even more humbled when I realize that the principles by which I am supposed to live my life are established at a higher level than the government, and my performance is evaluated by a higher power than the school principal. God evaluates us according to "The Law," a standard of perfect righteousness that is beyond our reach. Realizing that we could never check all the boxes by always doing and saying the right things required to be in His presence, God made it possible for us to become right with Him by accepting and applying the teachings of Jesus Christ.

Just doing our best and letting Jesus do the rest can go against our natural inclination to try to earn God's favor. Knowing the difference between right and wrong is both a blessing and a curse. Such knowledge can separate us from heathens, but it also tempts us to think "we got this" when it comes to doing right. However, relying on our own efforts to do good merely serves to magnify our shortcomings and guilt, and it treats the mercy and grace of God through Jesus Christ as meaningless (Galatians 2:16–21).

The purpose of God's Law is not to show us how to make ourselves right with God but rather to make us aware of our inability to meet God's standards of righteousness through our own efforts. It sets us up to fail. Accepting God's undeserved gift of salvation through Jesus Christ empowers us to resist sin and provides us with mercy when we fail. Ironically, we actually become lawbreakers by trying to achieve salvation through the Law, or our own efforts to be good. Salvation from our sins and right standing with God is a gift, not a reward or prize that we earn. Salvation gets us on the right road, and the additional rewards that God has in store for us will be determined

---

[29] Here is a word of advice for aspiring teachers: be nice to your students because they may one day be your bosses who evaluate you. I can attest to this from personal experience. They might also one day be operating the flashing lights that you see in your rearview mirror, drawing your blood, filling your cavities, giving you a prostate exam, or even arranging your funeral—so again, be nice

by the passion with which we seek to obey Him as we journey down that road in pursuit of our purpose.

I once read a story about a woman who, during the course of a remarkably busy day, parked her car at one of the destinations on her to do list, hopped out of the car, locked the door, and slammed it shut, only then realizing that she had left the keys in the ignition. She needed to be at work in just an hour, so in desperation she called her husband, whom she knew was in the middle of an especially important business meeting, to ask if he could bring her the spare key. He reluctantly agreed to excuse himself from the meeting, swing by the house to pick up the spare key, and bring it to her. He said he would be there in 30 minutes. After she had anxiously paced the sidewalk for about twenty-five minutes, a police officer walking his beat happened by and asked her what was wrong. The lady told him of her plight, almost crying. The police officer said, "Ma'am, don't worry, I have some good news for you. You see, the passenger door is unlocked. You can get in your car and be on your way." "Oh," the lady said as she thought for a moment. She realized that her highly inconvenienced husband would be arriving at any moment and that she would have some "splainin" to do. Much to the cop's amazement, she proceeded to walk to the other side of the car, open the passenger door, lock it, and then slam it shut. Sometimes we choose to live under the limitations and consequences of the law rather than "fessing up" and going forward in the freedom of Jesus Christ.

One of the first things that you learn in ~~torture~~ teacher college is to "lay down the law" on the first day of class, clearly establishing rules and expectations. There is an adage in the teaching business that you should not crack a smile until Christmas so that students do not perceive any cracks in your resolve to maintain an orderly classroom. God laid down the Law for us, and then Jesus Christ came to earth to lay down His life to make good what we could not. Now we can lay down the Law, the fulfillment of which is beyond our grasp, and take up the cause of Jesus Christ.

CHAPTER 13

HE KNOWS US FROM ADAM

I am a firm believer that timing is important in our lives and in God's plan for us. My place of employment for virtually all my adult life was determined by a sequence of events that seemed too exquisitely timed to be mere coincidence. Several times I have discerned God's direction to be in a certain place at a certain time, or His diversion from a place where I should not be. In pursuit of my quest to visit all the fifty nifty states, one summer break I decided to rent a car and just go west while still a young man to see what I could see.

I aspired to traverse the Great Plains and see the Rocky Mountains materialize in front of me, to gawk at as many scenic national parks as I could visit, to hike to the bottom of the Grand Canyon and hopefully make it back up again, and maybe even to step foot in the Pacific Ocean before making the return trip by some undetermined route. One day of travel took me to Kansas. Not much to see here (sorry Kansas). Another day's travel offered the first peek at the Rockies and even more high points passing through the ranges to descend into Utah. A rough night in the hotel made me wonder if my next site to see would be the emergency room. Fortunately, the worst passed during the night, and I could continue with my ambitious itinerary.

I must confess that this geography teacher grossly underestimated the time required to transit from Arches National Park to the Grand Canyon where I had lodging reservations for the next night, especially with plans to visit as many national parks along the way as possible. I can say that some of them looked just like in my dreams; just close your eyes and you can see about what I saw driving through Bryce Canyon in the dark of night. After necessary stops for purposes such as getting lotion to ease the consequences of too much sun exposure during hikes and dodging cattle and other creatures on mountainous highways through open range land, I rolled into Grand Canyon Village around 4:00 a.m. (and only rolled over only one rabbit along the way). I was still contemplating making my hike to the bottom of the Grand Canyon and back on the only day that I had allotted myself in the Park before moving on to some point yet unknown for my next night's lodging.

A quick check-in with my family confirmed a fear that my dying grandmother had taken a turn for the worse and that I needed to begin the homeward trek as quickly as possible if I was going to see her alive again. After having come so far, I thought that perhaps a day of hiking would provide a needed respite from driving before I made a beeline for home. Sad, sunburned, exhausted, and with little sleep and even less preparation, I proceeded to the Bright Angel Trailhead to assess whether the prospect of a day's round trip descent into the canyon allowed for a decent chance of success, or survival for that matter. I should note that the National Park Service strongly discourages hiking to the bottom of the Grand Canyon and back in one day, even in the best of condition and with the best of preparation. In contrast, I was barely conscious and half-cocked while contemplating taking a trail that could lead me into the National Park Service's annals of infamous, reckless tourist tales. Lo and behold, when I arrived at the trailhead at the rim of the canyon, I was greeted by a sign saying, "Trail Closed Today"—not the day before, not tomorrow, just today—just the day that I could have humiliated myself, or worse. I do not recall that there was any explanation offered for the closure. Perhaps my guardian angel was just winging it to save me from myself.

On another occasion, I had a half-baked plan to travel to Australia during a fall break, rent a car, and drive across as much of the continent as I could for a week or so with just the minimal preparation that I could muster while both teaching and taking classes. I suspect that God may have also had a hand in cancelling that trip at the last minute to keep me on the right side of the road and not down under in a grave.

God, in all His mercy and munificence, allowed me to eventually fulfill both of my aspirations: to journey to the center of the earth, or at least to the bottom of the Grand Canyon, and to venture down under to Australia under much safer and more satisfying circumstances. Upon successful completion of these journeys, I could more fully appreciate how close I came to disaster through my earlier plans, such as they were. On a later trip to the Grand Canyon, with somewhat better preparation and planning, I hiked to the bottom and then began my much more strenuous ascent in well over 100° heat. I avoided the rattlesnake coiled on the trail; my water lasted (barely); and I had one energy bar to spare, though it was melted and oozing from the package.

Switchback after switchback, one foot after the other, I made my way up to the rim of the canyon while passing many people along the way who were going to have difficulty making it to the top before dark. I remember one young woman who was exhausted beyond taking another step. She asked if I had any food to spare, and I offered her the leftover energy bar that looked like something the mule train had passed. Her eyes lit up like it was the most delectable morsel that she had ever seen. I made it over the rim just as the very last rays of twilight faded to black. I was thirsting for the twelve-pack of soft drinks in my car but found that most of the cans had burst in the heat (sorry rental car company), and the others were completely flat. After seventeen miles of hiking with almost a mile in elevation change down and another mile up, I had, in God's timing, successfully completed a major task on my bucket list without kicking the bucket.

Please bear with me as I take the time to tell but one more personal story that I believe illustrates God's auspicious timing. One summer I was down to my last state to visit in the lower forty-eight, so for a last hurrah of summer break I flew to Denver, Colorado, rented a car, and mapped out a circuitous route that would at least allow me to break the plane of the Nebraska state line. This trip also provided me with what I believe was a divine appointment to cross paths and share my faith with a wandering soul in the blink-and-you-miss-it town of Florissant, Colorado.

After notching Nebraska in my travel belt, I scheduled one of my ridiculously all-inclusive itineraries that works my guardian angels and my praying mother overtime.[30] My day's plans called for a 400-mile driving loop through the Rocky Mountains interspersed with as much hiking as I could squeeze in. To make it a trifecta of tests of God's protection, I also picked up a hitchhiker, or rather one picked me up.

Tired and thirsty after hiking nine miles in the Florissant Fossil Beds National Monument, and with many more mountainous miles to drive to complete my roundabout route back to my night's lodging, I pulled in to the first convenience store that I saw to buy a big, cold beverage. I was looking forward to a relaxing, quiet drive through the heart of Colorado, but as I walked back to my car from the store, I was approached by a hippyish young man who looked to be about 19 years old and who was carrying a backpack that was about as big as he was. I knew what was coming. "Are you heading west?" he asked. I affirmed that I was, and he asked if he could hitch a ride. Now like all good parents, mine taught me not to pick up hitchhikers, and I was not excited about giving up my solitude. My first response to his request was that my car was rather full. Indeed, my front seat was full of my navigation and photography paraphernalia. However, as the young man could plainly see, the rest of my car was completely empty. When he asked

---

[30] I rely on my belief in the protection afforded by a praying mother and guardian angels (Psalm 91:11) just to venture out of my house let alone to wander the globe, and I am sure that I work them all overtime with bouts of recklessness. Late one December night after wrapping up my semester and student council adviser homecoming responsibilities, I began my half-mile walk home in an unusually intense lightning storm. About halfway home, a man stopped his car to offer me a ride. Normally, I decline when drivers make a pity stop to offer me a ride during my therapy walks after a long, hard day, but given the flashes of lighting all around, I entertained the notion that perhaps God dispatched a guardian angel to deliver me safely home. So, I gratefully accepted the ride. The gentlemen introduced himself as someone from the neighborhood, but I could not recognize him in the dark car. He let me out in front of my home, and in a poor split-second decision on my part, I decided to pass in front of his car just as he began to pull forward without seeing me in the dark, rainy conditions. The upper half of my body was sprawled across the hood of his car, while my feet and legs were firmly grounded. Fortunately, the driver noticed his new hood ornament and hit the brakes just as the pressure must have come within a fraction of the pounds per square inch that would have snapped my legs. The gentleman was profusely apologetic, but the incident was entirely my fault. This book probably recounts more of my life story than is worth telling, but if I ever venture to write my official memoir, I may title it: *When Your Guardian Angel Runs You Down.*

if I was sure, I knew that I either had to say yes to his request or tell him the truth—that I just did not want to take him for a ride.

I felt a conviction to say yes, so we threw my stuff and his backpack into the back seat, and I headed west with the young man. Adam, he said his name was as we made introductions. Later the irony of that name would strike me. From the moment Adam asked for a ride, I felt that God wanted me to use the opportunity to share my faith with him. I do not often get to, or at least take the opportunity to share my Christian faith directly one-on-one, so I quietly and nervously sought the Lord's direction in how to steer the conversation to that end, not knowing for sure how long it would take to steer the car to where Adam and I would part company.

"Start with getting to know each other," seemed to be the Lord's direction. We made small talk for the first few miles. I learned that Adam was a high school dropout who had lost his license from driving under the influence. He frequently hitchhiked from the northern to the southern part of the state, although he virtually never came this route since it was not very direct. He just happened to have a ride from a friend to Florissant and decided to take advantage of the opportunity to get a start toward home. I was his ride to get him back on track.

It soon became clear to me that Adam was the stereotypical, alienated, young person with a lot of dreams but not much focus. He had a GED but worked odd jobs, not wanting to commit to a career or college. He talked about aspirations to ride horseback through Canada to Alaska, to travel with friends to Mongolia, or to convert a bus into a mobile music mecca to attract people to get together and just jam.

Concerned that we might be running out of miles together, I looked for an opportunity to get more spiritual mileage out of the conversation. I asked Adam if he went to church anywhere. He said that he leaned toward Zen Buddhism. "Ok Lord", I thought, "that isn't something I hear every day. So how do I respond to that." I knew that if I started to beat him over the head with the cross and tell him that he was on the highway to Hell, then he would probably start to wish that he had hitched a ride with an axe murderer. "Ask questions," seemed to be the Lord's instruction, and not snotty, confrontational ones like, "And so just where has Buddhism gotten you." Although Adam's life seemed to be pretty mixed up to me, he seemed to think of himself as more like a free spirit. So, I began to make some sincere inquiries.

First, I asked him what Buddhism was all about. I had a fairly good idea from teaching about world religions, but I wanted to see how much he knew about it. He seemed to be sincere in his beliefs and to have thought through Buddhism at least as well as anything else in his life. I asked him what attracted him to that belief system, and his answer was that basically its teachings seemed like wisdom to him. I asked him what the "end game" was in Buddhism, or what it would lead him to; he seemed to have given a little less thought to that. I then shared with him why I was a Christian and how the teachings of Jesus Christ provided me with not only daily spiritual guidance, but also with a purpose for existing, a means for making it through life, and a hope for the future.

I wish I could tell you that I was able to get Adam on the road to an eternal home in Heaven just as I was able to help get him back on his route to his earthly home. He did not seem ready for that though as we parted ways at another convenience store, where he hoped to pick up a ride south if, that is, he could avoid being mistaken for an escaped inmate from the nearby prison. I was confident that I was at least able to plant a seed that might one day sprout into salvation. I have hope that one day Adam and I will meet again, perhaps in Heaven, and then he can tell me about the rest of his trip home.

I was a little disappointed that it was somewhat rainy and overcast as I drove over the crest of the Rockies, just as I was initially annoyed by having an unexpected traveling companion for the previous leg of the journey. However, the good feeling that I had from sharing my faith more than compensated for the disruption to my plans, just as the beautiful rainbow that appeared as I crossed the continental divide made me grateful for the rain.

I pulled into a scenic overlook in Glenwood Canyon, in my estimation one of the most beautiful spots on earth, to use some of the last light of day to do my daily devotions before navigating another 150 dark, rainy, mountain miles to Denver. My daily Bible reading included First Corinthians 1:18–25 (NLT 1996) where Paul says:

> I know very well how foolish the message of the cross sounds to those who are on the road to destruction. But we who are being saved recognize this message as the very power of God. As the Scriptures say, "I will destroy human wisdom and discard their most brilliant ideas." So where does this

leave the philosophers, the scholars, and the world's brilliant debaters? God has made them all look foolish and has shown their wisdom to be useless nonsense. Since God in his wisdom saw to it that the world would never find him through human wisdom, he has used our foolish preaching to save all who believe. God's way seems foolish to the Jews because they want a sign from heaven to prove it is true. And it is foolish to the Greeks because they believe only what agrees with their own wisdom. So when we preach that Christ was crucified, the Jews are offended, and the Gentiles say it's all nonsense. But to those called by God to salvation, both Jews and Gentiles, Christ is the mighty power of God and the wonderful wisdom of God. This "foolish" plan of God is far wiser than the wisest of human plans, and God's weakness is far stronger than the greatest of human strength.

I began this chapter with reflections on God's perfect timing in offering provision and protection for our lives. The Bible says that at just the right time, while we were powerless sinners, God demonstrated His love for us by sending Jesus Christ to die for our sins so that we could be restored into relationship with our Creator. Through the disobedience of one man, the first Adam, the curse of sin and death fell upon all of humanity, but all of humanity was offered deliverance from the curse through the obedient sacrifice on the cross of the one man who the Bible describes as the second Adam, Jesus Christ (Romans 5:6–18).

Just like my hitchhiking friend Adam, we have a choice between the wisdom of God and what seems wise in our own understanding. Adam was examining his life through his own eyes and seemed to believe that he had found wisdom, even though his life would appear to most of us to be filled with foolishness. Our own wisdom and understanding will lead us down a road full of hitches that leads nowhere good. God sees what we are really like inside as well as seeing the road ahead of us. He has mapped out a route so that, by following Jesus Christ, we can dodge the destruction that we deserve due to our sinfulness and find His absolute best plan and provision for us. We can have a relationship with God because He knows us from Adam.

CHAPTER 14

THE MOTHER OF
ALL PROMISES

Now I know that young people are going to have a hard time relating to this, but in Old Testament society, children were treated almost like slaves by their parents, with all kinds of rules and regulations and few privileges regardless of what wealth their parents were grooming them to eventually receive. This fact can serve as a reminder that we are all born into this earthly existence in slavery to sin. "Hey Mom, thanks for bearing us into bondage." That is not a line that you will likely find on a Mother's Day card, but do not forget that our sinful condition is not Mom's fault. After all, she was born into the bondage of sin herself, as was every human being who has ever lived since Adam and Eve. An enslaved woman can only beget an enslaved child. And you mothers probably thought your children only made you feel like slaves.

Now mothers, please forgive me for comparing our natural birth to you with being born into slavery, but Paul, the New Testament writer, did it first (Galatians 4:21–31). Paul puts a new spin on the tale of two mothers, Hagar, a slave, and Sarah, a wife, both of whom bore children for Abraham, the patriarch of the Jewish people (see Chapters 16 and 21 of Genesis). A relationship of convenience between Abraham and his slave, Hagar, produced Ishmael in a premature attempt by Abraham to obtain God's promise of a perpetual line of descendants. The birth of Ishmael can represent the result of impatiently trying to do things our way instead of God's way. Poor Hagar loved and sacrificed dearly for her child; however, she was forced into the wilderness out of Abraham's presence and provision to make room for Isaac, Abraham's child by his wife, Sarah. Hagar was helpless to sustain her child's physical life, let alone provide for his destiny. Only God's merciful intervention to provide a spring of water in the desert allowed her offspring to survive. God loved Ishmael, the slave-born son, and blessed his physical existence for the rest of his life, but the promise for the future revolved around Isaac, the freeborn son.

Paul offers a parallel comparing the strained relationship between Ishmael and Isaac to the tension between our earthly existence and God's promise for our future. Ishmael represents our physical birth as specially created beings whom God loves, but with whom He can have limited relationship because of our enslavement to sin. Isaac represents our spiritual, second birth into freedom, which is made possible by our acceptance of the deliverance from the consequences of sinfulness that comes through the labor of Jesus Christ on our behalf. Galatians 4:4–7 (NLT 1996) explains it this way:

> But when the right time came, God sent his Son, born of a woman, subject to the law. God sent him to buy freedom for us who were slaves to the law, so that he could adopt us as his very own children. And because you Gentiles have become his children, God has sent the Spirit of his Son into your hearts, and now you can call God your dear Father. Now you are no longer a slave but God's own child. And since you are his child, everything he has belongs to you.

Once we change our will to serve God instead of sin, God changes His Will to include us as His children and heirs to everything that He has (Romans 8:15–17). God sustains and even blesses our physical existence on this earth because of His love for us, whether we are still enslaved to sin à la Ishmael, or free but not yet in a position to fully realize the fortune that He has in store for us like young Isaac. Not until a Jewish child reached adulthood was he treated as an heir to his father's wealth rather than as a lowly servant. Upon salvation, we become joint heirs with Jesus Christ, the Son of God, and the rest of our earthly existence is the opportunity to grow into the fullness of what God has in store for us (Galatians 4:19).

There was a lot of bad blood between Ishmael and Isaac, even though they both shared the blood of Abraham. Their father's world just wasn't big enough for the two of them. Both wanted to be heirs of their father, but only one could prevail. Despite their slave status, Hagar and Ishmael used Ishmael's position as the firstborn son to lord it over Sarah and Isaac, which is why Sarah said, "Get rid of that slave woman and her son, for that woman's son will never share in the inheritance with my son Isaac" (Genesis 21:10 NIV). That is not the kind of sentiment that you say with a Hallmark card, but it is exactly the message that Paul tells us to deliver to the old sinful nature that inhabits us from birth (Galatians 4:30). For the time being, we must still share some space with our original sinful human nature, which can give us a lot of grief. Sometimes you can still "call me Ishmael."[31] God will continue to sustain our physical needs through the remainder of our earthly lives, just as He did for Ishmael, but to our spirit, He has delivered a "Callmark" card welcoming us into His family as heirs to all that is His, which is pretty much every good thing that exists.

For my readers who are, or who one day will be parents, the physical birth that you offer to your children provides an essential start, but only by raising your children in the nurture and admonition of the Lord can you help to get them in line for the only inheritance that can sustain them for eternity. Imagine the legacy of raising godly children who will in turn spread their faith to others who will be born again into God's kingdom. To excel in every other aspect of our lives but to fail in prioritizing the spiritual instruction of our children is to risk leaving their promise unrealized.[32]

---

[31] Herman Melville, *Moby Dick; or, The Whale,* 1851.

[32] I speak here with the authority of someone who has never made a single parenting mistake. Granted, this could be due to my personal circumstances of being single with no children. Nonetheless, I have had parents, and I attribute much of whatever satisfaction and success that I have attained in life to their dependable and often sacrificial investment in both my physical and spiritual well-being. They served as a conduit for God's grace and mercy to me. I do not assert that any earthly parent can be perfect or entirely responsible for the decisions and outcomes of their children. I only propose that there is no greater way to leave a lasting legacy than by prioritizing godly parenting, and no greater failure than neglecting to do so and thereby contributing to the number of children with PDD (Parent Deficit Disorder). I have made the assertion to students that, even for Presidents of the United States, perhaps serving in the most impactful position in all of human history, to be great at their job and yet to fail their children would lead to more negative than positive consequences for humanity. There are many who can be great Presidents, but no one is more responsible to lead children into relationship with God than their own parents if they have the opportunity to do so. At least this seems apparent to me.

Of course, we must be free ourselves to help birth others into freedom. I am reminded of the safety presentations provided by flight attendants instructing passengers how to respond in the event of a loss of cabin pressure, in which case oxygen masks drop down from the overhead compartments of the airplane. Contrary to instinct, you are instructed to place the oxygen mask on yourself before helping others dependent upon you. Then, no pressure, just breathe. Evidently, you are no good to others if you pass out before helping them. Neglecting to tend to your own spiritual relationship with God, or to provide proper role modeling, and then expecting your kids to "find God" when you are not looking diligently for Him yourself will create a serious risk of losing altitude and missing the mark of God's high calling for both parents and their children.

We can all relate to how children yearn to be free from the rules and limitations of childhood. I am sure it is bittersweet for parents to watch their children grow up and become less dependent, yet as children get older, a whole new dimension opens up in the relationship between parents and their children as their sons and daughters mature into their brothers and sisters—all in the family of God. Children no longer approach their parents primarily as providers for their survival needs, but rather with a free expression of love and a desire for fellowship.

Our Heavenly Father also wants us, His children, to relate to Him willingly and joyfully, not out of a sense of obligation or dependence. Most people are familiar with the biblical story of the prodigal son, who abandoned his family and squandered his inheritance, only to return with a desperate plea for forgiveness that was unconditionally and lavishly granted by his father with great celebration. The prodigal son's equally flawed brother often receives less attention in the story. The "responsible" son complained that he had always been slavishly obedient to his father and was never treated with such fanfare. The prodigal's sibling was "stuck on slave," or obsessed with obligations rather than savoring the relationship of a son that his father so longingly desired for all his children (Luke 15:11–32).

The sacrifice that Jesus made for us is like the travails required of a woman giving birth before the joy of new life can be experienced. By taking upon Himself the consequences of our prodigal ways, Jesus delivered the opportunity for us to become children of God who are eligible to receive the fullness of what God desires for us (John 16:20–24). Our mortal enemy, Satan, believed that He could hijack and bring down God's special creation by tempting the mother of us all into disobedience, thereby sucking God's breath of life from her posterity and crushing it into the dust of the ground (Genesis 2:7). Our enemy then sought to ground God's plan for the redemption of humanity that required sending a Savior who would be born of a woman. In the ultimate plot twist, Satan's very act of orchestrating the natural death of Jesus Christ brought about what Eve prematurely tried to obtain, but what God intended for us to have all along—relationship with Him and a total access pass to His entire kingdom for all of eternity.

I do not think that I can offer any better conclusion than that presented in First Peter 1:23 (NLT 1996), which says: "For you have been born again. Your new life did not come from your earthly parents because the life they gave you will end in death. But this new life will last forever because it comes from the eternal, living word of God." Our saved identity will replace our enslaved identity, and we will live forevermore as heirs to a parent whose world is big enough for all. That is the mother of all promises.

CHAPTER 15

WALKING DEAD OR
WALKING IN HIS STEAD

Perhaps you have heard predictions of a zombie apocalypse. Perhaps you are not aware that it is happening right now, and you are living in the midst of it. Now that I have your attention, let me tell you what got me thinking about zombies. I assure you that I am not into the zombie craze in pop culture, but I was intrigued by an article in *National Geographic* magazine entitled, "Meet Nature's Nightmare Mindsuckers." The article describes how some organisms survive and reproduce by essentially making zombies out of other organisms.[33] Apparently, many kinds of critters can be zombified, including various species of insects, crustaceans, amphibians, and rodents. Zombification in this context is when parasites infest and begin controlling the behavior of their hosts.

Here is an example that probably routinely happens in your neighborhood. There are these tiny one-celled protozoa called *Toxoplasma gondii* that like to take up residence in other organisms. In fact, they can penetrate the brain of almost any other creature, to no good end for their host I assure you. Cats, however, seem immune to any harmful effects of *Toxoplasma*, and yet strangely, a cat's intestines are where these protozoa need to be to reproduce. To survive as a species, these pesky protozoa need a cat encounter. Maybe that is why rats and mice are among their favorite

---

[33] Carl Zimmer, "Meet Nature's Nightmare Mindsuckers," *National Geographic*, November 2014, 36.

hosts. Now normally, a mouse will avoid any trace of a cat, but *Toxoplasma* seems to trigger a change in the mouse's brain that makes it curious about cats, increasing its chances of becoming a cat's meal. When its mission to become cat chow is accomplished, the protozoa will have the guts to reproduce; then the cat will, shall we say, pass it on.

The article that awoke me to all of this acknowledges that, "How mutations and natural selection could give rise to such creepy powers is a particularly intriguing puzzle for evolutionary biologists,"[34] but then the author goes to great lengths to give an evolutionary explanation for this bank shot of organism survival. The author concludes that the lesson to be learned is that "Mother Nature's creativity has no limit."[35] Apparently, it is easier for some to attribute creative intelligence to impersonal forces rather than to a Creator God. Nonetheless, I also felt challenged to understand how the Creator might be speaking to us through such apparently callous complexity. Surely God did not originally design His creation to function in such a manipulative and destructive way. Perhaps this "mindsucking" is just more evidence that all of creation groans under the weight of sin and longs to be liberated from "bondage to decay" through a new birth (Romans 8:19–22).

A zombie is, as I understand it, the body of a dead person who appears to be alive, but whose mind is seemingly controlled by some other force. And oh yeah, zombies are usually up to no good. My assertion is that a zombie apocalypse began with the first sin of Adam and Eve in the Garden of Eden when God's pinnacle of creation, humankind, became the walking dead in sinful separation from God (Genesis 2:17). When I look around, I see dead people, as evidenced in their work obsession, sports fanaticism, or rapt attention to cultural influencers with apparently little attention to things that matter in the big picture of eternity. Each of us was spiritually stillborn, and our life's mission is to escape our slavery to sin and to restore communion with our Creator. Even a hall of famer of faith such as Paul, who wrote much of the New Testament of the Bible, found this to be the personal struggle of a lifetime. The frustration that he described in Romans 7:15–25 (NIV) borders on comic relief:

---

[34] Zimmer, "Mindsuckers," 43.

[35] Zimmer, "Mindsuckers," 54.

I do not understand what I do. For what I want to do I do not do, but what I hate I do. And if I do what I do not want to do, I agree that the law is good. As it is, it is no longer I myself who do it, but it is sin living in me. I know that nothing good lives in me, that is, in my sinful nature. For I have the desire to do what is good, but I cannot carry it out. For what I do is not the good I want to do; no, the evil I do not want to do—this I keep on doing. Now if I do what I do not want to do, it is no longer I who do it, but it is sin living in me that does it. So I find this law at work: When I want to do good, evil is right there with me. For in my inner being I delight in God's law; but I see another law at work in the members of my body, waging war against the law of my mind and making me a prisoner of the law of sin at work within my members. What a wretched man I am! Who will rescue me from this body of death? Thanks be to God, who delivers me through Jesus Christ our Lord!

An apparent theme of the zombie apocalypse in popular entertainment is that, when societal institutions and norms are threatened, people cannot be trusted to do what is right if the personal cost is too high. Selfishness supplants any sense of moral obligation to others.[36] Jesus Christ became flesh and blood and set into motion the events that allow us to escape from the zombie apocalypse. May I suggest to you that the most momentous free will decision that you will ever make is whether to accept Jesus Christ as Savior and Lord, or to reject Him. Either way, your choice will determine who will control you, and what you will live for. We were all born into the zombie apocalypse, but are you still consumed by brain dead pursuits? Are you mindlessly pursuing the meaningless, or are you seeking to live for a higher purpose than self-gratification?

If you have accepted Jesus Christ as Savior, congratulations, you are no longer a slave to sin, and you have been rescued from the zombie apocalypse.

---

[36] Kyle William Bishop, "Dead Man Still Walking: A Critical Investigation into the Rise and Fall . . . and Rise of Zombie Cinema" (PhD diss., The University of Arizona, 2009), 31.

You have escaped from the body of death and become part of the body of Christ. However, as Paul described, our quest is an ongoing struggle. Perhaps we can call it, the "zombie sanctification," in which we seek to become more like Christ and increasingly sacrifice ourselves in service to our Savior.

Zombies are often portrayed as having a hunger to consume human flesh, which also reminds me of people who are controlled by sin and who are described in the Bible as living according to the desires of the flesh (Romans 8:5). I think it is intriguing that two of the most popular cultural icons today are zombies, with a taste for flesh, and vampires with a taste for blood. Speaking of vampires, can you see your reflection in the Bible, God's Word to humanity (James 1:22–25)?

The ultimate taste test that life presents to us is deciding whether to pursue the flesh and blood of Jesus Christ or to chase our own desires. I am not proposing that we literally consume the body of Christ, but rather that we should strive to become part of His body, thoroughly consumed with pursuing the will of God for our lives. His will, of course, is for us to rescue others from the zombie apocalypse. Interestingly, according to Haitian voodoo lore, the taste of salt will break the zombie curse,[37] and who are Christians but the salt of the earth (Matthew 5:13)? Here is another morsel of spiritual brain food from the legendary zombie hunter, Saint Paul, who says in Ephesians 2:1–7 (NLT):

> Once you were dead because of your disobedience and your many sins. You used to live in sin, just like the rest of the world, obeying the devil—the commander of the powers in the unseen world. He is the spirit at work in the hearts of those who refuse to obey God. All of us used to live that way, following the passionate desires and inclinations of our sinful nature. By our very nature we were subject to God's anger, just like everyone else. But God is so rich in mercy, and he loved us so much, that even though we were dead because of our sins, he gave us life when he raised Christ from the dead. (It is only by God's grace that you

---

[37] Bishop, "Dead Man Still Walking," 70-71.

have been saved!) For he raised us from the dead along with Christ and seated us with him in the heavenly realms because we are united with Christ Jesus. So God can point to us in all future ages as examples of the incredible wealth of his grace and kindness toward us, as shown in all he has done for us who are united with Christ Jesus.

Will you survive the zombie apocalypse? Will you be consumed by the cares of the world, or will you consume the life of Jesus Christ? Will you be walking dead, or walking in His stead?

CHAPTER 16

BOND, JESUS BOND

Once again, I remind you of my proposition that God yearns for relationship, or communion, with each of us. Communion involves the intimate exchange of thoughts or emotions, and humans were God's special creation for this purpose. Sin separated man from God, and all human history from that time forward has been marked by the struggle to reconcile whosoever will into relationship with their Creator. In the Old Testament, we find the description of how God sought to restore relationship with mankind through a chosen group of people, the Israelites. At first, I thought of describing this as Plan A, and when that did not work, God went to Plan B, establishing relationship with individuals as set forth in the New Testament. But on second thought, I realized that, since the initial sinful separation in the Garden of Eden, there has only been one plan to restore relationship, but with two acts.

In Operation Communion, God sent His own agent, Jesus Christ, to dwell on earth with people, both to experience and to model existence as a human being while foiling an archvillain's plot to separate people from God for all of eternity. Perhaps we could call Him Agent 007, not because He was one of several agents licensed to kill people as was the case for James Bond, but because He was authorized to die for people. Plus, the number seven is often associated with perfection, fullness, completeness, accomplishment, and rest. Jesus certainly is not a secret agent. He is proclaimed to be Immanuel, or God with us, to all who will listen.

It seems natural to tell stories in trilogies, like *Lord of the Rings* and *Back to the Future*. Our existence will form a trilogy consisting of our past, present, and future. There is a third part to God's plan as well. It is yet to come, but the script is already written. Our Savior is coming back to earth in bodily form in the blockbuster conclusion of Operation Communion. Spoiler alert! The Bible provides an advance copy of the script. All the villains led by the Dark Invader are vanquished, and the good guys live happily ever after with God, their true Father (Revelation 21:3–7).

I know that I am mixing movie metaphors, but perhaps the trailer for the finale of God's plan, which is not for your eyes only but for whosoever believes it, might go something like this: "When the world is not enough, and you are facing an enemy with a license to kill your mortal body, and the spectre of death looms large, and Dr. No says that your fate is sealed, God provided a view to a kill of the Savior who loved you, who came from Heaven with love and whom God let die so that you could live with no time to die in His Majesty's Service, where you need never say never again. You may only live twice, but the next life is in the Quantum of Solace where, even though the sky fall, the diamonds are forever and tomorrow never dies due to the living daylight that illuminates relationship with your Creator forevermore. That's a bond, a Jesus bond."[38]

---

[38] I have never seen a James Bond movie, and I do not endorse them. I do highly recommend auditioning to be a Jesus bond girl or guy. You are a natural for the part and otherwise risk being cast out as a villain.

CHAPTER 17

CRY UNCLE

Because we could not earn our way into God's presence, God came into our presence in the form of Jesus Christ (John 1:14), an event called the incarnation that we celebrate every Christmas. Christmas was likely not recognized by Christians until a few hundred years after the main event of the birth of Jesus Christ. Apparently, early Christians were more likely to celebrate late Christians on the day of their death rather than of their birth.

Christmas was probably introduced as a commemoration among Roman Christians around the 4th century to counter the growing heresy, or false teaching, of Arianism. A church leader named Arius was teaching his followers that Jesus was a created being. Introducing the celebration of Christmas called attention to the traditional Christian belief that Jesus was a fully divine manifestation of God come to earth in human form. It often seems that for every error in human thinking, there is an equal and opposite error. For Arianism, that contrasting heresy was Gnosticism, or the belief that Jesus was not fully human like us. For Jesus to complete Operation Communion, however, He must be both completely human and completely God. To die for our sins, Jesus must be human. For His death to make a difference, He must be the perfect sacrifice, and only God can personify perfection.

Don't ask me how this works; I don't need to fully understand such a thing to live in the illumination of Jesus as the Light of the World (John 8:12). However, here is an illustration that may shed some light on this concept, even though it exceeds human understanding.[39] Imagine that you are completely bankrupt financially with no money to pay bills and accumulated debt—hopefully, a stretch for your imagination rather than a reflection of your reality. Anyway, because of your dire financial straits, no one will take a chance on you and loan you any more money. But wait, you have an extraordinarily rich uncle who loves you, and he agrees to pay off all your debts once and for all. Notice that a couple things must come together for this situation to play, or perhaps pay out, in your favor. First, your uncle must care enough about you to help you. Secondly, your uncle must be rich and have the resources to pay off your debts in a currency that your debtors will accept.

When it comes to spiritual bankruptcy, a musty old uncle will not fit the bill. Even if Bob's your uncle, you will not receive any credit. However, because Jesus is fully God, He has the resources, and the desire, to make perfect provision for your debt. Because Jesus is fully human, He can pay in the currency that you owe, and the denomination is death. The first step to salvation is to come to terms with your spiritually bankrupt human condition and insolvency and make good on your "sindebtedness." Cry uncle and claim the inheritance that will pay your debt in full and provide for you to have a brand-new start.

---

[39] For this illustration and much of the inspiration for this chapter I am indebted to: "The Christ of Christmas," in *Meditations on the Lord's Supper* (Becoming Closer Adult Bible Fellowship, n.d.), 70, http://www.becomingcloser.org/Downloads%20PDF/Communion%20Mediations.pdf.

CHAPTER 18

LIFE ON THE ROCKS

I have occasionally given tests that virtually all my students fail. I do my best to teach my pupils the material that, in my eyes, they need to know, but for whatever reason, sometimes most of them are not quite ready come test time. Perhaps my teaching was lacking, or my expectations were too high, or the test was too hard, or my students just let me down—or maybe all of the above are correct. Often teachers are expected to retest under such circumstances, but unless the teacher or the students, or both, make different decisions, the results are unlikely to get better.

When I return graded tests, I try to involve the students in what I call a "post-mortem" to determine why all the red. One of the strategies for improvement that I have found most difficult to instill in students is for them to take time to look over the questions they missed, determine the correct answers, try to figure out why they missed them, and then plan how to prepare better for the next time that they will be confronted with a similar test. I suspect that students often feel like I am rubbing their noses in exam excrement. Fortunately, there are always more tests to follow, and epic test fails serve to separate those students who consign themselves to perpetual failure, or at least the status quo, from those who resolve to learn from their mistakes and to do better the next time.

The night before Jesus died on the cross for our salvation, all His followers who were with Him were presented with a traumatic test of their faith in Jesus and of their determination to follow Him come what may. They all bombed in one way or another. There is a lot to learn from the subsequent destinies of two of those delinquent disciples, Judas Iscariot and Simon Peter.

After years of experiencing the ministry of Jesus Christ, a day of decision came for both men. Both Judas and Peter had spent years in the presence of Jesus—hearing His teaching, witnessing His miracles, and experiencing His love. But on this night, both would leave His presence. Judas rejected Jesus's love and turned Him over to those who would kill Him. Peter deserted Jesus because he was afraid of the consequences of following Him.

Like many of my students, Peter knew the answer going into the test, but he forgot it when it counted. Many of my exam questions are multiple choice (or multiple guess as the case may be). One of the best strategies for finding the true answer to such questions is to eliminate the wrong choices (distractors as they call them in the education business). Fortunately, when Jesus offered him a retest, Peter recognized the futility of life without Jesus and threw himself on the mercy of the Lord. There he found a purpose for living as well as the courage to live his life, and literally to give his life, for Jesus Christ. Such willingness to choose Jesus as Lord is the rock upon which Jesus builds His kingdom (Matthew 16:13–18).

Judas also discovered the futility of doing things his way. He rejected the mercy of the Lord and killed himself, with his body literally bursting open on the rocks of the earth (Acts 1:18).

Just as all of Jesus's disciples deserted Him on the night before His crucifixion, so all of us have sinned and departed from His presence. Only by confessing our sins and asking Jesus for His forgiveness can we enter eternal communion with the Rock of our salvation, and even become the very blocks from which He will build His kingdom (1 Peter 2:4–8). Each day you face a decision. You can be a blockhead and follow the path of Judas, doing things your way until you recognize the futility of your existence, and, possibly too late, that this path leads to self-destruction. Or you can choose the example of Peter and follow Jesus, fulfilling the purpose for which you were created, finding the hope of eternal life with your Creator, and sharing that hope with others. The choice is yours: life on the rocks, or life on the Rock.

CHAPTER 19

DON'T LIVE IN SUSPENDED ANIMATION

Consider a character with the following traits: highly motivated, focused, self-confident, persistent, courageous, willing to take risks, and smarter than any other of his species. What is not to admire? Surely such a creature would be a success story. The above description was inspired by Wile E. Coyote of *Looney Tunes'* Coyote and Road Runner cartoon fame, and multiple generations are now familiar with the Coyote as a case study of the consequences for obsession and recklessness, as well as for supreme overconfidence in oneself and in the latest and greatest gadgets and gizmos.[40]

Indeed, anyone unfamiliar with the running gags of the cartoon series would surely bet on Wile E. Coyote's latest ingenious scheme to catch the Road Runner, whose vocabulary seems limited to one word and whose only defenses seem to be speed and luck. And yet on every occasion in the time and space that these characters inhabit, the Coyote's elaborate efforts end with his own suffering while the Road Runner continues his merry way. What must be taken into consideration is that the Coyote and the Road Runner inhabit their own universe, with its own rules established by its creators. Among the rules that guided the animators are that the Road

---

[40] This chapter is inspired in part by:

"Genius," in *Meditations on the Lord's Supper* (Becoming Closer Adult Bible Fellowship, n.d.), 267, http://www.becomingcloser.org/Downloads%20PDF/Communion%20Mediations.pdf.

Runner can never go on the offensive or leave the road, all harm that befalls the coyote is a consequence of his fanatical obsession, and of course, the Coyote can never, ever prevail.

Wile E. Coyote is completely oblivious to His creators and to the rules that predestine the outcomes of his efforts to catch the Road Runner. No matter what his latest brilliant scheme or technology from ACME Corporation (a backronym for which could be "A Company that Makes Everything"), his efforts are doomed to abysmal failure. Similarly, any efforts of our own to obtain right standing with our Creator will be like filthy rags in the sight of God (Isaiah 64:6). In the spiritual universe that we inhabit, the Law dictates that the consequence of sin is spiritual death. Nothing that we could ever do could succeed in conquering our sinfulness, no matter how ingenious our efforts may appear to be.

Occasionally in an episode, the creators of the Coyote and the Road Runner cartoons suspend the rules, like allowing the Road Runner to leave the road or to go on the offensive. Yet they mercilessly never allow Wile E. Coyote to prevail or to know that all his efforts are doomed to fail. In contrast, our Creator God has made Himself known to us and has intervened on our behalf to allow us to gain victory over sin through Jesus Christ. When we were unforgiven sinners, we could be compared to Wile E. Coyote, always trying hopelessly to make ourselves right through our own efforts. Upon salvation, there is a cosmic shift in the rules of the universe in our favor. Christians take on the part of the Road Runner, escaping all the wiles of the Devil (Ephesians 6:11), whose schemes seem unassailable, but whose efforts are doomed to failure because our Creator wrote the rules.

Unlike the Road Runner, who seems to rely a lot on luck and the ineptitude of the Coyote, Christians do have some responsibility for spiritual self-preservation. The Bible describes the Devil as an adversary who roams around like a roaring lion seeking whom He can devour, which should give us some pause. Christians are advised to be clearheaded and ever vigilant to resist the temptations that will come our way. Then such attacks will only serve to make us stronger (1 Peter 5:8–11).

Here is a deep philosophical question inspired by the Coyote and the Road Runner cartoons: would Wile E. Coyote have been more successful if he relied on his natural instincts instead of absurdly elaborate contraptions? God implants within all people a basic human instinct to recognize their emptiness before Him as well as their inability to fill that God-shaped hole with anything other than their Creator. Our conscience is programmed to detect right and wrong, but it can be hardened by faulty thinking or blocked by any number of distractions that fill our minds (Romans 2:14–16).

Gravity was often the Coyote's greatest threat, and ours can be the failure to recognize the gravity of our situation on the road to ruin. If you have never accepted Jesus Christ as Savior, perhaps this can be the moment of realization that there is no ground under the pinnacle of human achievement, and you are in a free fall. Jesus is the go-to source to equip you with everything that you need to prevail over all forces seeking to interfere with your relationship with God (Philippians 4:19). As Christ Makes Everything possible, the only word that you need in your vocabulary is Jesus, since all who call upon His name shall be saved (Romans 10:13). Do not live any more in suspended animation; fall into the arms of a loving and forgiving God.

CHAPTER 20

IT'S IN YOUR BLOOD

One of my ancillary duties as a public servant schoolteacher is to coordinate a few blood drives each year for students, school employees, and the community. This duty is also a privilege in that the thousands of units of blood that we have collected over the years have no doubt helped to save countless lives. Our local blood center's motto is, "blood is life, just give it." The Holy Bible agrees. Leviticus 17:11 (NIV) says, "For the life of a creature is in the blood, and I have given it to you to make atonement for yourselves on the altar; it is the blood that makes atonement for one's life." Atonement is making right one's wrong behavior. It is an essential part of communion, or being "at one" with, our Creator God.

Blood donation is essential for sustaining the lives of people who do not have enough of their own healthy blood coursing through their veins. Often blood centers put out notice that there is a critical shortage in the blood supply that is anticipated to be needed in the community. However, donors must be screened to avoid infusing blood that could harm the recipient. Deferrals, or rejections, of willing donors could be necessary due to natural health limitations, or due to impurities that may have been introduced into the blood of donors through their behaviors—hence all the personal questions that needle prospective donors before their donation is in the bag.

Blood, our own or that of a donor, will circulate through the bloodstream to every nook and cranny of our bodies, carrying both the good and the bad elements. Our behavior can affect what circulates through our bodies by introducing impure elements, such as alcohol, drugs, or diseases. What circulates through our blood can also affect our behavior, which is why blood alcohol content can be an indicator of the level of impairment of someone who has consumed alcohol. Some people will seek such impairment as a way of distracting themselves from the stresses and strains of life.

Humans also have different blood types, and as a result, another important consideration of blood donation is to make sure that the donor and recipient are of compatible types. Fortunately, Type O, the most common, can be received by people of any blood type, and thus people with Type O blood are called universal donors.

In a spiritual sense, our blood is filled with impurities, both from the sin condition inherited from our parents and from our own bad behaviors, and this contamination makes us incompatible with a holy, righteous God. The blood from animal sacrifices as described in the Old Testament was at best a stopgap measure to call people's attention to the consequences of sin, and sacrificing our own blood would kill the patient.

In the battle against sin and death, the forces of darkness drew first blood when Jesus Christ was crucified, but that shedding of blood makes possible our release from the consequences of our sins. Jesus Christ was the perfect sacrifice whose blood had no impurities, either from inheritance or from His own iniquity. He is the universal donor (Type O for omnipotent, omniscient, and omnipresent), and His blood is never in short supply when needed to infuse any person with an otherwise incurable sin disorder. When His blood gets in your blood, the consequences of your past behaviors will be eliminated, and your future behavior will be directed to fulfilling the purpose for which you are so wonderfully made.

CHAPTER 21

DAYLIGHT SAVING TIME

At the beginning of a recent new year, which also happened to mark a new decade by many reckonings, I decided to reread a book that I had first read at the dawn of the 21st century. In this book, entitled *Calendar: Humanity's Epic Struggle to Determine a True and Accurate Year*, David Ewing Duncan distinguishes between clock time, which is a cycle that repeats itself indefinitely with no progression, and calendar time, which is linear and "made up of small boxes that contain everything that happens in a day, but no more. And when the day is over, you can't return to that box again." In other words, it has been and will be the time of day that you are reading these words many times. However, it will never again be the day that I am writing this, February 2, 2020 (even if it does coincidently happen to be Groundhog Day), nor will it ever again be the day that you are reading this. Duncan goes on to say, "Calendar time has a past, present, and future, ultimately ending in death when the little boxes run out." The calendar reflects "the human compulsion to comprehend the passing of time, to wrestle down the forward motion of life and impose on it some sense of order," like casting a net of thousands of squares to capture a lifetime.[41]

It seems like God designed our solar system to confound our efforts to create a consistent calendar. Because the amount of time that it takes for the earth to complete a revolution around the sun (a solar year of approximately

---

[41] David E. Duncan, *Calendar: Humanity's Epic Struggle To Determine A True And Accurate Year* (New York: Avon Books, Inc., 1998), xviii-xix.

365.242189 days) is not evenly divisible by the approximate 24 hours that it takes for the earth to complete a rotation, a fixed pattern of days year in and year out is likely impossible to establish. Pope Gregory and the Catholic Church were instrumental in creating our current Gregorian calendar in 1582. Even with the system of leap years and leap year exceptions, our calendar mismatches the solar year by 27 seconds per year and will be a day off from the solar year every 3236 years. Believe it or not, earlier cultures may have had more accurately calibrated calendars a few thousand years ago. Maybe that is why they were early.

People spend a lot of time thinking about time. Ray Cummings proposed that "time is what keeps everything from happening at once," while Lucille Harper described time as "a great healer, but poor beautician." Henry David Thoreau cautioned, "as if you could kill time without injuring eternity," and Hector Louis Berlioz stated that "time is a great teacher, but unfortunately it kills all its pupils."

Measuring the annual passage of time seems to have been particularly important in the system of worship that God instituted among the Jews as described in the Old Testament. There were prescribed days and years for special commemorations of their relationship with their Creator. However, after a quick word study of the Bible, I found it remarkable how unremarkable calendar events seem to be in the teachings of Jesus Christ and the New Testament writers. In fact, Paul, who wrote much of the New Testament, discouraged obsessing over the observation of special days, months, seasons, or years (Galatians 4:10–12). Holy days and Sabbaths only cast shadows of the reality of what Jesus Christ has done, is doing, and will continue to do in our lives (Colossians 2:16–17).

First century Christians seemed to pay little attention to days, weeks, or years, apparently because they expected the return of Jesus Christ to be imminent. The way Duncan described this in the book *Calendar* caught my attention. He states, "When Jesus *failed* to return immediately, Christians realized that they needed some system for dating" [emphasis added],[42] and apparently ChristianMingle.com was not around yet. I understand the author's point, but I am reminded of Second Peter 3:8–9 (NIV), which says, "But do not forget this one thing, dear friends: With the Lord a day is like a thousand years, and a thousand years are like a day. The Lord is not slow

---

[42] Duncan, *Calendar*, 63.

in keeping his promise, as some understand slowness. Instead, he is patient with you, not wanting anyone to perish, but everyone to come to repentance." What we had here was a failure of human understanding, not divine tardiness.

Nonetheless, as Duncan says, "Christianity became a religion of history and the calendar."[43] After a couple hundred years of intense persecution and martyrdom, many secret and scattered communities of Christians began to be welcomed into the Roman mainstream as the Emperor Constantine called for church leaders to gather at the Council of Nicaea in 325 AD to unify their doctrine and practices. Establishing a uniform date for the celebration of Easter each year was apparently the most pressing problem and remained for centuries one of the driving forces of the Church's efforts to calendarize Christianity.

It seems like Christians lost sight of Paul's admonition to not be consumed by such things. Christianity in real time according to Paul is found in Ephesians 5:15–17 (NIV): "Be very careful, then, how you live—not as unwise but as wise, making the most of every opportunity, because the days are evil. Therefore do not be foolish, but understand what the Lord's will is."

Do you want to fulfill the purpose for which you were created? It is about time. God's expectations for us are the same 24/7/365, yet there is no time like the present to spring forward in pursuit of His direction. In Second Corinthians 6:2 (NLT), God says: "At just the right time I heard you. On the day of salvation, I helped you." Indeed, the 'right time' is now. Today is the day of salvation." Daylight saving time has begun.[44]

---

[43] Ibid.

[44] When these remarks were originally presented, I concluded with the following prayer:
Dear Heavenly Father of Time,
We recognize that our life on this earth is like a mist that appears for a little time and then vanishes, and that we do not yet know what tomorrow will bring other than your perfect will for our lives (James 4:13–15). We thank you that, once upon a time, the infinite became an infant and entered our time and place—that all in good time you sent forth your Son, born of a woman, born under the law like us (Galatians 4:4) to unite all things in Heaven and on earth in Jesus (Ephesians 1:10). For as long as it is called today, we dedicate ourselves to following you and encouraging each other to avoid the deceitfulness of sin (Hebrews 3:12–15). Although the message of the cross may seem to be foolishness to those who are perishing (1 Corinthians 1:18), we will seek to make the best use of whatever time you have allotted us on this earth to walk in wisdom (Colossians 4:5) as we proclaim the timeless message of your death on the cross for our sins, so that whosoever believes on you will not perish but have eternal life (John 3:16). Amen.

CHAPTER 22

LET IT RIP

I think I have always had a morbid streak in me. I remember that, as a child, one of my favorite TV shows was *Quincy, M.E.* about a crusading medical examiner. It was just to die for. One of many things that I wanted to be when I grew up was a forensic pathologist that determined how people died. I also always liked the board game *Clue*, trying to figure out who killed Mr. Body—like Colonel Mustard in the kitchen, with the knife. I have at times found myself wandering around in graveyards thinking about the lives represented by the tombstones—and occasionally wondering what expiration date would be carved on mine. In one local cemetery I observed an old grave marker for a married couple with no death date inscribed for the husband, who was born in 1872. Perhaps the man had a happy life with another wife and was buried elsewhere than where he intended when his first wife died. Otherwise, the man is either the oldest person alive, or sadly, no one thought to mark his exit.

As I progress through the stages of life, I find myself increasingly scanning obituaries, a curious behavior that I once only associated with old people. Perhaps this is to satisfy a compelling need before we start our day to know who is not starting theirs, or perhaps confirming that we are not listed in the obituaries is how we determine that we are indeed alive for another day. I remember my grandparents talking about how they knew more people in Heaven than on earth and telling me to never get old as they moaned about their aches and pains. I usually responded that I thought growing old beat the alternative, decaying young. With each passing year, however, I can better relate to my parents and grandparents. [45]

As I grew up, I realized that autopsies and crime scene investigations were more appropriately entertainment than employment for me, but I still find determining the time, manner, and place of death to be a fascinating endeavor. Christianity may also seem to have a morbid streak. Christians are encouraged to die to self and to remember the crucifixion of Jesus by symbolically consuming His flesh and blood through the observance of the Communion sacrament. Ultimately, however, Christianity is a celebration of new life as it presents parallels between what must die and what can live forever.

Everyone is born with one life to live, a physical existence that generally plays out as birth, growth, decline, and then death. About the best this life can give us is some temporal pleasure capped by a nice obituary and a tombstone. It was not meant to be this way. Genesis describes how people were created for an eternity of communion with and service to their Creator and His creation. When sin entered the picture, the life of service ended, and one of survival began. Creation turned into a hostile environment, and scraping together basic needs of food, clothing, and shelter became an all-consuming requirement just to prolong a physical life that was inevitably in a slow fade to death.

When we accept Jesus Christ as our Savior from the consequences of sinfulness, we are born again into a new, eternal life that, for a while, runs parallel to our dying physical existence until it takes a sharp turn at the ~~coroner~~ corner of life and death, where we take our last breath on earth and our first in Heaven.[46] During the period of our overlapping lives, the task at hand is to transition back from survival to service, and that requires killing our old self. We may not know what expiration date will be etched on our

---

[45] Once I develop a compulsive need to share the hour-by-hour weather forecast for the next ten days with anyone in earshot, then I will know that I have fully arrived in the golden years of life.

[46] This reminds me of when students run the hallowed hallways of the school building for sports conditioning after classes during inclement weather. Sometimes it sounds to me like they are yelling "coroner," and I cannot help but think, "Wow, our students must be in bad shape." Then I remember that they are yelling "corner" to alert anyone coming from an unseen direction.

tombstone, but we can know the time, manner, and place of death of our old, sinful self. If we have truly been born again, then I suspect that we can identify the date, note the details, and describe the setting of the demise of our former life.

I still remember the essential elements of a story from Sunday School literature that I read when I was just a boy. As I recall, it told of a young girl who brought a boyfriend to visit her godly grandmother. The grandmother asked the young man if he was a Christian. "Oh yes," he said as the granddaughter began to redden in anticipation of the third degree she knew was coming. "Tell me about when you became a Christian," the grandmother said. "Um well," the young man replied, "I don't remember exactly when, I guess I just always have been a Christian. I have gone to church all of my life." "Well," the grandmother said, "if you have never asked Jesus Christ to be your Savior, then you are not a Christian." I think one reason that I remember this story is because this bluntness reminded me of my own godly grandmother.

Of course, by this time, the boy was extremely uncomfortable, and the girl was deeply embarrassed, and even angry, at her grandmother's confrontational approach to a getting-to-know-you conversation. She was sure this relationship was going nowhere. Later, when they were alone, she apologized to the boy for her grandmother's provocative comment. The boy replied, "You know, I have been thinking all day about what your grandmother said, and maybe she is right. I just always assumed that I was a Christian because my family says that we are Christians. I think I would like to go back and talk to your grandmother about how I can be sure that I am right with God."[47]

I remember the time, manner, and place of my old sinful self's demise. It was when I was seven, with a confession of my sinfulness, in my bedroom, and my mother was an accomplice. I do not think that we recorded the exact date, but I remember kneeling at my bed as my mother led me in a prayer asking Jesus to be the Lord of my life. I can even remember what the bedspread looked like. My salvation date was stamped on the death certificate of my old life, and thus began a new life and a new reason for living. It was then that I could say, like Paul in Galatians 2:20 (NIV), "I have

---

[47] This is a reconstruction of the story as I remember it from over 40 years ago. Unfortunately, I have no means to credit the original source.

been crucified with Christ, and I no longer live, but Christ lives in me. The life I live in the body, I live by faith in the Son of God, who loved me, and gave himself for me."

I hope to have a few more years of physical life left in me, only now as a new creation running in sync with my spiritual existence. When my temporal life disappears like a vapor, I have the assurance that to be absent from the body is to be present with Jesus Christ (2 Corinthians 5:8). Romans 14:7–9 (NLT 1996) says: "For we are not our own masters when we live or when we die. While we live, we live to please the Lord. And when we die, we go to be with the Lord. So in life and in death, we belong to the Lord. Christ died and rose again for this very purpose, so that he might be Lord of those who are alive and of those who have died."

My old sinful self may still have a few gasps of breath left in him, and the obituary for my physical life is still being written. But now I know that my obituary on earth will be my introduction in Heaven. Christianity does not come in mother's milk. It is not just a club that we join or some cultural construct. It requires that we consciously choose a second birth that delivers us from our doomed physical existence on this earth into a new life as a child of God.

If you desire relationship with your Creator, do not assume that it is a given; you need to be forgiven. Assume the position of prayer and sincerely tell God in your own words and from the heart that you know that you have sinned, or disobeyed Him, and that you realize that you need to be saved from the consequences of disobedience so that you will not be eternally separated from Him. Ask God to forgive you of your sins and to apply the sacrificial death of Jesus Christ to your life to pay the penalty for the wrong that you have done. Repent, or state your intent to avoid sinful disobedience with God's help from this point forward. Invite Jesus to be the Lord, or Master of your life, and to direct your path ever forward in service to and in relationship with your Heavenly Father. If you have done this, your stock has just risen, so go public with your commitment to serve Jesus Christ. Let others know that you have made this commitment.[48]

Rest assured that if you declare with your mouth and believe in your heart that Jesus died for your sins, rose from the dead, and is now Lord of your life (Romans 10:9–13), then regardless of your past, you are in a right relationship with God from which nothing or no one can separate you (Romans 8:38–39). However, if you have already been born again into a new life in Jesus Christ but feel that you may need to hit refresh, then welcome to the club; I am a charter member. I try to repent, rinse, and repeat the above steps almost daily to cleanse sins and to rededicate myself to serving my Savior. When it comes to killing your old sinful self, let it RIP.

---

[48] Commitment is a key word. This is a life-altering decision to dedicate the rest of your life to serving and becoming more like Jesus Christ in pursuit of an ever-closer relationship with your Creator and Heavenly Father. Please read on into Part Two for thoughts about what comes next.

PART TWO
WHAT IS ~ STRONG FINISH

But all these things that I once thought very worthwhile—now I've thrown them all away so that I can put my trust and hope in Christ alone. Yes, everything else is worthless when compared with the priceless gain of knowing Christ Jesus my Lord. I have put aside all else, counting it worth less than nothing, in order that I can have Christ, and become one with him, no longer counting on being saved by being good enough or by obeying God's laws, but by trusting Christ to save me; for God's way of making us right with himself depends on faith—counting on Christ alone. Now I have given up everything else—I have found it to be the only way to really know Christ and to experience the mighty power that brought him back to life again, and to find out what it means to suffer and to die with him. So whatever it takes, I will be one who lives in the fresh newness of life of those who are alive from the dead.

I don't mean to say I am perfect. I haven't learned all I should even yet, but I keep working toward that day when I will finally be all that Christ saved me for and wants me to be.

No, dear brothers, I am still not all I should be, but I am bringing all my energies to bear on this one thing: Forgetting the past and looking forward to what lies ahead, I strain to reach the end of the race and receive the prize for which God is calling us up to heaven because of what Christ Jesus did for us. ~ Philippians 3:7–14 (TLB)

CHAPTER 23

LIGHTS! CAMERA! ACTION!

I believe that each of us plays a role in the greatest story ever told, and like most good stories, this one has a setting, a cast of characters, and an action-packed plot with a great love story to boot—something for everyone. Like many movies and even true-to-life stories that catch our attention, this drama is a rescue story of helpless victims in dire straits. Such stories draw us into empathizing with the plight of the victims, admiring the risk and sacrifice of the rescuers, and rejoicing in the second chance given to the people in peril. What is seldom given any attention, however, is what comes after the climactic rescue, and yet what really makes a rescue significant is that it provides a person with a renewed opportunity to live and to make an impact on the world.

I will use one reportedly true story to illustrate. Leif Olafson was a fisherman in Alaska. He was a good but not a godly man. One day, just like every day, he took his small boat out into the icy waters along the coast of Alaska to catch fish as doing so was his livelihood. He eventually hooked a big one, a grand king salmon, perhaps fifty pounds or more. After a couple hours of tiresome struggle, Leif landed the fish on the boat. This was when he noticed that his boat had drifted dangerously close to a large iceberg. He quickly moved to start the motor, but before he could move the boat out of harm's way, the iceberg shifted. A submerged portion of the iceberg rose above the water, leaving Leif and his boat dangling precariously thirty feet in the air. Any movement at all would likely dump Leif into the icy waters below.

Leif had no recourse but to hope for a rescue. In the evening, a mail plane flying over dipped its wings to signal that Leif's plight had been noticed, but Leif knew that it was too late in the day for rescue to come until morning. So, he settled in for a long, cold night. It was during this time that Leif began to reflect on the godly influences of his wife and mother as well as of the Sunday School lessons that he heard as a boy. In this time of great peril, the distractions of earthly living faded away, and the ultimate purpose of life became as clear to Leif as the star-studded heavens above. He called out to God, promising to serve Him if only God would deliver him from his perilous circumstances. In this instance, the God who can move heaven and earth moved an iceberg to capture a lost soul's attention. It might not have been apparent to Leif, but at the point of calling out to God, his salvation was accomplished even before his rescue ship came in. If you want to hear the rest of the story, I will not Leif, or I mean leave you hanging.

In the morning, a Coast Guard cutter came on the scene, but God was not finished with His role in the rescue. At this very moment, the iceberg miraculously shifted back to its original position, shooting the little boat and Leif back into the water, upright and unharmed. The Coast Guard captain who gave Leif a ride back to shore and safety exclaimed, "If I hadn't seen it myself, I wouldn't believe it." Leif had the first of many opportunities to share his new-found faith that day, and by all accounts Leif was thereafter known as a good and a godly man.[49]

Now that is reportedly the actual conclusion to this story, but let us consider for a moment an alternate ending as they sometimes do in the movies. What if Leif never shared or lived by his newfound faith? What if immediately upon disembarking from the Coast Guard cutter, full of faith and enthusiasm, Leif slipped on some ice, cracked his head open, and died before ever getting a chance to live a godly life. The physical rescue from the iceberg would certainly seem diminished in significance in the ultimate scheme of things if Leif did not have an opportunity to make good on his rescue.

The point that I would like to make is that the rescue is important,

---

[49] The source of this story is:
DeVern Fromke, *Life's Ultimate Privilege* (Indianapolis: Sure Foundation, Inc., 1986), 1-7.

especially to the individual involved, but it is what comes afterward that makes the deliverance from danger significant on a greater stage to a larger audience. I doubt that any of us would be entertained for long by a movie chronicling the routine, daily life of someone after a dramatic rescue.[50] In the movies, the rescue is usually the climax, but in a Christian's life, the adventure really begins after the deliverance. Salvation is not just an end, but it also a means to an even greater end. After the rescue comes the race, and it is the race that gives purpose to our lives (1 Corinthians 9:24–27).

I am probably one of the few people of my generation who never saw *Star Wars*, but even I know the memes, including the opening scroll that begins: "A long time ago in a galaxy far, far away." I think that Paul, as a "special agent" of Jesus Christ, describes a star search for a much more dramatic scene in the following select verses from Ephesians 1:4–22 (MSG):

> Long before he [God] laid down earth's foundations, he had us in mind, had settled on us as the focus of his love, to be made whole and holy by his love. Long, long ago he decided to adopt us into his family through Jesus Christ. (What pleasure he took in planning this!)[51] He wanted us to enter into the celebration of his lavish gift-giving by the hand of his beloved Son.
>
> Because of the sacrifice of the Messiah, his blood poured out on the altar of the Cross, we're a free people—free of penalties and punishments chalked up by all our misdeeds. And not just barely free, either. *Abundantly* free! He thought of everything, provided for everything we could possibly need, letting us in on the plans he took such delight in making. He set it all out before us in Christ, a long-range plan in which everything would be brought

---

[50] I have had occasion to watch a couple movies being filmed, and although there is a lot of glamour associated with movie stardom, the process of filming the same scenes over and over seemed downright boring and monotonous to me. Any given day in real-life service to the Creator of the Universe is potentially much more exciting and momentous than merely putting on an act.

[51] In other words, God is saying, "Look, I am your Father," and I would much rather hear this from God than Darth Vader.

together and summed up in him, everything in deepest heaven, everything on planet earth.

It's in Christ that we find out who we are and what we are living for. Long before we first heard of Christ and got our hopes up, he had his eye on us, had designs on us for glorious living, part of the overall purpose he is working out in everything and everyone. . . .

I ask—ask the God of our Master, Jesus Christ, the God of glory—to make you intelligent and discerning in knowing him personally, your eyes focused and clear, so that you can see exactly what it is he is calling you to do, grasp the immensity of this glorious way of life he has for Christians, oh, the utter extravagance of his work in us who trust him—endless energy, boundless strength!

All this energy issues from Christ: God raised him from death and set him on a throne in deep heaven, in charge of running the universe, everything from galaxies to governments, no name and no power exempt from his rule. And not just for the time being, but forever. He is in charge of it all, has the final word on everything.

Act two of our story offers a plot twist; the rescued become the rescuers, racing against time to save others from the dark side, which is destined for destruction. Hebrews 12:1–4 (MSG) offers us a peek at the director's notes for our story:

. . . we'd better get on with it. Strip down, start running—and never quit! No extra spiritual fat, no parasitic sins. Keep your eyes on Jesus, who both began and finished this race we're in. Study how he did it. Because he never lost sight of where he was headed—that exhilarating finish in and with God—he could put up with anything along the way: cross, shame, whatever. And now he's there, in the place of honor, right alongside God. When you find yourselves flagging in your faith, go over that story again, item by item, that long litany of hostility he plowed through. That will shoot adrenaline into your souls! In this all-out match against sin, others have suffered far worse than you, to say nothing of what Jesus went through—all that bloodshed!

The setting of a story includes time and place, and the setting of our story is, well, everywhere, and it encompasses all time—past, present, and future. The cast of characters includes everyone who ever lived, and some are protagonists while others are antagonists. You do not need to settle for a bit part, but you only get to be in a few scenes in the first installment of this dramatic story. You do get to decide whether you are cast as a hero or a villain in the greatest story ever told.

There may be some parallels between movies and God's plan for us, but the former inevitably involves dramatic license, while the latter presents us with a real choice with dramatic consequences. My word of the day app once delivered a doozy of a term that I may never have occasion to use other in this context. It seems that the ancient Geeks, I mean Greeks, needed a fancy word to describe the moment in a dramatic story when the protagonist suddenly recognizes another character's true identity, and the true reality of his own circumstances—hence the term anagnorisis.

God is neither a nag, nor is He one to refuse assistance in overcoming the Devil, who seeks to deceive and destroy us. God created us for the purpose of relationship with Him, yet sinfulness makes it impossible to realize our reason for being. The rescue provided by the death and resurrection of Jesus Christ gives us a second chance to choose to fulfill our purpose. Then our attention must turn to our second act, running the amazing race of living and serving like our leading man, Jesus Christ, until we finally finish in the lap of a loving God.

Many people try to run the race without first being rescued from the iceberg dead ahead. They try to be good, but they cannot be godly. Essentially, they are living on thin ice, frozen in place. Like Leif Olafson, they are unaware of their need to be rescued until God gets their attention. As Paul says in First Corinthians 9:26, they are running aimlessly, or fighting like a man beating the air, and such an act is not likely to score any box office hits.

On the other hand, some of those who have been rescued are so focused on the amazing grace that they are not running the amazing race. Jesus

Christ did not lay down his life to create a dramatic story. God's purpose for creating us was not just so that we could be rescued from the dark side. The rescue is an essential plot point to put us back on the path to fulfilling our original purpose—serving God and bringing the world's attention to Him.

The script of God's Word is ultimately not just about what God did for us, but also about what we are to do for Him. You can have a supporting role as a sidekick to Jesus Christ, the greatest action hero ever. He is fighting the Dark Invader in the most epic action-adventure of all time, an inspired true story of the battle between good and evil. The events depicted are true to life, and the stakes are eternal life or death. SPOILER ALERT! If you end up on the winning side, in the sequel to our story you become a sky walker in an eternal, recurring role (yes, with even greater longevity than the *Star Wars* franchise). And you thought your life was boring. It is "take two" of your life. The Force is with you. Get ready to play your part. You are a star in the scene now playing out. Steal the scene. Lights! Camera! Action!

CHAPTER 24

SECONDS COUNT

There is a tried-and-true formula for a great action-adventure story: people in danger, a hero who puts himself at risk, and a great rescue that gives people a chance to go on with their lives. Consider the story of Marine Sergeant Rafael Peralta. Sergeant Peralta was a Mexican immigrant who enlisted in the Marines on the day he received his green card. On November 15, 2004, he was a part of a squad going house-to-house trying to cleanse Fallujah, Iraq of terrorists. In one house that they entered, Sergeant Peralta was shot several times. His fellow Marines had to step over his injured body to confront the terrorists, one of whom released a grenade into the room. Sergeant Peralta gathered his remaining energy to grab the grenade and tuck it under his body where it exploded. In his last act of heroism, he saved the lives of several of his friends. One of them said, "We will never forget the second chance at life that Sergeant Peralta gave us."[52]

In the formulaic, Hollywood version of rescue dramas, it often seems like the people in need of help are not always the most receptive or cooperative. Many of them are obstinate and resistant to following the hero's direction.

---

[52] Based on original reporting in news sources such as:
Tony Perry and Richard Marosi, "A Hero's Courageous Sacrifice," *Los Angeles Times*, December 6, 2004, accessed 2020, https://www.latimes.com/archives/la-xpm-2004-dec-06-me-marine6-story.html.
Although some controversy as to the exact circumstances of Sergeant Peralta's death has arisen since I first prepared these remarks, his willingness to sacrifice himself for his adopted nation, for US, is undisputed.

Some may even be enthralled by the bad guys until they are convinced that there is a better way. There is usually at least one obnoxious individual in the mix who leads the resistance to the rescuer as the plot unfolds, making the rescuer's patient determination to help the undeserving seem even more noble and longsuffering. There are generally a few points in the plot at which the hapless victims question the ability of the rescuer to deliver them from their plight, and perhaps some bad decisions are thrown in to intensify the drama. Often the obnoxious resister in the group gets a chance at redemption, generally by self-sacrifice.

The Bible states that, while we were hopeless, and even still His enemies, God sent Jesus to die for our sins[53] at the perfect time so that we could have a second chance to live happily ever after (Romans 5:6–11). Fortunately for us, God rescues the needy, not the deserving. Once we have made the decision to break our allegiance to the forces leading us to destruction, the rescue will still need to play out through the rest of our earthly existence as the enemy will continually try to exploit our weaknesses to thwart our deliverance. Dumb decisions to resist the direction of our Rescuer will prolong the drama and interfere with us becoming a constructive part of the plot to redeem all of humanity. However, if we can endure opposition to the end (Matthew 24:13), then as the credits for our life roll, top billing will go to the One who gave us a second chance to live for Him, and seconds count.

---

[53] Call it the ultimate plot de-vice.

CHAPTER 25

THE CAT'S IN THE TOILET AND THE SHOWER SOON

Once upon a time I had a cat. I took her in as a kitten when her mother disappeared. She became my first, last, and only house pet. My mother called her Stormy because she was often like a tempest in a teapot. At nights she would sometimes calm down and snuggle up with me in bed. I think that one of the most relaxing experiences in life is to have a cat lying on your chest, purring to your heart's content.

In her waking hours, Stormy would often jump up on things, seeking the highest ground from which to survey her domain. One of her favorite perches was the toilet stool, or sometimes that was just a steppingstone to the vanity and beyond. Occasionally, she would not look before she leaped, and in a couple of instances, she did not notice that the toilet seat was up.

Now I know what you ladies are thinking. If you guys would just put the toilet seat down, then the world would be a better place for felines and females alike. Suffice it to say that there are certain times when it is completely impractical to have the toilet seat down. Of course, the greater trauma for both of us was yet to come, giving Stormy a bath. I think that bathing cats may have inspired the origin of the word catastrophe. A while back there was a popular essay attributed to Bud Herron entitled "Cat Bathing as a Martial Art." Here is some of the advice that he offers for bathing cats:

- Know that although the cat has the advantage of quickness and lack of concern for human life, you have the advantage of strength.

Capitalize on that advantage by selecting the battlefield. Don't try to bathe him in an open area where he can force you to chase him. Pick a very small bathroom. If your bathroom is more than four feet square, I recommend that you get in the tub with the cat and close the sliding-glass doors as if you were about to take a shower. (A simple shower curtain will not do. A berserk cat can shred a three-ply rubber shower curtain quicker than a politician can shift positions.)

- Know that a cat has claws and will not hesitate to remove all the skin from your body. Your advantage here is that you are smart and know how to dress to protect yourself. I recommend canvas overalls tucked into high-top construction boots, a pair of steel-mesh gloves, an army helmet, a hockey face mask, and a long-sleeve flak jacket.
- Prepare everything in advance. There is no time to go out for a towel when you have a cat digging a hole in your flak jacket.... Make sure the towel can be reached, even if you are lying on your back in the water. ...
- Once you are inside the bathroom, speed is essential to survival.... You have begun one of the wildest 45 seconds of your life. Cats have no handles. ...

I would say that this advice was offered tongue in cheek, but the cat probably had his tongue also. I have heard that there is a less traumatic way to give a cat a bath, but all that hair on your tongue would present its own problems. I remember briefly thinking upon each of Stormy's splashdowns in the toilet that she would never again be clean enough to be anywhere close to me, but after the bath, and as I recall a little bloodshed on my part, I had enough confidence in my cleansing ability to welcome her into my presence.

There was a popular folk song in the 1970s called "Cat's in the Cradle." Perhaps you have heard the lyrics that speak of the longing for relationship between a father and son through all the busyness of life:

And the cat's in the cradle and the silver spoon
Little boy blue and the man in the moon
"When you coming home, son?" "I don't know when"
But we'll get together then, dad
You know we'll have a good time then.[54]

I tried to write my own lyrics to this song from my life experiences, but since I have no children, the only line that I could come up with was, "and the cat's in the toilet and the shower soon." Like the father in the song, our Heavenly Father longs to spend time with us, but unlike the father lamenting lost opportunities to spend time with his son while he was growing up, our Heavenly Father is never too busy for us. He is fully satisfied with the cleansing we receive through the blood of Jesus Christ. Stormy eventually bit me and ran away, and I was not even trying to bathe her at the time. Hopefully, our longing to spend time with and to be like Jesus will never wane.

We have been, and occasionally may still be, contaminated creatures. Whether your life is in the toilet, or has merely absorbed some of the world's odor, every moment presents an opportunity to resolve to be more like Jesus. Satan was trying to give us a swirlie, but God plunged to our rescue. Rest assured that the blood of Jesus offers sufficient cleansing no matter how soiled your past—if you will only apply it to your life. The shedding of blood at the crucifixion that made us worthy of fellowship with our Creator happened long ago, but regular occasions of self-examination and cleansing are still warranted so that we can snuggle ever closer with our Savior.

---

[54] Harry Chapin, "Cat's in the Cradle," track 1 on *Verities & Balderdash*, Elektra, 1974.

CHAPTER 26

NEVER LEAVE HOME
WITHOUT HIM

Here is a saying that offers some good advice for life: "give credit to whom credit is due." I should note that I cannot take credit for being the first to say this. Our school administrators are understandably excited when the State awards the schools in our corporation "A" grades, which indicate that we are hitting our marks when it comes to educating our students. Such achievement reflects well on their leadership. As a social science teacher, I tend to take such recognition with a grain of salt. Significant though my efforts may be to our school's overall mission statement, I do not consider them to contribute greatly to meeting the specific criteria that determine our school grade.[55] For decades now, I have come to work every day just trying to do my best that day, and better than the day before—regardless of what recognition the powers that be give to our school, or to me. I figure that if I pat myself on the back when our school grade goes up, then I will also have to shoulder some of the responsibility when it goes down. And there are just too many variables in play that are beyond my control for me to assume too much responsibility for so much that happens, good or bad.

Our school once received recognition for being among the top schools in the State when it comes to the percentage of students earning dual credits, which allow students to receive both high school and college

---

[55] Math and English standardized test scores as well as graduation and attendance rates have generally been emphasized.

credit for courses that they take at our high school. Many of our students are graduating with enough credits to be college sophomores. When our school administrators announced that they would be taking a victory lap to Indianapolis to receive the award, I do remember a passing thought that this was made possible through the work of a few teachers who took a lot of extra graduate college courses to receive the dual credit instructor certification. Upon their return to our hallowed halls, our administrators were diligent to express their pleasure with the teachers who made the recognition possible, thus giving credit where credit is due.

I also remember a student popping into my classroom during a passing period wanting to know if I would answer a personal question. He said that he was trying to figure out what to do with his life. He observed that I seemed to enjoy my job more than most people that he knew, and he wondered how I came to do what I do. I gave him the best tick-tock for my career path that I could in a short timeframe. Then he said thank you, shook my hand, and was off to lunch. He was no sooner out the door than I realized that I was out-to-lunch when it came to explaining the fundamental reason for my career contentment. The most significant contributor to my passion for teaching is the meaning derived from the opportunities that it presents to serve Jesus Christ by serving others. So, note to self, the next time that I have a short time to answer a momentous question, do not bury the lead; give credit where credit is due.

No matter what occupies us, so much of what we do daily can lay the groundwork for opportunities to give credit to our Lord and Savior for what He is able to accomplish through our lives. God also offers dual credit for our efforts in His institution of higher yearning. Our sacrificial labors will be rewarded many times over, both in the present age (with some troubles) as well as in eternity with no troubles at all (Mark 10:29–30).

So far, I have referenced credit as acknowledgment of responsibility as well as recognition of educational attainment, so allow me to extend credit to one more definition. In my economics class, I emphasize the difference between using credit and investing. Credit in this context is using someone else's resources to meet our immediate wants and needs with a promise to repay them using our future resources. Investing, on the other hand, is not using our current resources for ourselves in the present, but rather offering them to others to use with reasonable assurance that they will be returned to us with interest in the future. One person's use of credit is another person's investment in the borrower's endeavors.

As sinners, we had no resources to satisfy our most fundamental need for the righteousness required to be in communion with our Creator, and unfortunately, we all had a horrible credit score. Titus 3:3–5 (NIV) says:

> At one time we too were foolish, disobedient, deceived and enslaved by all kinds of passions and pleasures. We lived in malice and envy, being hated and hating one another.[56] But when the kindness and love of God our Savior appeared, he saved us, not because of righteous things we had done, but because of his mercy. He saved us through the washing of rebirth and renewal by the Holy Spirit, whom he poured out on us generously through Jesus Christ our Savior, so that, having been justified by his grace, we might become heirs having the hope of eternal life.

Perhaps you have seen the bumper sticker that says, "Jesus is my copilot." Maybe a more apt description of our situation would be, "Jesus is my cosigner." And just like most cosigners, He had to make good on our debt. It is our faith in Jesus Christ that is credited to us as righteousness (Romans 4:4–5). Jesus freely and willingly invested His life in us knowing that we would never be able to fully repay Him—although we can make some humble down payments in the currency of sacrifice and service to others. Today, and every day, give credit to whom credit is due, Jesus. He extended His credit to us, thereby allowing us to obtain credit from God's Institution of Highest Learning toward receiving a Master's degree in Christlikeness. To appropriate an old marketing tagline for American Express credit cards, "Never leave home without Him."

---

[56] I suppose you could say that the only return on investment that we were yielding was double trouble.

CHAPTER 27

THE BATTLE OF
BENDED KNEE

Columbus Day, the commemoration of when Christopher Columbus first laid eyes on the New World, seems to be the Rodney Dangerfield of holidays; it just doesn't get any respect anymore. Perhaps this is due to political correctness run amuck, or maybe it reflects Western civilization's guilty conscience arising from the impact of European encroachment on Native American space. It seems that nowadays the holiday serves merely as an opportunity for a good sale. Perhaps even this association will fall into disrepute if it is ever deemed insensitive in light of all the bargains the palefaces got over the years by buying a whole lot of land from the Indians for a little bit of nothing.

By happenstance, one Columbus Day I found myself at the Wounded Knee Battlefield on a Native American reservation in South Dakota. The site is generally considered to be the location of the last battle of the Indian Wars, although it could more fittingly be described as a massacre site. As late as 1890, Native Americans were still being forced off their little remaining land to make room for the whites. Not surprisingly, the natives were getting restless as they were losing their way of life. Word began to spread of an Indian prophet who had a vision that the Christian Messiah, Jesus Christ, had come to Earth as an Indian who would restore native lands and remove the white people. A dance craze swept the Indian nations—a silent shuffle to a slow, single drumbeat that was supposed to bring back their dead to share in this pending peaceful existence, hence it was called the Ghost Dance.

The American government was worried that this was the beginning of another violent Indian uprising, so the 7th U.S. Cavalry was tasked with assuring that the Indians were kept in their place (yes, that same 7th U.S. Cavalry from Custer's famous last stand). Amid the tension, as the soldiers were trying to confiscate the weapons of the Indians gathered at Wounded Knee, shots of uncertain origin were fired. The cavalry unloaded a barrage of rifle and cannon fire that killed or wounded over two hundred native men, women, and children, most of whom were offering no resistance. Even most of the U.S. soldier casualties were likely the result of friendly fire.

I could not help but note the irony of standing on this site on Columbus Day as Native American children were approaching me with trinkets to sell to raise money for school pictures while a man claiming to be a direct descendent of one of the Ghost Dancer Indian chiefs was describing the Wounded Knee massacre to me and soliciting a donation to a Native American school that he ran. Because of sympathies for the large Indian population in the state, South Dakota does not even recognize Columbus Day; they call it Native American Day.

It is understandable to have mixed feelings about the events that transpired after Christopher Columbus first laid eyes on the New World on October 12, 1492, but perhaps Columbus Day should be celebrated for reasons other than merely as an opportunity for a good sale, or as a day off work, or yet another obscure date that people in my profession make students memorize. I believe that it was a part of God's plan to establish a new nation founded on religious freedom. Unfortunately, He only had at His disposal imperfect people who sometimes seemed determined to match the so-called "heathen savages" brutality for brutality. However, we do not need to ignore the bad things to appreciate the blessings that God had in store for all His children in the New World—red and yellow, black, and white.

Remember that Columbus Day is a prerequisite for virtually every secular holiday that we celebrate. Martin Luther King, Jr. Day, President's Day, Independence Day, Veterans Day, and even Thanksgiving Day would be nonexistent without the events set in motion when, "in fourteen hundred and ninety-two, Columbus sailed the ocean blue." Indeed, our very lives as we know them in the Western world would not exist.

October 12, 1492 set in motion events that would make possible the exodus of many of our ancestors from lands of religious oppression to a land of freedom. Columbus Day reminds me of another exodus to a land of freedom. The ancient Israelites were once in bondage in the land of Egypt. God instituted the Passover both to initiate and to commemorate His deliverance of His chosen people, as well as to reaffirm a covenant with them (Exodus 12:14). October 12, 1492 also set in motion the events that led to the Battle of Wounded Knee on December 29, 1890, when the United States Cavalry completely subdued the Native Americans and, sadly, virtually ended their way of life. In the wake of Columbus sailing the ocean blue in 1492, God's provision led to the founding of America the beautiful, a brotherhood of Native, Asian, African, and European-Americans from sea to shining sea. Columbus Day helped to determine the destiny of all Americans to live in the New World, not the Old.

One day a couple thousand years ago, Calvary came to our rescue and vanquished our savage sinfulness. The death of Jesus for the sins of humanity converted the Passover into the Lord's Supper and thereby transformed the Creator's limited Old Covenant relationship with humanity into an opportunity to discover a New Covenant with an unlimited horizon. God's grace made Jews and Gentiles alike citizens and heirs of His eternal kingdom.

One time a replica of one of Columbus's ships passed by our area. Some people like to re-enact history, but in reality, through our commemorations we live history. Past events shape our destiny, and all our present activities flow from what came before. We do not just remember the past; we participate in extending it into the future. Columbus Day celebrates the discovery of the New World that we inhabit. Every day we can celebrate new life through Jesus Christ who inhabits us. On bended knee we can prayerfully fight the good fight of faith and progress toward that glorious day when we lay eyes and feet on the New World that God is preparing for us.

CHAPTER 28
BE WHAT YOU ARE
CRACKED UP TO BE

The Liberty Bell, with its very prominent crack, has become an icon of American independence as well as of the freedoms enjoyed by the citizens of the United States of America. Throughout most of its existence, it has been on display in Philadelphia, hanging from its original yoke made of American Elm. It is a popular tourist attraction for freedom-loving people from everywhere.

The Liberty Bell was originally commissioned by and for the colony of Pennsylvania in 1751, perhaps to celebrate the 50th anniversary of the Charter of Privileges granted to Pennsylvania colonists. The Bell was forged in England but cracked on its first test ring. So, a couple American metalworkers melted the bell down, adjusted the composition of its metallic elements, and recast it into its present existence. The Bell weighs a little over one ton and was originally just known as the State House Bell since it was regularly rung to call colonial Pennsylvania legislators into session. Once the Pennsylvania State House became Independence Hall upon the birth of a new nation in 1776, the Bell's peel rang out to the Founding Fathers during the nation's formative years.

The historical record seems to indicate that the Bell did not have any obvious defects during its early days and did not become popularly known as the Liberty Bell until around the 1830s. Its new name was probably not so much a reference to American independence as to the growing movement to abolish slavery. Abolitionists found inspiration in the Bell's inscription, which quoted God's instructions to the Israelites in Leviticus 25:10 to: "Proclaim Liberty Throughout All the Land Unto All the Inhabitants thereof" to commemorate a "year of jubilee" every fifty years. This semicentennial event would be a time to free slaves and to return property pledged for debt.

No one seems to have recorded the actual date when a hairline crack formed in the Liberty Bell after decades of hard use, but it was probably in the 1830s or 40s. The very visible, nearly one-inch-wide crack that the Bell is known for today was intentionally created to preserve the tone of the Bell. That may not sound like a visually aesthetic fix, but remember that the Bell was intended to sit high atop a tower and to be heard and not seen. Alas, the repair job did not work. Another crack formed and the bell has been sound off ever since, other than from occasional gentle taps with a mallet to mark special events. No one alive today has ever heard the Liberty Bell ring freely with its clapper.

Throughout history and even into the modern day, some have suggested recasting the Liberty Bell to repair the crack, but most agree that such an effort would probably destroy its greater significance. After all, many bells are older, bigger, and ring louder and more mellifluously, but they are largely unheard of. Besides, reports from those who actually heard the bell ring in its pristine form, including those who commissioned its creation, did not find its E-flat ring very appealing, and the bell's tone apparently even became a town joke.

The value of the Liberty Bell is in its symbolic representation of the priceless freedoms offered by the United States of America despite its flaws. Christians have also been made free from sin through Jesus Christ, despite their lingering imperfections. Efforts to repair ourselves will fall flat, and even make things worse. Even though Jesus has introduced some new elements into our composition and recast us, we are still far from perfect form. Yet when we rise above our weaknesses through the power of Jesus Christ within us, then we demonstrate that He is the only source of perfection (2 Corinthians 12:9–10).

Freedom is not free. Satan once rang our bell, but Jesus has signed in His blood the declaration of our independence from sin. And when the Son of God has set you free, you are free indeed to be a part of the family of God

(John 8:35–36). Paul instructs us to stand firm in the freedom that Jesus Christ died to secure for us and to make sure that we do not allow ourselves to become burdened again by the yoke of slavery to sin (Galatians 5:1). We will be in eternity in no time flat, but for now Jesus sets the tone for how we live our lives. We are far from perfect, but the Spirit of the Lord within us has overcome the forces separating us from God and has placed us at liberty to demonstrate to others the prospects of redemption and relationship with our Creator (2 Corinthians 3:16–18).

Be what you are cracked up to be—the imperfect but improving visual representation of Jesus Christ on earth, yoked with the task of making His Word heard throughout the land. He is tuning you up and preparing you to ring out loud and clear a call to repentance and to the business at hand of helping to form God's new kingdom of Heaven and Earth (Revelation 21:1–7). Your life is cast to resonate with a proclamation to everyone for whom the name of Jesus Christ does not ring a bell that this is the year of the Lord's favor and of deliverance from the death toll of enslavement to sin (Luke 4:18–19).

CHAPTER 29

THE GOSPEL ADDRESS

President Abraham Lincoln certainly played a pivotal role in the elimination of the evil of slavery in the United States. He led our great nation through a civil war to preserve our Union against those fighting for the right to do wrong, to enslave other people. By April of 1865, the writing was on the wall, and the South knew that it was beat. In a desperate attempt to revive the Confederate cause, John Wilkes Booth tried to throw the victorious Union into disarray by taking out its leader. On Good Friday, President Lincoln attended a play with his wife. According to one account, his last words to her were a suggestion that they visit the Holy Land after his Presidency. "There is no place I so much desire to see as Jerusalem," he reportedly said moments before the fatal shot was fired.

Because he was killed for leading a fight against a great national sin, Abraham Lincoln has been described as our "Redeemer President." A freed slave was overheard saying at his funeral procession, "he died for us." His wife, Mary Todd Lincoln, called him "the immortal Savior and Martyr for Freedom."

Ok, maybe that is a little much. Lincoln's dead body was viewed by tens of thousands of people in the weeks before his burial. His body was moved 17 times until finding a permanent resting place. Five times his coffin was opened to make sure his body was still there. It was, every time. Lincoln may have defeated an insurrection, but resurrection was beyond his power. Today, the body of Abraham Lincoln is entombed under 10 feet of concrete, yet I have hope to meet him some day in the New Jerusalem that God has prepared for those who know Him.

The untimely demise of Abraham Lincoln presents some reminders of the immortal Savior and Martyr for freedom from sin, Jesus Christ. The crucifixion was a last-ditch effort by a defeated enemy to keep all of humanity in bondage by taking out its rightful Leader and thereby thwarting a union with the Creator. Jesus died for the cause of restoring our communion with God. Through His death and resurrection, at precisely the right time, Jesus proclaimed us emancipated from slavery to sin and death and issued the battle cry of freedmen. First Corinthians 7:22–23 (NLT) says: "And remember, if you were a slave when the Lord called you, you are now free in the Lord. And if you were free when the Lord called you, you are now a slave of Christ. God paid a high price for you, so don't be enslaved by the world."

In November of 1863, President Abraham Lincoln was invited to Gettysburg, Pennsylvania to say "a few appropriate remarks" for the dedication of a national cemetery for the fallen Union soldiers. I hope that President Lincoln would not mind if I appropriate a few of his remarks in dedication to our place of eternal rest. I will call it "The Gospel Address."

Two thousand and more years ago, our Father brought forth on this earth, a new nature, conceived in liberty from sin, and dedicated to the proposition that all men are created for communion with their Creator. Now we are engaged in a great struggle, testing whether I, or anyone so conceived and so dedicated, can endure to the end and be saved. We are met on a great battlefield of that struggle. We have come to dedicate our lives to Him who gave His life so that we may live. It is altogether fitting and proper that we should do this. But, in a larger sense, we cannot dedicate—we cannot consecrate—we cannot hallow this dust of the ground. The One who died and came to life again, who conquered sin and death, has consecrated it, far above our poor power to add or detract. The world will little note, nor understand what we say here, but we can never let it forget what He did here. It is for us with eternal life, rather, to be dedicated here to the work that He who died for us has thus far so nobly advanced. It is rather for us to be here dedicated to the great task remaining before us—that from His honored death we take increased devotion to that cause for which He gave the last full measure of devotion—that we here highly resolve that His death shall not be in vain—that the government shall be upon His shoulders, that human nature, under God, shall have a new birth of freedom—and that whosoever believeth in Him, shall not perish, but have eternal life.[57]

---

[57] The actual Gettysburg Address, delivered by Abraham Lincoln on November 19, 1863, reads as follows:

Fourscore and seven years ago our fathers brought forth on this continent a new nation, conceived in liberty and dedicated to the proposition that all men are created equal. Now we are engaged in a great civil war, testing whether that nation, or any nation so conceived and so dedicated, can long endure. We are met on a great battlefield of that war. We have come to dedicate a portion of that field as a final resting-place for those who here gave their lives that that nation might live. It is altogether fitting and proper that we should do this. But, in a larger sense, we cannot dedicate—we cannot consecrate—we cannot hallow—this ground. The brave men, living and dead, who struggled here have consecrated it, far above our poor power to add or detract. The world will little note, nor long remember what we say here, but it can never forget what they did here. It is for us the living, rather, to be dedicated here to the unfinished work which they who fought here have thus far so nobly advanced. It is rather for us to be here dedicated to the great task remaining before us—that from these honored dead we take increased devotion to that cause for which they gave the last full measure of devotion—that we here highly resolve that these dead shall not have died in vain—that this nation shall have a new birth of freedom and that government of the people, by the people, for the people, shall not perish from the earth.

CHAPTER 30

SLAVISH LIFESTYLE

Slavery was officially abolished in the United States after the Civil War, and legal rights for former slaves were established upon passage of the Thirteenth, Fourteenth, and Fifteenth Amendments to the United States Constitution. Yet slavery left a legacy that required decades of hard-fought social struggle to overcome, and its repercussions linger even into the present day. In some ways, it seems like slavery was our nation's original sin that has cursed the implementation of the inspired and ingenious government that our nation's founders designed to be based on the equality of all individuals, regardless of race, color, or creed. Christians have also been emancipated from slavery to sin through the redemption provided by the sacrifice of Jesus Christ. Better yet, Christians are adopted into the family of God, with the full rights of His children (John 8:34–36).

Civil liberties and civil rights are touchstones of the American experience and are ideally guaranteed for every citizen. We often use the terms civil liberties and civil rights interchangeably, but there is a meaningful distinction that demands our attention to protect both as our birthrights as American citizens. Both concepts are also critical to our citizenship in the kingdom of God.

Civil liberties are the protections that we enjoy from the government passing laws that place unreasonable limitations on our fundamental freedoms, such as the freedoms of speech and religion. As Christians, we have civil liberties too; we are set free from the law that demands perfection and that decrees death for our sinful behaviors. Romans 6:14 (NLT 1996) says: "Sin is no longer your master, for you are no longer subject to the law, which enslaves you to sin. Instead, you are free by God's grace."

Civil rights, on the other hand, refer to the obligations that the government has to us, such as guaranteeing the right to vote and assuring equal opportunity to succeed. Christians also have civil rights, including the rights to become children of God (John 1:12) and to eat and drink from God's bountiful provision (Luke 22:29–30).

Americans are rightfully attuned to both their civil liberties and civil rights, although perhaps sometimes at the expense of their civil responsibilities. One of the most destructive forces in our nation may be the demand for individual rights and freedoms without a sense of responsibility to accept restraints on behavior for the sake of others—or a willingness to accept responsibility for the consequences of mistakes. Instead, Americans may sometimes feel entitled to government intervention to compensate for their failures. And yes, Christians have civil responsibilities that we can tend to neglect. Our good lives, even in the face of unfair treatment, should silence critics. Although Christians are free from the consequences of sin, this freedom is not an excuse for doing wrong. Instead, Christians have a responsibility to live in obedience to God and thus to lead others to righteousness by following the example of Jesus Christ in showing integrity, love, and respect toward everyone—including people in authority over us, even when they do not deserve it (1 Peter 2:15–25).

Freedom is a wonderful concept, but it would seem to have its limits. We are not free from the consequences of our behaviors, for ourselves or for others. One of the polarizing issues of political science is whether it is the responsibility of government to protect us from our own self-destructive decisions, or rather to maximize individual freedom, even to the point of allowing people to act in "freedumb." In the ultimate scheme of things, our only true freedom may be choosing between righteousness or wretchedness, and whichever we choose will be our slave master. Our choice will lead to either holiness or helplessness—either to God's approval and presence in our lives or to separation from Him (Romans 6:6–23).

After the Civil War, some slaves chose to continue to serve their masters. This decision may have been in part due to their limited options, but sometimes it may have reflected either a degree of trust that their masters cared about them, or a lack of trust in their own ability to fend for themselves in a world that could still be very dark and cruel. Slavery and its successors of racial segregation and discrimination have been largely eradicated in our nation, thanks in part to civil rights leaders like Martin Luther King, Jr., who advocated for nonviolent and patient persistence in demanding full equality. King became a martyr for the cause of civil rights. He truly made very noteworthy contributions to and sacrifices for this nation, but just like the rest of us, he was a flawed human being.

Jesus Christ, however, was the perfect sacrifice for our sins, and by giving His life for us, He set us free from the power of sin to control our lives. Whereas before salvation we had no choice but to be enslaved to sin, we now get to choose our master. The deed that Jesus did on the cross set Christians free indeed (John 8:36), but the deeds that we choose to do will reflect whose property we are. Although our freedom from sin is bought and paid for, there is still an effort required on our part to preserve our spiritual freedom. Second Peter 2:19–20 (NLT 1996) states: "… For you are a slave to whatever controls you. And when people escape from the wicked ways of the world by learning about our Lord and Savior Jesus Christ and then get tangled up with sin and become its slave again, they are worse off than before."

Freedom from domination by other people is a cause worth fighting for, and even dying for. Freedom from service to our Creator is only the freedom to pursue self-destruction. We are free in our deeds but responsible for the consequences. You have no doubt heard about the Underground Railroad that helped slaves escape to freedom; well, if we press for the right to run our own railroad, then it will no doubt be underground, because we will run it right into the ground.

A choice between slavery and, well slavery, might not seem like much of a choice, but only through slavish obedience to our Lord and Savior, Jesus Christ, will we be free to fulfill the purpose for which we were created (Romans 6:16–23). Our fundamental right is the right to be righteous, which allows us to be in relationship with a Master who knows our needs even before we do and who longs to take care of them, with a Master who is a loving Heavenly Father rather than a slave driver, with a Master who also serves us, and with a Master who submitted Himself to be beaten and to die in our place just so that we could live with Him forever. Enslaved to sin or saved from sin—the choice is ours. I choose the abundance of living the slavish lifestyle of service to the Master of the universe.

CHAPTER 31

THIS IS WHY WE CAN HAVE NICE THINGS

There is probably always a reason for everything that we do, no matter how seemingly trivial and insignificant. Earlier, I explained why I was writing this book. There are reasons why you are reading it; perhaps you are battling insomnia. I often watch what other people do and ask, "why?"—like watching virtually anything on daytime TV and "reality shows," or paying attention to celebrities, athletes, or the "cultural influencers" on social media. I am sure that I give occasion to others to question why I do what I do. The motives for many behaviors may be mysterious or misunderstood, even to the person doing them, but this does not mean that underlying motives are not present. Whether our motives are noble, ignoble, or inconsequential, most everything that we do is for a reason rather than at random.

Motivations generally fall into the categories of push factors or pull factors. Push factors originate from those things that we want to leave behind, like changing jobs because of a cantankerous boss. Pull factors arise from those things that we are seeking, like a higher paying or more satisfying job. We can also pursue relationships to avoid loneliness or to contribute toward someone else's happiness. I am far from qualified to speak about such things, but perhaps the problem with many people's love life is that they love their own life more than that of their partner.

Spiritual motivations include push and pull factors as well. We may want to escape a momentarily gratifying, yet destructive sinful lifestyle in order to embrace a more purposeful existence. We may want to avoid punishment, or to pursue the unimaginable pleasures eventually awaiting those who serve God. Just like anyone else in a personal relationship, God wants us to want a relationship with Him, and He created us with the free will to choose our daily motivation and our destiny.

Why ask why? Routinely examining our thoughts and intents, or better yet, letting God evaluate them and instruct us accordingly, will determine the motivating force for our time-limited lives (Psalm 26:2). Are we seeking to make our own way in the world, or to follow God's way? Giving attention to the needs and wants of ourselves and our families is a necessary part of human existence, but is the driving force or our lives self-gratification or fulfilling our divine destiny? For many, maybe most people, it would seem that life is consumed with pursuing personal satisfaction. Someone once said Confucius-style, "He who thinks himself number one thinks of next to nothing" (which parallels Galatians 6:3 nicely[58]). I would add that living for oneself is a lost cause.

The Bible would advise a more eternity-encompassing focus. In Matthew 16:24–27 (NIV), Jesus told His disciples that:

> Whoever wants to be my disciple must deny themselves and take up their cross and follow me. For whoever wants to save their life will lose it, but whoever loses their life for me will find it. What good will it be for someone to gain the whole world, yet forfeit their soul? Or what can anyone give in exchange for their soul? For the Son of Man is going to come in his Father's glory with his angels, and then he will reward each person according to what they have done.

Jim Elliot, a Christian missionary, said: "He is no fool who gives up what he cannot keep to gain what he cannot lose." Elliot was later killed in Ecuador by members of a native tribe to whom he was attempting to introduce the Gospel, but many of those natives eventually came to accept Jesus Christ as their Savior and Lord. If there is nothing worth dying for,

---

[58] Galatians 6:3 (NIV) says: "If anyone thinks they are something when they are not, they deceive themselves."

then maybe there is nothing worth living for—and dying for something is better than living for nothing. Perhaps our to do list should take second place to our "to die" list, the self-sacrifices that we are willing to make in service to God and people.[59] This may include a bucket list of those to whom we want to introduce the Gospel before they kick the bucket. Be the cultural influencer introducing people to the greatest celebrity of all time, Jesus Christ. WARNING: Some sacrifice of our immediate gratification is required, but Jesus set the example by laying down His life for us. Dying to follow Christ is an out of this world motivation. By dying vicariously through Jesus, we can live victoriously. After all, it is only because of Him that we can have the nicest of things.

---

[59] Doug Redford, "Mission Accomplished," *Christian Standard*, Christian Standard Media, February 10, 2017, https://christianstandard.com/2017/02/mission-accomplished.

CHAPTER 32

JOBS FOR LIFE

Steve Jobs was one of the greatest technology and business leaders of the 20th and 21st centuries. His life and philosophy left a provocative legacy. An article in *The Wall Street Journal* by Andy Crouch described Jobs as "a secular prophet" who presented the hope that "technology promises to relieve us of the burden of being finite creatures in a harsh and unyielding world."[60] In fact, the original Apple logo of a rainbow-colored apple with a bite out of it is perceived by some as symbolic of the promise of technology to save humanity from the curse earned in the Garden of Eden. From what I can ascertain, the creator of the logo had no such symbolism in mind. He chose an apple because, well the company was called Apple, the rainbow showed the color capability of the product, and the bite offered size perspective so that people did not mistake it for a cherry. So I suppose Christians can partake of Apple products without committing sacrilege.

Crouch asserts that hope is the oxygen of human societies, and he references an adage that "human beings can live for 40 days without food, four days without water, and four minutes without air. But we cannot live for four seconds without hope." Here is the version of hope offered by Steve Jobs in an address to Stanford University graduates on June 12, 2005:

---

[60] Background for this chapter came from:
Andy Crouch, "The Secular Prophet," *The Wall Street Journal*, October 8, 2011.

No one wants to die. Even people who want to go to heaven don't want to die to get there. And yet death is the destination we all share. No one has ever escaped it. And that is as it should be, because Death is very likely the single best invention of Life. It is Life's change agent. It clears out the old to make way for the new. Right now the new is you, but someday not too long from now, you will gradually become the old and be cleared away.

The world view of Steve Jobs was informed by a career in which the latest technology is being replaced at lighting speed by the new and vastly improved. From his perspective, the fate of individuals is to be discarded like an "old" iPhone rendered obsolete by a fifth generation model in four years. I prefer the biblical perspective presented in First Corinthians 15:19–20 and continued in verses 54–57 (NLT 1996). Here Paul agrees that we all face death, but he adds that, in God's operating system, death presents the ultimate upgrade:

And if we have hope in Christ only for this life, we are the most miserable people in the world. But the fact is that Christ has been raised from the dead. He has become the first of a great harvest of those who will be raised to life again. . . .

When this happens—when our perishable earthly bodies have been transformed into heavenly bodies that will never die—then at last the Scriptures will come true: "Death is swallowed up in victory. O death, where is your victory? O death, where is your sting?" For sin is the sting that results in death, and the law gives sin its power. How we thank God, who gives us victory over sin and death through Jesus Christ our Lord!

Mr. Jobs was a Zen Buddhist who believed that this life is all there is for us, and that there is no source of hope outside of ourselves or what our knowledge can produce. His conclusion for the Stanford graduates was:

"Your time is limited, so don't waste it living someone else's life." Mr. Jobs had a lot of faith in knowledge to make our daily existence better, but he had no hope for any meaning for his life other than perhaps, as he put it, to "put a ding in the universe." In the Garden of Eden, Adam's appetite for knowledge cost him, and all of us, access to the tree of life. Through the death and resurrection of Jesus Christ, sinners get another "bite at the apple" representing the knowledge of good and evil, and this apple today keeps the sting of death away—if we choose to run God's program for our lives. With all due respect to Mr. Jobs's faith in pursuing "bytes at the apple," I propose that the greatest waste of human life is to miss the opportunity to live for Jesus Christ and thus to reign with the King of the Universe forever (2 Timothy 2:11–12).

Comparing the sacred and the secular perspectives on existence is like comparing apples and orangutans—both can be found in trees, but one is fruit and the other eats fruit. We have heard the gospel according to Steve Jobs, but my hope is in the Gospel according to Job 19:25–26 (NLT 1996) which says, "But as for me, I know that my Redeemer lives, and that he will stand upon the earth at last. And after my body has decayed, yet in my body I will see God!" We have a job for life, and beyond.

CHAPTER 33

TAKE THIS JOB AND LOVE IT

For most Americans, it seems like their occupation comprises much of their identity. Young people are asked ad nauseam some version of the question: "So what do you want to be when you grow up?" The implication is that we are defined by our career. When we meet someone for the first time, one of our leading questions is likely to be, "so what do you do for a living?" Before the age of fifty, a typical American might spend over 56,000 hours working full time. Obviously, there is danger for Christians to become so wrapped up in what they do, that they forget whom they serve. The challenge for Christians is to make what they do for a living a reflection of their reason for living.

No doubt many Americans have a preoccupation with occupation as a means to accumulate wealth, power, and prestige. For those so motivated, I recommend careful consideration of Ecclesiastes 2:21–26 (NLT 1996), which states:

> For though I do my work with wisdom, knowledge, and skill, I must leave everything I gain to people who haven't worked to earn it. This is not only foolish but highly unfair. So what do people get for all their hard work? Their days of labor are filled with pain and grief; even at night they cannot rest. It is all utterly meaningless. So I decided there is nothing better than to enjoy food and drink and to find satisfaction in work. Then I realized that this pleasure is

from the hand of God. For who can eat or enjoy anything apart from him? God gives wisdom, knowledge, and joy to those who please him. . . .

At every stage of our lives, ultimate meaning only comes through laboring for God's kingdom, and any other activity is just marking time without leaving a mark. A theme Scripture for my life is Colossians 3:23–24 (NLT 1996): "Work hard and cheerfully at whatever you do, as though you were working for the Lord rather than for people. Remember that the Lord will give you an inheritance as your reward, and the Master you are serving is Christ." These verses are apropos to every period and endeavor of our lives, whether we are a child, a parent, a student, an employee, an employer, or even a retiree. This Scripture likely does its best work when it inspires us to give our best effort toward those responsibilities that we find least desirable.

On many occasions when I am going above and beyond the call of duty to my career, I try to evaluate my motivations to make sure that my due diligence to my job is not a distraction from my reasonable service to my Lord. I volunteered to be a representative of our school on the governing board of a consortium of schools and was asked to be the secretary. Although I find preparing the minutes of each meeting to be a tedious task and a distraction from other things that I would rather do, for over twenty years now I have tried to be as diligent and dependable as possible in my service as secretary. I have occasionally received some compliments on my efforts, including one e-mail that the consultant for our consortium sent out to all members making some very flattering remarks. I appreciated the feedback that colleagues were pleased with my performance, but I felt uncomfortable receiving the praise of people. Although minutes count, the true reason for my dedicated effort was to please God, and I felt that perhaps I should use such recognition as an opportunity to bring attention to my Role Model.

I decided to "reply to all" of the e-mail recipients with a brief statement that I was just trying to be a Christ-like servant. I do not know what most of the recipients thought, but I did receive one reply from a colleague that said, "nice testimony through your actions, brother." I did not know before that this person was a brother in the family of God, but it did not surprise me because of the work ethic and character that I had observed in him.

No matter how important our job might seem to be, its temporal impact will likely fade relatively soon, and no doubt any number of people could, and one eventually will, replace us. No matter how menial our job may seem to us, it takes on exemplary eternal value when it is done for God. I cannot think of any better attitude to bring satisfaction to our job than recognizing that our employer is God, our paycheck is our reward in Heaven, and our retirement plan is eternal life.

I cannot promise that this attitude will prevent workplace frustrations, but I do propose that it will help to keep them in perspective. I read a story about an airline worker whose job was to address the concerns of passengers during a long flight delay. As the delay grew longer, the passengers became angrier. One observer marveled at how the employee was able to remain so kind and patient with all of the irate passengers. When the passengers were at long last boarding, the observer asked the airline employee for her name so that he could write a letter of commendation to the airline. "Oh, I don't work for this airline," she replied. "I work for Jesus Christ."

Indeed, Jesus Christ provides the inspirational example for us to follow in navigating the amazing rat race from start to finish. No one has ever tackled a tougher job with better endurance and attitude despite all the horrible things that people said about Him and did to Him. He was even willing to lay down His life on a shameful cross because He knew what joy would follow for both Him and for us (Hebrews 12:1–4).

Working for Jesus Christ provides the most gainful employment possible. One of my previous bosses once told me that whenever someone from work called his cell phone, his designated ring tone was the tune "Take This Job and Shove It." When my Heavenly Boss calls me to service, even if it involves sacrifice and suffering, I want my tune to be the same as His tone when I call upon Him. Take this job and live it. Take this job and love it.

CHAPTER 34

WILL WORK FOR FOOD

If you are like me, you think a lot about food. I think about food when I get up in the morning. I think about food throughout the day in anticipation of the evening meal when I will at last reward myself for a hard day's work with a microwave masterpiece. I suspect that I am not alone in my food infatuation given how much calories count in our culture. God also serves up many scriptural references to food as spiritual appetizers.

The Old Testament tells of the strict dietary laws that God set for the Jewish people at a certain time and place in their existence as a group of people set apart by God to call the attention of the rest of the world to the God of Creation. Animals were classified as either clean for eating, like oxen and sheep, or unclean and not to be eaten, like pigs and shellfish. The New Testament seems to make it rather clear that the sacrifice of Jesus for our sins made such dietary restrictions unnecessary. As I once heard someone say, Jesus really saved our bacon, in more ways than one.

The Book of Acts tells the story of Peter, a disciple of Jesus who was hanging out on the roof of a house in the town of Joppa on the shore of the Mediterranean Sea one day around lunchtime. Peter was praying and feeling hungry when God presented him with a takeout menu of sorts in the form of a vision of a bunch of unclean animals being lowered from the sky on a large sheet. A voice told him to kill and eat them (probably history's first serving of pigs in a blanket). When Peter objected on the grounds that he had never before eaten unclean animals, the voice instructed him that He should not consider as unclean what God had declared to be clean. This was the beginning of the "see food diet" for Christians—as in see food and eat it. More significantly, the point of the story is that God was calling Peter to take the Gospel message, the good news of salvation through Jesus Christ, to "unclean" Gentiles—the non-Jewish people of the world (Acts 10:9–15).

I am not much into historical reenactment, but I inadvertently recreated this scene to a certain extent during a trip to Israel. After a kosher (prepared according to Jewish dietary laws) breakfast at my hotel in Tel Aviv, only about two miles from where Peter saw his dream food, I went up to the rooftop lounge area to plan my day's explorations. I first read through the Bible passages set in Joppa, and with this food for thought, I also found myself dreaming about bacon.

You have probably heard the saying, "you are what you eat." Our bodies are literally formed from the nutrients that we ingest in our food and drink, which basically replenish the dust of the ground from which God made us. As I was chewing on this thought, I was reminded of a book I bought years ago for geography students to use as a reference in preparing food projects from different cultures. I stopped assigning those because I was gaining too much weight. However, I was inspired to dig into my classroom closet and dust off this book by Thelma Barer-Stein that is titled *You Eat What You Are*. The author's thesis is: "What we select to eat, how we prepare it, serve it and even how we eat it are all factors profoundly touched by our individual cultural inheritance." She proposes that food provides more than sustenance for us. It is also a source of pleasure, comfort, and security as well as a symbol of hospitality, social status, and religious significance. She states that "certain foods are given symbolic and even transformative connotations, and there is still no shortage of publications promising that a 'magic food' will alleviate pain . . . and promise almost everything but life after death."[61]

If we are followers of Jesus Christ, we are people on the move. I was struck by the spiritual parallels with another comment in *You Eat What You Are*. The author states that "migration to find food results in the necessity of relinquishing customary tastes according to what foods, seasonings, and even cooking methods are available . . . in the new location."[62] Before our

---

[61] Thelma Barer-Stein, *You Eat what You are: People, Culture and Food Traditions* (Buffalo: Firefly Books, 1999), 14.
[62] Ibid.

salvation, we sought to satisfy our worldly, sinful appetites. As immigrants to the kingdom of God, we are filled by hungering and thirsting for righteousness (Matthew 5:6).

Whereas natural food reflects cultural diversity, Christians all share the same food, doing the work that God has called them to do. Jesus told His disciples that His nourishment came from doing the will of God who sent Him to finish God's redemptive work for humanity (John 4:31–34). Jesus set the table for us when He told us to turn from our selfish ways, take up our cross daily, and follow Him (Luke 9:23). One of the most familiar and frequently recited passages of Scripture is the Lord's prayer (Matthew 6:9–13). "Give us this day our daily bread" is usually presumed to be a request for divine provision of the food that we need to keep our physical bodies functioning, but perhaps this portion of the prayer is also to be offered as a request to nourish our spirit through our daily work assignment to help in the harvesting of souls for the kingdom of God. I suppose you could call this "soul food."

African slaves in the United States were often only provided with the cheapest, least desirable, cast off food that other people did not want. The slaves had to learn creative ways to prepare these leftovers with whatever resources they could scrounge up. This was the origin of soul food, which can be described as humble food prepared with imagination. That sounds kind of like Christians—people who are often despised and cast off by the world, but who, through the imagination of God, expose how insignificant is that which the world considers important (1 Corinthians 1:27–28).

I read an account of a man introducing himself as a Christian in a conversation with a Hindu. The Hindu responded, "I know Christians. You are the people who swallow God."[63] He was probably making an association with the Communion sacrament, apparently with limited understanding of what it means. But maybe at some level he was about right. Christians are those who can swallow the foolish-to-the-world concept that the Author and Creator of the Universe desires a personal relationship with each of us.

Natural food both regenerates and energizes our physical bodies for a relatively brief time, but the nourishment provided by doing the will of God

---

[63] Robert Benson, *That We May Perfectly Love Thee: Preparing Our Hearts for Holy Communion* (Nashville: Upper Room Books, 2011), 59.

actually prepares us for life after death. We are what we eat; Christians have partaken of the Bread of Life and have become the body of Christ. We eat what we are; Christians nourish themselves by becoming more like Jesus. What we consume, consumes us. The will of our Father is for us to serve the Bread of Life, Jesus, to those who are starving for salvation (John 6:33–40). If you are waiting for a sign from Heaven, here it is: "Will work for food."

CHAPTER 35

FEEL THE BURN

I am rather a local fixture when it comes to riding my bicycle for exercise on county roads when weather permits. To keep in shape during the not-so-nice weather, I invested in an elliptical machine, which is kind of like a walking bicycle. It will schedule a walk or run for me anywhere in the world, or it will let me map out my own. It will then show pictures of what I would actually see if setting foot there. I have been using it relatively faithfully, although some may think that I am just spinning my heels.

I am pleased that I have been able to walk or to jog at least as far and as fast now as ever before in my life, but I have been a little disappointed in how increasingly difficult it has become to take off the seemingly inevitable winter weight gain. Perhaps I will have to schedule a walk around Jericho to have such a breakthrough (see Hebrews 11:30). The formula for weight loss is simple: burn more calories than you consume. Unfortunately, we just don't burn as many calories as we get older. I read that metabolism begins to slow down in our twenties. I suppose that could be good in that, as people get older, they do not have to work as hard to get food since they do not require as much. But I like food, and I do not want to eat less at any age. Hence my many hours on the elliptical machine going nowhere fast.

My exercise efforts have given me reason to think about metabolism, which can be defined as the life-sustaining cellular transformation of food or fuel into energy and into the substances that our bodies are made of—all while eliminating waste products. Metabolism is essential for organisms to grow, to reproduce, to maintain structure, and to react to their environments.

There are actually two types of metabolism. One involves breaking down substances, such as fats and carbohydrates, to produce energy, and the other uses energy to build up substances, such as the proteins of which our bodies are made. Interestingly, substances that can be metabolized for nutrition in some organisms can be poisonous to others.

We have a spiritual metabolism as well; what we fill our soul and spirit with provides us with energy to sustain ourselves. Once while Jesus's disciples were on a food run to get some physical nourishment, He had an opportunity to minister to a woman enmeshed in a hopeless, sinful lifestyle. When His disciples returned and encouraged Him to eat something, Jesus replied that He had food that they did not know about. Confused, His disciples wondered if someone else had brought Him food. Perhaps He had a pizza delivered from Little Caesars. Jesus explained that His food was to do the will of God and to complete the work of delivering people from their sinfulness, one soul at a time (John 4:32–34).

Our spiritual metabolism is the process by which consuming God's will for our lives sustains us by generating the energy that we need to grow in our relationship with Jesus Christ, to reproduce by sharing our faith with others, to maintain our part in the body of Christ, and to serve those around us. Our spiritual metabolism is also a two-way process. As we consume the Word of God (Matthew 4:4), we obtain energy to build our spiritual lives in the body of Christ while expelling our old sinful nature. Romans 6:19 says that if we present our bodies as slaves to righteousness, then we will purge impurities that separate us from God. The people of the world may seem to be having a good run sustaining themselves with the lust of the eyes and of the flesh and the pride of life, but the empty calories of such junk food is all passing. What the world offers may taste great, but it is less fulfilling—and the aftertaste will eventually sour you on life. Yet those who are energized by doing the will of God will enjoy the sweetness of life with God forever (I John 2:15–17).

Consuming the will of God is a meal designed for losing weight. Binging on the will of God allows us to purge the weight of sin from our lives, and the burden God offers is much lighter (Matthew 11:28–30). To paraphrase an old Doritos slogan, eat all you want, God will make more opportunities to serve Him. In the natural world, food is burned through exercise, but in serving Jesus Christ, spiritual exercise is food. We have the opportunity to schedule walks with Jesus, and the scenery can be heavenly. Feel the burn of running toward the prize of the high calling of Heaven (Philippians 3:14). If you run the other direction, the burn you feel will cause you to lose a lot more than weight.

CHAPTER 36

FOOD FIGHT!

Sometimes it seems that Thanksgiving celebrations in our culture are all about food without reflection on the provision required to set the table for such feasting, but food is seldom provided without sacrifice. Our physical nourishment often requires the death of other living organisms. In some primitive cultures, people expressed remorse to creatures that they killed for food. Because they did not have the revealed truth of God's word, they likely did not understand the connection between sin and death, but they instinctively understood and regretted that some things must die so that others may live.

The ability to give thanks for provision is something that separates us from animals. Now I do not want to poke at anyone's pet peeves, but I doubt that any animals gracing your household are able to feel gratitude for the provision made for them. And if you are absolutely convinced that those puppy dog eyes reflect deep thankfulness for filling their bellies, then perhaps you will at least grant me this: your pets probably cannot appreciate that their sustenance came at a cost to you. When we partake of God's bountiful provision for our physical and spiritual needs without thankfulness, we fall short of being the distinctive creation that He intended for us to be. As Romans 1:21 (NIV) says, "For although they knew God, they neither glorified him as God nor gave thanks to him, but their thinking became futile and their foolish hearts were darkened."

Whenever we pig out on food for our physical sustenance, it is good to remind ourselves of the sacrifices required to satisfy our appetite. Every time we sustain ourselves through the death of another organism, we can be thankful for God's physical provision as well as for His spiritual provision through the death of Jesus Christ. That is why praying over a meal is often called "returning thanks" or "saying grace."

So, if you occasionally feel a little guilty about all the food that you consume, I can at least offer you this absolution—feasting is described in the Bible as a divinely ordained means of showing thankfulness for God's provision for all our needs from His abundant riches (Philippians 4:19). Here is some food for thought: in the food fight for physical survival, you won, and your food lost. When our spiritual food is doing the Lord's work, we help to generate new life; we become much needed harvesters reaping souls to join us in the kingdom of God (Matthew 9:37–38).

CHAPTER 37

THE GOOD TASTE OF DEATH

Christianity, more so than many religions, emphasizes proclamation—telling others what we believe and why we believe it. It is worthwhile to contemplate the content of what Christians are to proclaim. The Gospel, or Good News, tells of the life, death, and resurrection of the Savior of humanity, Jesus Christ. Surprisingly, the Gospel puts a lot of emphasis on the death of our Savior, even though, as Paul noted, preaching Christ crucified can seem offensive and foolish to those who do not understand (1 Corinthians 1:22–31).

Preaching about pain, suffering, and death is not exactly something that people are dying to hear. It can even repel some people from the Faith. In our society, we go to great lengths to prolong our lives and to distract ourselves from the inevitability of death, but we should avoid the temptation to downplay sacrifice and death in order to make the proclamation of the Gospel more palatable for people to swallow. It is easy to tell people how much God can do for them if they only believe; it is another matter to tell them that truly serving God means that they must also die to their own desires. However, a conversion to Jesus Christ that is grounded in this reality is much more likely to endure the inevitable challenges to the faith required for lifelong relationship with God.

One reason why we find death to be such a downer is that we perceive it as loss. However, the death that the Gospel presents is not a net loss, but rather an exchange—an exchange of what we cannot keep for something of infinitely greater value that we cannot lose. For most Christians, the path before them does not lead to literal martyrdom, just to the death of sinful, selfish desires. Jesus died and then was resurrected for a time back into this world in a bodily form before He ascended to Heaven. Similarly, after we accept Jesus Christ as Savior and crucify our old, sinful self, we experience a spiritual resurrection of sorts within a continuing physical existence. During our remaining days left in the dust that shapes our earthly lives, we can proclaim to others the blessed hope of renewed relationship with God (Titus 2:13) before we take up permanent residence in Heaven in a new and improved form.

Although we can know that physical death merely anticipates resurrection into eternal life, until we actually die a physical death, we cannot experience what it is like to get up on the other side of dead. Even for those of us who do not fear death because of our assurance of eternal life, we probably are not dying to experience the process of dying. Yet only upon the pronouncement of death can we say goodbye to all pain and suffering and hear the welcome to Heaven. Dying to self is a lifelong process, but the slower the gasps of our sinful self, the deeper our breath of Heaven—and the more fulfilling the rewards of living for Jesus Christ.

There is nothing like the prospect of death to encourage us to evaluate ourselves. Evangelistic ministers find funerals to be an excellent occasion to encourage mourners to reflect upon their own eternal destiny. As I watched my grandparents grow old in their physical bodies and approach their eternal reward, I observed them becoming more comfortable with the prospect of death. They became increasingly exposed to it through the deaths of their loved ones and friends. It may at times have seemed to them as if they knew more people who were already dead than still alive. Perhaps one reason that God allows us to experience the ravages of aging, if we are so fortunate to live to a ripe old age, is so that we can more easily let go of our inevitably rotting bodies and take hold of the fruit of the Tree of Life, which offers pure sweetness with no sourness or bitterness. We are following Jesus Christ, who took the bite out of death by blazing the trail from physical death to eternal life so that we can enjoy the good taste of death (Hebrews 2:9–10).

CHAPTER 38
SPITTING IMAGE

One summer I made my first venture off the North American continent to help tend to a friend recovering from surgery near the picturesque city of Bremen, Germany. With minimal mastery of the German language, and with little knowledge of how to get around in Germany, but with a lot of chutzpah, I set off on my first intercontinental adventure. A plane, a few trains and buses, and finally a walk of a couple miles brought me to my friend's hospital bedside. When I could get away from my caretaking duties, I would venture out on the town to see the sites.

One of Bremen's most famous associations is with a story from *Grimm's Fairy Tales* about a rooster, a cat, a dog, and a donkey—all past their prime and about to be disposed of by their human masters. To avoid this fate, the dog hops on the back of the donkey, the cat jumps on the back of the dog, and the rooster perches on top of the cat—then off they go together on the road to Bremen to become the town musicians. I am not sure why Bremen claims these critters since, according to the story, the animals end up chasing human robbers out of a house along the way and living there happily ever after without ever even reaching the city. Nonetheless, statues of these town musician wannabes are an easy find for tourists. More obscure is a Bremen landmark called the *spuckstein,* or the spitting stone.

Town Musicians of Bremen (Photo by author)

As the presumably true story goes, in the early 1800s, Gesche Gottfried became known as the "angel of Bremen" due to her diligent care for several of her friends and family as they died slow and agonizing deaths. Eventually, people realized that she was in fact responsible for the deaths of at least fifteen of these poor souls by slowly poisoning them with arsenic. In 1831, Ms. Gottfried earned the dubious distinction of becoming the last person publicly executed in Bremen. According to legend, the cobblestones where her head was chopped off, or where her head quit rolling after it was chopped off (depending on which version you believe) were replaced with a stone marked with a cross. To this day, locals and tourists in the know will manifest their disgust by spitting on the spot.

Because of my morbid curiosity, finding the spitting stone was near the top of my must-see list, but that was easier said than done since much of the downtown is paved with cobblestones. After two failed attempts to see the stone, and with little time before my scheduled departure from the city, my third sortie was a success. Lo and behold, there it was, the spitting stone, living up to great expectorations.

The *Spuckstein* or Spitting Stone (Photo by author)

It is interesting to note the different take that people tend to have regarding saliva depending on whether it is inside or outside the body. Anyone who has suffered from dry mouth knows how welcome saliva is in its proper place, yet most people would find spitting in a cup and then immediately drinking their own saliva to be grossly distasteful.

The Bible also presents some different perspectives on saliva. In the culture of biblical times, spitting on someone, or even in the presence of someone, was a great insult. Old Testament passages indicate that such exposure made someone unclean. Isaiah 50:6 prophesied the suffering of Jesus Christ, who would give His back to be beaten, His beard to be pulled out, and His face to be spat upon. Matthew 26:67–68 (NLT 1996) records the fulfillment of this prophecy: "Then they spit in Jesus' face and hit him with their fists. And some slapped him, saying, "Prophesy to us, you Messiah! Who hit you that time?"

I was struck, however, by how differently Jesus used spit. Jesus spat on His fingers and touched a man's tongue to heal his deafness and muteness (Mark 7:31–37). On another occasion, Jesus spat on the ground to make mud, which He smoothed over a blind man's eyes. He then told the man to go and wash off the mud, and after the man did so, he could see (John 9:6–7). Note the contrast—people used spit to hurt, but Jesus used spit to heal. Jesus touched the people He healed, but He spat on the infirmity to show His disgust with and dominance over disease.[64]

Perhaps one reason that people avoid the first row of seats in church (or my classroom) is because it can become the baptismal row if the preacher (or teacher) gets especially enthusiastic. Speaking and saliva sometimes proceed forth together. Notice how in Gospel accounts, healing comes from the mouth of the Lord—from speech and from saliva. The conception of Jesus's saliva mixing with the dirt for a creative miracle reminds me of how God originally brought forth man from the dust of the ground and breathed into him the breath of life (Genesis 2:7).

The Bible explains that people also have the power to hurt or to heal through what proceeds out of their mouths (James 3:5–10). Some animals have chemicals with healing properties in their saliva. Although human saliva has not been shown to have the same healing compounds, it is thought to have potential disinfectants. So, licking our wounds may not be such a bad idea. On the other hand, saliva can be contaminated. The Bible describes how Satan, speaking through a serpent, contributed to the fall of humankind (Genesis 3:1). Snakes have saliva too; it is called venom.

Overzealous Christians sometimes become venomous. Around the same time that I went upon my German excursion, there were news accounts of a church in the United States that was making public displays of burning the Muslim holy book, the Quran. That seems like spitting to wound rather than to heal. Let the words of the Quran speak for Muslims. Let Christians use the loving words of Jesus Christ to heal and to restore relationships with the Creator.

It is important to get our priorities right lest we become spit wads, the bane of every teacher's classroom. Jesus said that He would spit out of His mouth lukewarm Christians—those who think that they are in right relationship with Him but who do not acknowledge their dependence on God. Such people may refuse to respond to divine discipline or to accept

---

[64] Bob Yandian, "The Miracle of Spit and Sight," Bob Yandian Ministries, June 27, 2018, https://www.bobyandian.com/bible-topics/the-miracle-of-spit-and-sight-still-working-on.

the invitation to live for their intended purpose of fulfilling fellowship and friendship with their Creator (Revelation 3:15–21). Such a spit-take is no laughing matter.

The prophet Isaiah served as a forerunner of Jesus Christ by bringing God's Word to a sinful people. Rather than recognizing the mouthwatering sweetness of what God was serving up to them (Psalm 119:103) most people spat upon the messenger (Isaiah 50:6). Jesus was spat upon for being the foundation stone upon which to build relationship with God (1 Peter 2:4–8). As followers of Jesus Christ, we may sometimes be received as a voice of hope, and at other times, we may be rejected as a spitting stone. When the latter happens, we can take inspiration from Isaiah's reaction to being spit upon, "Because the Sovereign LORD helps me, I will not be dismayed. Therefore, I have set my face like a stone, determined to do his will. And I know that I will triumph" (Isaiah 50:7, NLT 1996).

The entire story of Jesus healing the blind man with His saliva illustrates the point that His ultimate mission on earth was to spit on the forces causing our spiritual blindness and to speak the words that would allow us to see the Light of the World. Like a scuba diver will rub his mask with saliva to keep it from fogging up, so applying the words of the Gospel to our lives will keep our vision clear.

Salivation serves as the first step in the digestion process. It begins breaking food down into smaller particles of nutrients that will be absorbed into our bodies to give us energy to live. Salvation is the first step in absorbing Jesus Christ into our lives, which gives us a new and vastly improved reason to live. We find a new home, like the outcast town musicians of Bremen. Salivate at the opportunities to absorb the words of Jesus into your life, to make His ways your ways, and to become His spitting image.

CHAPTER 39

HOW SWEET IT IS!

Consider the Reese's Peanut Butter Cup Classic, an American original dating back to 1928. It is hands down my favorite candy, and it is also one of the nation's bestselling confections. Dozens of variations have been offered over the decades, but I dare say that none have improved upon the original. This reminds me that Jesus is the classic Christ; He is the same yesterday, today, and forever (Hebrews 13:8). Nothing needs to be added or changed to improve the savor of our Savior. I propose some additional comparisons so that perhaps we can see ourselves in a Reese's Cup—before, that is, the cup is in us.[65]

There is a fancy, flashy wrapper on the Reese's Peanut Butter Cup, but it is what is inside that people really crave. Sometimes when you take off the wrapper, you might find a product that is smooshed or damaged, just like people who may put on a good appearance but be hurt on the inside. If you can get past the imperfections though, the taste is likely to be uncompromised. What is inside us is what is truly important, and the value of people is not diminished by their flaws.

The original peanut butter cup is packaged to sit upon a stiff card to protect it and keep it stable. The card is bright white, kind of like a clean and pure foundation of righteousness surrounded by darkness. Before you try

---

[65] The original inspiration for this topic was: Lauren Surprenant, "Reese's Cup Communion Devotional," Kidology Inc, accessed 2017, https://kidology.org/zones/zone_post.asp?post_id=8942.

to consume the good stuff, look out for the inner wrapper. There is a layer of sin that separates us from the righteousness of God. When you take off that wrapper, some of the good stuff might stick to it. I always look at that paper and resent every little crumb that remains there. I have been known to lick the wrapper to get at every last morsel. Sin also takes something out of us, but we should discard everything that slows, obstructs, or distracts us from the race to relationship with God (Hebrews 12:1). When it comes to sin, we can lick it.

Notice the bumps and ridges on the outer shell; even when we are delivered from sin, life is not all smooth sailing. The cup is round, which can symbolize eternity. Jesus is always around and has no beginning or end. Just as we can enjoy a Reese's Cup, so can we enjoy eternal life. But consider what the candy bar is made of. There is a hard shell of chocolate surrounding a soft interior of peanut butter—like our bodies are a physical shell containing our blood and our being. Jesus's body was broken, and His blood was shed.

The crown shape is reminiscent of the crown of thorns placed on Jesus's head before he was crucified. Every time Christians partake of the sacrament of Communion, they proclaim the death of Jesus until He comes again (1 Corinthians 11:26), upon which time Jesus will be proclaimed King of Kings and Lord of Lords (1 Timothy 6:14–16). Second Timothy 4:8 (NIV) says, "Now there is in store for me the crown of righteousness, which the Lord, the righteous Judge, will award to me on that day—and not only to me, but also to all who have longed for his appearing."

A few decades ago, there was a Reese's Cup advertising campaign in which someone would be walking along eating a chocolate bar and bump into someone eating from a jar of peanut butter. The chocolate bar would end up in the jar of peanut butter. One person would say, "Hey, you got your chocolate in my peanut butter," and the other would say, "Well you got your peanut butter on my chocolate." Then they both would taste the blended product with great satisfaction followed by the tag line: "Two great tastes that taste great together." A later advertising theme was, "There's no wrong way to eat a Reese's," and an even more recent slogan was simply, "Perfect." As of this writing, the slogan for the Reese's Cup is "not sorry." The sacrifice of Jesus, in whom there was no wrong (1 Peter 2:22), for the sorriness of our sinfulness, brings us together with Him in a perfect combination forever (Hebrews 10:14).

Another vintage series of commercials for Reese's was its "and so the world would have to wait" advertising campaign from the 1980s. My personal favorite of these commercials was set in biblical times—2104 B.C. to be precise. One guy is dipping chocolate in peanut butter and says to his friend, "Here taste this." His friend says, "Hey, this is great, you know who would like this, Noah." "You mean the guy building the ark." "Yeah, he likes chocolate, and he likes peanut butter, let's go tell him." Then two giraffes walk by the window as there is a flash of lightning and a rumble of thunder. One of the guys suggests to the other, "Let's wait until after it stops raining." A voice-over then adds, "and so the world would have to wait to learn about the two great tastes that taste great together."

So, I suggest to you that the Reese's Peanut Butter Cup, this confection of my affection, is the perfect communion between two great tastes. But today, if you have bumped into Jesus Christ and allowed Him into your life, then you can celebrate a far more significant communion, albeit one that is bittersweet. Hebrews 2:9 (NIV) says, "But we do see Jesus, who was made lower than the angels for a little while, now crowned with glory and honor because he suffered death, so that by the grace of God he might taste death for everyone," and it was His suffering, the righteous for the unrighteous, that brings people into communion with God (1 Peter 3:18). Romans 8:10 (NIV) adds, "But if Christ is in you, then even though your body is subject to death because of sin, the Spirit gives life because of righteousness."

Once we accept Jesus Christ as the Lord or our lives, there is no wrong way in us as far as God is concerned (Ephesians 1:4–5). God does not want the world to have to wait to hear the message that Jesus Christ in us is the perfect combination. How sweet it is!

CHAPTER 40

MAKE YOURSELF SCARCE

The very essence of being a Christian is to be "Christ-like," for this is what the label "Christian" literally means. Although accepting Jesus Christ as Savior is all that is required to get on the right road to relationship with our Creator, becoming a Christian, or more like Jesus Christ, is a lifelong journey. Just as every song composed in our culture derives from the notes on the musical scale, so every consequential aspect of our existence is composed by the call of Jesus on our lives. The components of our physical existence are sometimes reduced to flesh and blood, but more broadly speaking, flesh and blood can represent the physical and spiritual components of our being. Just as the binary code of 1's and 0's, switches that are either open or closed, drives every possible computer operation, so the interaction of our physical and spiritual components will direct our lives.[66] There is a binary choice; we either run God's program or our own program. To get with the program that generates eternal life rather than the blue screen of death, our function must be to replace our own flesh and blood with the flesh and blood of Jesus Christ.

The sacraments most universally practiced in Christian churches today—baptism, marriage, and Communion—all have a common theme. Each of these church ordinances serves as a symbolic reminder that to become a Christian is to become the body of Christ. Through baptism, we

---

[66] Greg Allen and Dennis Kaufman, *Come to the Table: Fifty-Two Meditations for the Lord's Supper* (Joplin: College Press, 2003), 56-57.

identify with the death, burial, and resurrection of Jesus Christ. In marriage, two people become one flesh as a model of the relationship between Jesus and His Church. During Communion, we ingest representations of the tortured flesh and shed blood of Jesus into our physical and spiritual being to proclaim the death of Jesus and of our sinful self. John the Baptist, whose mission was to prepare the way for humanity to receive its Savior, summed up the objective for all followers of Jesus Christ in John 3:30 (KJV): "He must increase, but I must decrease."

When we nourish ourselves with physical food, the products of the earth, we are just replenishing the dust from which we were created. We all are, or will become, painfully aware of the limitations of what our natural bodies can do and for how long they can endure. They are perishing from the moment of conception with the seeds of their eventual self-destruction planted into our very genes. Our consumption of food and drink merely delays the decay as our bodies become consumed by the ravages of aging. Hebrews 2:14–15 (NLT 1996) assures us that: "Because God's children are human beings—made of flesh and blood—Jesus also became flesh and blood by being born in human form. For only as a human being could he die, and only by dying could he break the power of the Devil, who had the power of death. Only in this way could he deliver those who have lived all their lives as slaves to the fear of dying."

Fortunately, unlike the original Adam who was the ancestor of us all, our existence is not limited to our natural bodies made from the dust of the ground with physical ailments multiplying like dust bunnies as we get older. Upon salvation, a new life is conceived, and the process of sanctification, or becoming more like Jesus Christ, begins. We are born again into a spiritual body that should gradually grow to mirror "the last Adam," Jesus Christ. Someday, even our physical bodies will catch up and be transformed into heavenly bodies that will leave all our limitations and lamentations in the dust (1 Corinthians 15:44–49). The culmination of our new life in Jesus Christ is not a return to dust but rather a return to Eden, only better. The new and improved communion with our Creator that is coming soon will far exceed the Garden variety available to Adam and Eve in that it will be closer, constant, and eternal.

Christmas is a special holy day to celebrate the Incarnation, when the Son of God became human flesh and blood to serve as a sacrificial offering for our sins. Jesus crossed our path, providing not only the necessary course correction, but also the course construction required to lead us into the presence of God. By becoming human flesh and blood that could be sacrificed in our stead, Jesus established a reverse route for us to become His flesh and blood. This gives an entirely new meaning to the concept of "working at cross purposes." While I am taking liberties with the meaning of words, let me invent one. If Jesus taking on human form is called the Incarnation, then perhaps our objective is "deincarnation," crucifying or denying the demands of our human flesh and blood and morphing into the form of Jesus Christ through exemplary words and actions.

I believe it was that great moral philosopher, Garfield, who said that diet is "die with a 't'." Our spiritual diet is to die with a cross by doing the will of the Deity rather than our own—kind of like being a tree hugger by embracing the cross. Symbolically, we replace our own flesh and blood with that of Jesus Christ, who gets under our skin and so that we can get over our sin. He must increase and we must decrease. We should seek to make ourselves scarce. Becoming a Christian is to become more like Jesus Christ, and that truly becomes us.

CHAPTER 41

LET ME DWELL ON THAT

During the Christmas season, we reflect on how God came to earth in the form of Jesus Christ to dwell among us. He was crucified for our sins, rose from the dead, and ascended into Heaven to prepare a dwelling place for us in His eternal presence. The conventional interpretation of the Gospel is that, when we accept Jesus Christ as Savior, we are born again, and a new spiritual self is conceived and begins to grow inside of us as our old self continues to decay away. I think this is a very valid conception, but perhaps there is another way to connect the dots of Scripture into an illustration of God's plan to restore relationship with humanity. Maybe it is fitting to view salvation, not just as the spiritual birth of a new and improved version of us, but also as the birth of Jesus Christ in us. The day of our salvation becomes our own personal Christmas, when our very being becomes Bethlehem and our heart a cradle for Immanuel, God with us.[67]

First Peter 1:23 (NLT 1996) says, "For you have been born again. Your new life did not come from your earthly parents because the life they gave you will end in death. But this new life will last forever because it comes from the eternal, living word of God." John 1:14 (KJV) states that the Word of God is Jesus Christ, who "was made flesh, and dwelt among us." The Son of God had to take on the limitations of human form on this earth so that He could lay down His life as the sacrifice for our sinfulness.

---

[67] Oswald Chambers, *My Utmost for His Highest* (Grand Rapids: Discovery House Publishers, 1992), May 31.

Jesus told His followers that, upon His ascension back to Heaven, He would prepare a place for us. I have generally envisioned this as Jesus the carpenter building fabulous new digs for me in Heaven to accommodate me after someone digs my grave on earth. Indeed, I do believe that Jesus is, at this very moment, preparing to receive His followers into Heaven to live with Him forever; however, we do not need to wait until then for Jesus to dwell in us in the form of God's comforting Holy Spirit. Jesus may no longer be physically present with His followers with all the limitations that involves, but better yet, He maintains a perpetual presence within them (1 John 2:24–27). Jesus cohabitating with us in our earthly existence is a down payment on the residence that He is preparing to share with us, but in the meantime, there is much more that we can do to make room for Him in our hearts by following His instructions for a life well-lived (John 14).

For some who make a profession of faith in Jesus Christ, it seems like Jesus is stillborn in their lives, or perhaps kept in swaddling clothes in the stable with growth in the relationship apparently stalled. Certainly, the selfish human nature that previously ruled tries to extinguish the new life of promise. Wilderness temptations seek to distract from God's plan and purpose and to arrest the development of Christ in new Believers. In Galatians 4:19 (NLT 1996) Paul says, "But oh my dear children! I feel as if I'm going through labor pains for you again, and they will continue until Christ is fully developed in your lives." It is incumbent upon us to strive to grow in the nurture and admonition of the Lord by loving, serving, and obeying.

Second Peter 1:3–4 (NLT) assures that:

> By his divine power, God has given us everything we need for living a godly life. We have received all of this by coming to know him, the one who called us to himself by means of his marvelous glory and excellence. And because of his glory and excellence, he has given us great and precious promises. These are the promises that enable you to share his divine nature and escape the world's corruption caused by human desires.

Angelus Silesius, a 17th century Catholic priest from Germany, said: "Were Christ born a thousand times in Bethlehem, and not in thee, thou art lost eternally." We consume food and drink into our physical bodies for energy to function. We consume the flesh and blood of Jesus Christ by doing His work, and the Lord's work in turn consumes us, energizing us for eternal life (John 6:54). Like the Energizer Bunny, we can keep going and going. Jesus becomes more, and we become less. Someday indeed we will dwell with God in Heaven, but in the meantime, He will dwell in us. Let us dwell on that.

CHAPTER 42

MUSIC TO MY YEARS

After celebrating the birth of Jesus Christ each year, tis the season for new year resolutions. As soon as the Christmas merchandise is removed from store shelves, it is replaced by exercise equipment, diet products, organizational aids, and money management tools. Retailers have done their research and know that the top new year resolutions include: losing weight and getting in better physical condition, reducing debt and sticking to a budget, enjoying more quality time with family and friends, breaking bad habits, and getting organized.

There is certainly nothing wrong with trying to improve oneself, but you probably would not be surprised by statistics that indicate that 97% of new year resolutions are not kept. Generally, before the January page is turned on the calendar, the exercise equipment is wasting away, and the organizational aids are buried under stacks of clutter. Does this sound like the typical history of one of your new year resolutions?

> Three years ago: I will diet to get my weight down below 180.
> Two years ago: I won't let my weight get above 200.
> One year ago: I won't eat dessert until I get my weight below 200.
> This year: I will try to develop a more realistic attitude about my weight.

Or how about this one?

Three years ago: I will go to church every Sunday.
Two years ago: I will go to church as often as possible.
One year ago: I will get to church on the important holidays.
This year: I will listen to worship music while I am getting
ready for work.

I hope this one does not hit too close to home.

Three years ago: I will try to be a better boyfriend to Amber.
Two years ago: I will not break up with Amber.
One year ago: I will try to make up with Amber.
This year: I will try to be a better boyfriend to Ashley.

If your failure to meet your new year resolutions frustrates you, at least take comfort that you are not alone. Robert Paul summed up the outcome of his new year resolutions like this, "I'm a little bit older, a little bit rounder, but still none the wiser." An anonymous person described new year resolutions as something that goes in one year and out the other.

It is no mystery why new year resolutions generally do not work; there is nothing magical about January 1. There is not even any logical reason for it to be the beginning of a new year. By the happenstance of history, it was picked by the Romans to be the beginning of the year on the calendar they developed. Furthermore, as Christians know, we have a limited capacity to overcome our weaknesses through our own strength. Even people who are not generally remembered for their religiosity recognized this. Mark Twain said, "New Year's Day is the time to make your resolutions. Next week you can begin paving the road to Hell with them as usual." Oscar Wilde suggested that, "Good resolutions are simply checks that men draw on a bank where they have no account."

It is natural for the beginning of a new year to inspire us to think about the possibilities of new beginnings, especially if we have had a bad year. Perhaps you have had one of those years where you will stay up until midnight on New Year's Eve, not to see the new year in, but rather to make sure that the old year leaves (Bill Vaughan). If that is the type of year that you have had, then may your troubles last as long as a typical new year resolution (Joey Adams).

I have been extremely blessed in that I have never had a truly bad year that I couldn't wait to end, but each of us who has asked Jesus Christ to forgive us of our sins has recognized that we have a sinful past that we want to put behind us. Interestingly, the pagan Romans saw the new year as an opportunity to seek forgiveness from their enemies and to start over again in relationships. However, we need not wait until January 1st to seek forgiveness, to restore relationship with our Creator, or to resolve to improve our Christlikeness.

The significance of new year resolutions is not that the year changes, but rather that we change (G.K. Chesterton). I know that it is a cliché of motivational speakers, but I think there can be real power in reminding ourselves that each day is truly the first day of the rest of our lives. Each day is an opportunity to put our past behind us and to renew our resolution to serve the Lord with all our heart, soul, and mind.

If you ever think that you have had a bad year, consider the plight of the prophet Jeremiah, who wrote a whole book of the Bible pouring out his miseries to God. Here is a brief excerpt from Lamentations 3:17–26 (NLT 1996): "Peace has been stripped away, and I have forgotten what prosperity is. I cry out, 'My splendor is gone! Everything I had hoped for from the Lord is lost!' The thought of my suffering and homelessness is bitter beyond words. I will never forget this awful time, as I grieve over my loss." But amazingly, Jeremiah goes right on to say:

> Yet I still dare to hope when I remember this: The unfailing love of the Lord never ends! By his mercies we have been kept from complete destruction. Great is his faithfulness; his mercies begin afresh each day. I say to myself, 'The Lord is my inheritance; therefore, I will hope in him!' The Lord is wonderfully good to those who wait for him and seek him. So it is good to wait quietly for salvation from the Lord.

There may be a season for new year resolutions, but any day that you are alive is a great day for making a "new life resolution." I cannot describe this any better than Paul does in Philippians 3:12–14 (TLB):

I don't mean to say I am perfect. I haven't learned all I should even yet, but I keep working toward that day when I will finally be all that Christ saved me for and wants me to be. No, dear brothers, I am still not all I should be, but I am bringing all my energies to bear on this one thing: Forgetting the past and looking forward to what lies ahead, I strain to reach the end of the race and receive the prize for which God is calling us up to heaven because of what Christ Jesus did for us.

For many, the stroke of midnight marking the beginning of New Year's Day is an occasion to make a toast with a glass of wine and sing *Auld Lang Syne*. Psalm 116:13 (NLT 1996) says, "I will lift up a cup symbolizing his salvation; I will praise the Lord's name for saving me." *Auld Lang Syne* is a classic Scottish song that more or less translates to "old long ago." It has been described as a song that nobody knows since apparently hardly anybody sings it without butchering the lyrics. I think that is understandable as most of the actual translated lyrics look like gibberish to me; however, a couple lines remind me of our new shot at relationship with our Creator.

> Should auld acquaintance be forgot,
> and never brought to mind?
> Should auld acquaintance be forgot
> and days of auld lang syne?
> For auld lang syne, my dear,
> For auld lang syne,
> We'll take a cup o' kindness yet
> For auld lang syne

Auld Lang Syne was probably written to reflect a longing for "the good old days," but now we can sing a different tune. Like Jeremiah, we can sing a lament for our previous cup of suffering. Yet in Philippians 3, Paul offers a resounding yes to the question, "Should auld acquaintance be forgot, and never brought to mind?" In the same song, second verse of our lives, Jesus offers a cup of kindness to save us from our old long ago. Psalm 119:54 assures us that God has offered us His principles by which to live our lives day by day, and these principles will provide the very best soundtrack to our lives until we join the heavenly chorus. That sounds like music to my years.

CHAPTER 43

OUR EARS OLD STRUGGLE

Birthdays are highly symbolic occasions to reflect upon the past, present, and future of one's existence. A birthday celebration usually involves a gathering of people **present** to commemorate a **past** event with cake and candles, perhaps funny hats and party favors, gifts, games, that insipid *Happy Birthday* song, and the very unhygienic practice of someone blowing out candles while making a wish for the **future** and spewing germs all over cake about to be served to other people.

Many birthday party traditions as we practice them in our culture seem to have originated in Europe many centuries ago. At first, apparently only kings merited such celebrations, but over time the tradition trickled down to the common folks. People feared that evil spirits were especially wanting to bring mischief against people on their birthdays. Friends and family would gather with a person turning a year older to bring good thoughts, wishes, and cheer—party favors.

Much of the symbolism of birthdays would no doubt be lost on a foreign observer; perhaps the meaning of many of the practices has even become lost on us today. Birthday party games show what abilities children have developed and improved upon over the previous year. Candles symbolize carrying our wishes upward to God. Gifts help to set up a person for a more prosperous future. Birthday punches, pinches, or whacks indicate that the worst is behind, and the best is yet to come. In Hungary and some other European nations, the tradition is to make a tug on the ear lobe for each year passed with a wish for God to bless with such a long life that the ears grow to reach the ankles.

There is also an intersection of past, present, and future when it comes to restoring relationship with our Creator. In describing the sacrament of Communion, which symbolizes our relationship with God, First Corinthians 11:26 (NLT 1996) says, "For every time you eat this bread and drink this cup [in the present], you are announcing the Lord's death [in the past] until He comes again [in the future]. Indeed, God does not seem to make distinctions between the past, present, and future in the way that we do. Revelation 13:8 (KJV) describes Jesus as "the Lamb slain from the foundation of the world." That syntax can make an English teacher tense, but God operates outside of grammatical constraints.

God has no beginning or end, but He is always looking forward. The years of our earthly existence may be numbered, but our spirit is intended to live forever in communion with its Creator. Sinfulness diverted humanity into this temporal existence, and the wages of sin for everyone have been spiritual death, or separation from the Creator, since the day that Adam first disobeyed God. Through His birth and death, Jesus entered our present predicament, and through His resurrection, He leads us back to the future that God has always planned for us. Philippians 3:16 instructs us to realize our God-given potential through the death and resurrection of Jesus Christ. Verb tenses indicate time, continuance, and completion in relation to the present moment. God's plan for humanity merges past, present, and future into one tense—a completed work that continues at this very moment toward full realization in the future.

Each birthday is merely a milestone on our journey. If your birthdays are leaving unwelcome marks and contributing to making you past tense, remember that Jesus speaks to us in a truly future perfect tense. We can be confident that, since Jesus began a good work in us, then He will continue it until completion upon His return (Philippians 1:6). With each passing year, may the call of your Creator tug on your ears, yielding more acuity in hearing His call on your life and making you ever more hungry to hear Him say, "well done my good and faithful servant, enter into the joys of the Lord" (Matthew 25:21).

CHAPTER 44

SIMPLY TO DIE FOR

Once upon a time as a child, I remember seeing a crucifix in a jewelry display in a store and telling my mother that I would like to have one. She used the occasion to explain to me the significance of the empty cross, and even more so of the empty tomb of Jesus Christ. I do not think there is necessarily anything wrong with a crucifix depicting Jesus on the cross, but I understand the point.

Christians commemorate the Incarnation, the Crucifixion, and the Resurrection of Jesus Christ all as critical to restoring communion between God and humanity. Is one more crucial to God's plan to redeem humankind? Should we commemorate one more than the others? The easy answer of course is that they are all equally important, a trilogy of interdependent events. The Resurrection could not have happened without Jesus being born and dying, but without the Resurrection, His life and death would have been no different than any other. Yet at times, the Bible seems to emphasize one of these events in the absence of the others. For instance, First Corinthians 11:26 indicates that, when we partake of the Communion sacrament, we proclaim the Lord's death until He comes. There is no reference to the Resurrection.

Perhaps crucifixion and resurrection are like flip sides of the same coin, each contributing a unique aspect toward understanding God's grand plan. In the biblical book of Song of Solomon, there may be a clue as to the relationship between these two events that are so foundational to Christianity. Now normally, when I get to Song of Solomon in my annual read-through-the-Bible, the mushy-gushy language makes me blush and move on as quickly as possible. I have found the book to be one of the most challenging portions of Scripture in which to find meaning and application. I know some cite the book as instructive inspiration for romantic love between a man and a woman, but since I do not exactly put the "man" in romance, the notion of the book as a love potion does not do much for me. I have also heard that Song of Solomon can be interpreted as an allegory of the divine love shared between God and His people. This perspective is more intriguing to me, but I still struggle with understanding many of the allusions.

So, I invested in a commentary[68] that explains the symbolism and found much to love about this portion of Scripture that allows us to listen in on some of the sweet nothings whispered between Solomon, a king of ancient Israel, and his lover (his dove). Or maybe the passages describe the sweet everything that God wants to speak to people loud and clear—how crucifixion makes possible resurrection to new, eternal life in His presence. After describing the bursting forth of spring after winter, Song of Solomon 2:14 (NIV), quotes Solomon (perhaps representing God) saying to his lover (perhaps referring to Christians): "My dove in the clefts of the rock, in the hiding places on the mountainside, show me your face, let me hear your voice; for your voice is sweet, and your face is lovely."

The "cleft in the rocks" can be interpreted as a reference to the Cross of Christ. In other words, our old, barren sinful life (winter) ends when we accept the salvation from our sins made possible through the death of Jesus Christ (spring). We cleave from our old sinful life that we nail to the Cross of Christ, and we cleave to life in Christ evidenced by our new and improved words and countenance (see also Galatians 2:20). In Song of Solomon 2:15, Solomon encourages getting rid of the foxes that spoil the blooming vineyards. The foxes are interpreted to represent sins that persist in our new relationship with God. God is not seeking "a foxy lover," but rather one who can outfox the forces that seek to interfere with our relationship with Him.

So here is an interpretation, inspired by Song of Solomon, as to how the resurrection and the crucifixion are distinct, yet linked. Those who are dead in sin need the message of the resurrection. If Jesus Christ was not raised

---

[68] Watchman Nee, *The Song of Songs* (Anaheim: Living Stream Ministry, 1995).

from the dead, then our faith is meaningless, and we remain condemned for our sinfulness (1 Corinthians 15:17). After resurrection to the new life that comes with salvation, the crucifixion comes back into play as we pursue sanctification, the process by which we strive to become ever closer to whom God wants us to be. This requires keeping our old sinful passions and inclinations nailed down to keep them from perpetually crossing our path to God (Galatians 5:24).

It can be frustrating to try to encourage godly living among those who are not yet resurrected into new life, and even among those of us who are. I often feel the frustration of encouraging those who are young of age, but old in their sinful nature, to make wise decisions that deny themselves immediate gratification that can obstruct their long-term prospects. Many teachers aspire to be miracle workers who, with enough hard work and dedication, will inspire every student to rise above the fallen world around them, and within them. Teachers have many standards to teach in their curriculum, but the standard by which to live one's life often receives scant attention. My experience and biblical perspective make me a realist when it comes to relying on what education alone can accomplish in making a better world, especially with moral instruction stripped of any absolute standard of right and wrong, as seems to be commonplace today. I will step down from my soapbox now given my limitations in cleaning up the world.[69]

The Holy Bible is the only authoritative textbook to offer instruction in righteousness (2 Timothy 3:16), and it introduces the living hope of eternal relationship with God found only through the interjection of Jesus Christ into human history (1 Peter 1:3–6). The Incarnation and the Crucifixion were a means to the end of restoring the relationship between God and humanity, but even the Resurrection is a means to this end rather than an end in itself. Jesus did not live, die, or come to life again just for the sake of these events happening, but because of the end result of eternal fellowship with God that they collectively make possible. My mission as a teacher, and your mission as a Christian in your corner of the kingdom, is to bring

---

[69] I sometimes tease my students that spending more time in Sunday School would result in less time in Friday School, with Friday School being one of our after-school detention periods generally supervised by yours truly. The detentions are three hours long, although the students will swear that they seem interminable.

the attention of others to Jesus Christ through our voices and through our countenance so that He can draw people to Him (John 12:32). This mission is only made possible by:

1. avoiding acts of the flesh, or temporary pleasures of sin that cause us to self-destruct[70] (Galatians 5:13–21)
2. demonstrating the fruit of God's Spirit inside of us, which refers to the positive character traits that exemplify God's love for others[71] (Galatians 5:22–26) and
3. giving reason for the hope that is within us with gentle respect (1 Peter 3:15).

The interjection of Jesus Christ into humanity through the Incarnation, the Crucifixion, and the Resurrection established a pattern. A complete life cycle for a Christian consists of being born in flesh, living for self, being born spiritually into a new life in Jesus Christ, dying to selfish pursuits while growing into the body of Christ, dying a natural death, and finally being resurrected into eternal life. If you are a Christian with a pulse, then you are likely in stage four—dying to self while living for Christ and eagerly anticipating eternal life. Once again, as Philippians 3:7–11 (TLB) says it:

> But all these things that I once thought very worthwhile— now I've thrown them all away so that I can put my trust and hope in Christ alone. Yes, everything else is worthless when compared with the priceless gain of knowing Christ Jesus my Lord. I have put aside all else, counting it worth less than nothing, in order that I can have Christ, and become one with him, no longer counting on being saved by being good enough or by obeying God's laws, but by trusting Christ to save me; for God's way of making us right with himself depends on faith—counting on Christ alone. Now I have given up everything else—I have found it to

[70] Among these are sexual immorality, irresponsibility, misplaced priorities, conflict, anger, jealousy, drunkenness, and the like.

[71] Among these are sacrificial love for people, happiness, contentment, patience, compassion, decency, dependability, gentleness, self-control, and the like.

be the only way to really know Christ and to experience
the mighty power that brought him back to life again, and
to find out what it means to suffer and to die with him.
So whatever it takes, I will be one who lives in the fresh
newness of life of those who are alive from the dead.

Song of Solomon alludes to the symbiotic relationship between
resurrection and crucifixion. The resurrection is for sinners; the cross is for
saints. Resurrection is about how much we gain in our new life; crucifixion
is about how much we lose from our old one. Resurrection is about Jesus
living for us; crucifixion is about us living for Him. Resurrection is about
what Jesus did for us; the cross is about what we will do for Jesus. Our new
life serving Jesus Christ is simply to die for.

CHAPTER 45

LIFE OUTSIDE THE TOMB

One of my international expeditions gave me a chance to do some navel gazing. No, I was not on a beach looking at scantily clad people. I was in Cusco, Peru, which for the Incas was the belly button of their empire, and as far as they were concerned, of the world. The navel probably seems like a novel topic for a book such as this, or any book for that matter, but apparently contemplation of the navel is common enough to require a word for it, omphaloskepsis. If you will bear with me, I will try to get to the point and make some connections to communion with our Creator.

One observation that I have made in my travels and studies is that there is a tendency for people to customize some aspects of Christianity to their culture—for better or for worse. In the Cathedral of Cusco, I saw a painting from the 18th century depicting the Last Supper. Judas was painted in the image of Francisco Pizarro, the brutal conquistador who brought down the Incan Empire. In place of the Passover Lamb was a guinea pig, which is a great delicacy in Peru. Maybe this is not an entirely inappropriate representation of sacrificial substitution; as the firstborn from the dead, Jesus was kind of the guinea pig in experiencing what awaits us all (Colossians 1:18).

The Last Supper by Marcos Zapata—circa 1753 (Public Domain)

Back to the belly button. For the Inca, referring to Cusco as the navel indicated that it was the origin and center of their empire and of the world. Other ancient cultures also shared the presumption that they existed in the center of everything. An ancient Jewish interpretation of Scripture (Midrash) states that "God created the world like an embryo. Just as the embryo begins at the navel and continues to grow from that point, so too the world. The Holy One, blessed be he, began the world from its navel. From there it was stretched hither and yon. Where is its navel? Jerusalem. And Jerusalem's navel itself? The altar [of the temple]."

Here are some of the ins and outs of what I discovered in my navel research. The navel, or belly button, is the attachment point of the umbilical cord, or at least it is for everyone born of a woman. I remember a riddle someone told me when I was a kid. If you came across a naked couple in the woods who claimed to be Adam and Eve, how could you know if they were lying? Just look to see if they have belly buttons.

The umbilical cord is the conduit by which the baby receives nutrient and oxygen-rich blood and then expels the blood depleted of these essential elements. Where the cord attaches to the baby is the point from which development proceeds within the womb. The mark that forms as the umbilical cord detaches is considered to be the very first scar on the body. As such, it is a great place for later abdominal incisions to minimize additional scarring. The navel marks the approximate center mass of our bodies throughout the remainder of our lives.

John 3:3 proclaims that we must be born again to enter the kingdom of God, so I wonder if we have a spiritual belly button. Does being born of the spirit leave a mark on us? Romans 1:16 says that the Gospel is the power of God that brings us to salvation, our biblical cord so to speak. The Word of God connects us with our Creator and helps us to expel the old, depleted and contaminated parts of us (2 Timothy 3:16). Jesus Christ, who is the Word made flesh (John 1:14), delivers us from the law of sin and death (Romans 8:2), after which our development is to proceed in a different fashion. First Peter 2:1–3 (NLT) advises: "So get rid of all evil behavior. Be done with all deceit, hypocrisy, jealousy, and all unkind speech. Like newborn babies, you must crave pure spiritual milk so that you will grow into a full experience of salvation. Cry out for this nourishment, now that you have had a taste of the Lord's kindness."

Growing in relationship with our Creator is a developmental process. Naturally, our new life requires a period of learning to walk with Jesus. During this time, we are likely to require more care from others than we can give to them. If we are disciplined to seek time with our Creator through reading the Bible, praying, and play dates with other Believers, then our communion should progress from passive reception to active service.

It is always good to take a little time for reflection on our relationship with the One who truly brought us into this world and who will one day take us out. Are we still living like the spiritually dead of the world? Are we still jealous of and quarreling with our siblings in the family of God (1 Corinthians 3:1–3)? Have we found our spiritual legs of service in God's kingdom, facilitating the birth of and nurturing the development of other Christians? Or are we still spiritually sucking? Hebrews 5:11–14 (NLT) speaks to the developmental norms for Christians:

> There is much more we would like to say about this, but it is difficult to explain, especially since you are spiritually dull and don't seem to listen. You have been believers so long now that you ought to be teaching others. Instead, you need someone to teach you again the basic things about God's word. You are like babies who need milk and cannot eat

> solid food. For someone who lives on milk is still an infant and doesn't know how to do what is right. Solid food is for those who are mature, who through training have the skill to recognize the difference between right and wrong.

Perhaps gazing at your spiritual belly button is a bare necessity for maintaining Jesus Christ as the center of gravity for your existence. Is your belly button showing? Can others see the scar of your salvation? Have you allowed God to cut the cord and feed you the solid food of service to Him? If you still see a need to grow up to be more like Jesus, then pursue more spiritual discipline and self-denial, and not just for the forty days before Easter as some denominations practice. Perhaps the consistent appearance of Lent in our spiritual belly button assures that it is a mark of maturity.

First Peter 1:23 (NLT 1996) says, "For you have been born again. Your new life did not come from your earthly parents because the life they gave you will end in death. But this new life will last forever because it comes from the eternal, living word of God." You have been delivered from sin and death into new life. You may still be developing spiritually, but this is your time to live outside the womb. This is your time to live outside the tomb.

CHAPTER 46
MISTAKEN IDENTITY

I once took a graduate psychology course on personality. The experience provided an opportunity for me to study the biographical backgrounds and ideas of several people who contributed prominent theories to explain how people form their personalities. I am still striving to develop a personality, let alone a personality theory of my own, but I am fascinated by the developmental forces that helped to shape each theorist into a textbook example of personality development. A common denominator for many of these individuals, who dedicated themselves to understanding how we become who we are, is that they had relatively troubled childhoods. Most of them were not inspired by any particular religious orientation, and yet I can see occasional glimpses of spiritual insight in each of their theories.

Although there is no universally agreed upon definition of personality, a commonly accepted one would be "a pattern of relatively permanent traits and unique characteristics that give both consistency and individuality to a person's behavior."[72] The term probably derives from the Latin word *persona*, which referred to a mask worn by actors in ancient Rome.

One concept that especially caught my attention comes from the personality theory of Erik Erikson. Erikson was unique in a couple ways. First, he was a blonde-haired, blue-eyed son of a Jewish woman in Germany. For most of his life, he was troubled by the uncertainty as to who is father

---

[72] Tomi-Ann Roberts, Gregory Feist, and Jess Feist, *Theories of Personality* (New York: McGraw-Hill Education, 2012), 4.

was, as well as by a feeling that he did not quite fit in to either the Jewish or Gentile world of Germany prior to World War Two. A second unique characteristic of Erikson was that he went from being a wandering artist and poet to a world-renowned expert in many fields, including psychology, with no college education to speak of.

Erikson is probably best known for his identification of eight developmental stages that people progress through during their lives. Each stage involves a basic conflict that must be successfully resolved to develop a healthy personality in order to progress onto the next stage. For instance, during the first year of life, infants are in oral-sensory mode, constantly incorporating the world into their experience through the mouth and through visual and other sensory stimuli. During their first year, children instinctively learn to receive passively what their environment naturally provides to them, like air to breathe. However, they depend on other people to provide many necessities, such as food, clothing, and shelter. Children must learn how to act in ways that inspire others to provide for them the resources that they cannot obtain by themselves. They must also learn to accept the assistance others offer to them, even if it does not quite meet their expectations.

For instance, children may learn to ask, or to cooperate, or to give in order to receive from others. If they are not able to dependably get others to provide what they need in a way that they are prepared to receive, then children will develop a basic mistrust that will cause them to withdrawal from people in later stages of life. If, however, children learn to receive what they need and to accept what others have to offer, even if it is not entirely to their tastes, then they will develop a sense of basic trust in the world around them with less anxiety about provision for their future needs. What most caught my attention was Erikson's suggestion that it is not the avoidance of hunger, pain, and discomfort in the formative years that makes for healthy personality development. Instead, receiving from others the necessary provision that allows one to make it through difficult experiences is what creates a sense of hope and trust in the future.

Erikson's stages of development help to inform our understanding of human personality development, but perhaps there is also a spiritual personality formation through which our most fundamental developmental task is to take on the persona, or person, of Jesus Christ. Paul declares in

Second Corinthians 4:6 (NIV): "For God, who said, 'Let light shine out of darkness,' made his light shine in our hearts to give us the light of the knowledge of God's glory displayed in the face of Christ." Paul goes on to acknowledge that:

> We are hard pressed on every side, but not crushed; perplexed, but not in despair; persecuted, but not abandoned; struck down, but not destroyed. We always carry around in our body the death of Jesus, so that the life of Jesus may also be revealed in our body. For we who are alive are always being given over to death for Jesus' sake, so that his life may also be revealed in our mortal body.....
>
> Therefore we do not lose heart. Though outwardly we are wasting away, yet inwardly we are being renewed day by day. For our light and momentary troubles are achieving for us an eternal glory that far outweighs them all. So we fix our eyes not on what is seen, but on what is unseen, since what is seen is temporary, but what is unseen is eternal (2 Corinthians 4:8–11; 16–18 from the NIV).

Erik Erikson contributed the concept of "identity crisis," although its original meaning may be lost in common usage. Each stage of life presents an identity crisis to each person, a turning point that will either strengthen or weaken one's personality going forward. The ultimate identity crisis is when we decide whether to trust in ourselves or to identify with Jesus Christ by trusting Him for provision and by accepting His form of provision through whatever life throws our way (Luke 11:9–13). Each day of our lives presents us with an opportunity to pursue relationship with our Heavenly Father. Unlike Erikson and his earthly father, our Father in Heaven is one that we can know and one who seeks to know us. All the world's a stage for taking on the persona of Jesus Christ, and every act is an opportunity to press forward in making an ever more perfect impression of Jesus Christ for all the world to see. Anything else would be a case of mistaken identity.

CHAPTER 47

GET YOUR BEARINGS

Just like for our homes, our cars, our bodies, and pretty much everything else in this world, there is a natural tendency for our relationship with God to deteriorate over time unless we apply consistent maintenance. We would be well advised to inspect the quality of our relationship routinely and to confront any problems that we find as quickly as possible to make sure that we are on the course that God set for us to follow to be in relationship with Him.

If an airplane pilot gets off his course by even a fraction of a degree, the variation from his intended flight plan may not be evident immediately, but over time and distance, he would likely miss his intended destination by dozens or perhaps even hundreds of miles or more. By taking our bearings often, we only need to make slight, occasional corrections to get back on course.

One way or another, the Lord has a way of correcting those whom He loves (Hebrews 12:6). Regular self-examination provides an opportunity for self-correction through the gentle and private nudging of God's Holy Spirit living within us. The farther we get off course, the more dramatic and traumatic the correction that is likely to be required.

I cannot sugarcoat this fact: serving Jesus Christ as Lord of your life requires self-denial, sacrifice, and plain hard work. Every day we can see people who lose their bearings, or who make choices that take them away from God. Surveys of Christians often reveal little difference in their behaviors from those of everyone else in the world. When we examine ourselves, we must look beyond specific sins to the underlying roots of our disobedience, whether it be neglect, undue worldly influences and desires, selfishness, self-gratification, or stubbornness. The purpose of self-examination is not to find reasons to beat ourselves up, but rather to refocus and rededicate ourselves to strengthening our relationship with our Creator. We are on approach to a place of rest and relaxation that offers far more than must be given up to get there. Soul-searching provides an opportunity to get our true bearing—the cross on which we crucify our selfish, sinful desires so that we can follow Jesus Christ to our final destination, our heavenly home for all of eternity (Matthew 16:24–26).

CHAPTER 48

SIN SCAN

As we progress through our natural lives, it seems like there is so much more that can go wrong in our physical health as aging takes its toll. Some of us are inclined to live in denial of our decline; if we are not diagnosed with a problem, then it does not exist, right? At least that is the wishful thinking that drives my inclination to avoid MDs (medical deities) who might prescribe unpleasant procedures to look for problems or who might recommend undesirable changes in my lifestyle. It would be at one's peril, however, to completely ignore the warning signs that might indicate a health issue that is best addressed sooner rather than later. At any age, routine self-examination of our physical and mental health is advisable, along with seeking medical intervention, at the very least when symptoms warrant doing so.[73]

We must overcome the fear of what may follow if our self-examination raises a concern that necessitates a visit to a medical professional—with all the paperwork, expense, and generally awkward, unpleasant, and perhaps even downright painful probing and testing that may come when you darken the door of a doctor's office. Maybe even surgery will be required. I have heard surgery described as a friendly attack with a knife. The pain really sets

---

[73] Part of this chapter was inspired by:

"Self-Examination," in *Meditations on the Lord's Supper* (Becoming Closer Adult Bible Fellowship, n.d.), 37, http://www.becomingcloser.org/Downloads%20PDF/Communion%20Mediations.pdf.

in when payment is due for services rendered. Nonetheless, the prognosis for what ails us is likely to be better, and the interventions less invasive, if health issues are addressed at early stages. Self-examination may not prevent the onset of diseases, but it may help to improve and even prolong life down the road if it allows for health problems to be dealt with before they spread or do more permanent damage. Similarly, regularly examining our spiritual health may not allow us to avoid every sin, but it can help us to treat the source and symptoms of sins before they cause a decline in the health of our relationship with our Creator.

Before we can recognize any abnormalities in our physical or spiritual wellbeing, we must know what is normal or expected so that we can compare what we find in our self-examination with what should be. This requires consulting the Great Physician's reference for righteousness, the Holy Bible interpreted through the Spirit of God living within us. We cannot ignore whatever problems that we find and expect them to just go away on their own. Maybe improvements in spiritual diet or exercise by incorporating more service to God and people into our lives will increase resistance to or recovery from spiritual health "failments." Maybe we will need a more invasive intervention to cut out some self-indulgences or self-righteousness. Regular prayer appointments with God, the Great Physician, offer both preventive and ameliorative care. He has no need for a waiting room, He makes house calls, and He offers the gentlest of bedside manners. Best of all, His bill has already been paid in full.

Medical doctors do amazing things to facilitate our health and healing, but they are not truly miracle workers. Their greatest limitation can be uncooperative patients who deny that there is anything wrong or that any changes are needed. Similarly, if Christians do not examine themselves, they will not recognize their "sintoms," and they will not be at "dis ease" as they should be with the spiritual health problems deteriorating their relationship with God. They will not make the changes necessary to fulfill the purpose for which they were created, and they will fall short of the glory that God has in store for them.

Modern medicine increasingly offers us less intrusive ways to diagnose what ails us. A CAT scan can show any structural abnormalities in our bodies. A PET scan can show any abnormal functioning in our tissues or organs. A DOG scan can show "Who's a good boy." My apologies for trying to be doggone funny, but a GOD scan can certainly reveal if there be any wicked way in us (Psalm 139:23–24). A daily dose of God's Word is much more friendly and effective than any cutting instrument when it comes to separating unhealthy attitudes and desires from the healthy parts of our soul and spirit (Hebrews 4:12).

If you have accepted Jesus Christ as your Savior, then you have been healed of the terminal condition of sinful separation from God through a transfusion of the blood of Jesus Christ and through an ongoing transplant of His body into yours. A regular diagnostic sin scan will detect any signs of rejection that you can then treat before it is too late, and such iniquity imaging will thus assure you of a prognosis of eternal health and life in Heaven in the care of your Creator. One of the more advanced medical imaging techniques is functional magnetic resonance imaging (fMRI), which can show brain activity by measuring blood flow as people do various tasks. I prescribe frequent fMRI scans to determine if you are functioning in your Master's righteous image.

CHAPTER 49

FIREPROOF

I once saw a news headline proclaiming that the Indiana Department of Homeland Security rolled out its "Get Alarmed" program to distribute 10,000 smoke alarms to high risk populations in the State. Apparently, this was in response to an uptick in fire fatalities and to the fact that two-thirds of fatal fires occur in homes without working smoke alarms.[74] Around the same time, there were a couple grass fires near where I live. Given the large amount of rain that had recently fallen, I could not help but wonder how reckless one had to be to burn a whole hillside in such conditions, but then I have had some family members meet their match a few times and almost set the world afire with ill-conceived efforts to purge what seemed unsightly.

Fire has a way of capturing our attention, whether it be for good or for ill. I doubt that any of us burns to be the victim requiring a dramatic fire rescue, but we all likely marvel at the exploits of those who feel the burn to save others. Firefighting is no doubt one of the most admired and aspired to professions, not to mention one of the most dangerous. Firefighters are among those public servants who run toward what the rest of us run from.[75]

---

[74] Indiana Department of Homeland Security, "Fire Fatality Map," *The Hoosier Responder*, June 2020, 9, https://www.in.gov/dhs/files/Hoosier-Responder-2020-06.pdf.

[75] Part of this chapter was inspired by:
"The Fireman," in *Meditations on the Lord's Supper* (Becoming Closer Adult Bible Fellowship, n.d.), 112, http://www.becomingcloser.org/Downloads%20PDF/Communion%20Mediations.pdf.

Contrast this with the public persona of the fire inspector or fire marshal, who is in the business of telling us what we must do or cannot do in the name of personal or public safety. I used to take student council members to conventions in various high schools across the state. One time we had indoor fireworks in the gymnasium, which was a real crowd pleaser not repeated after the fire inspector weighed in. Thanks to fire codes, the indoor candle lighting ceremony that was the traditional highlight of the closing session was also extinguished. So there were a couple bad reactions between an open candle flame and a hairspray drenched hairdo. Nothing was permanently singed except for a little dignity. Nonetheless, such ceremonies were allowed no more indoors. More recently, students in our school were told that they would need to keep all backpacks and bags in their lockers, in part due to concerns of what the fire inspector might say about halls or classrooms with too much baggage.

Those fire marshals can be such a wet blanket when you are just trying to have a blast, and they are never so admired as those who come to the rescue when things go up in flames. Nonetheless, who likely saves more lives: the firefighter or the fire marshal? As the old saying goes—an ounce of prevention is worth a pound of cure.

Some inspection of our spiritual surroundings and service can also help to prevent some unwelcome fires in our future, some of our own making and some thrown at us by a spiritual enemy who shoots fiery darts of destruction our way (Ephesians 6:16). We should fear the fire, not the fire inspector. It is also advisable to regularly recharge the batteries of our sin detectors to warn of any smoldering cinders of our past infernal life. After all, we will not be able to mount heroic rescues of those at risk of perishing in the fires of Hell if our own house is burning. The Bible sets the standard for being a firefighter in God's company and tells us to expect trial by fire to test the foundation and structure of our lives. Our own fire protection may be secured by accepting Jesus Christ as Savior, but our commendations will be determined by our service (1 Corinthians 3:10–15).

The lives of even the best of people are a dumpster fire until they call for salvation from the first and only Responder who not only rescues but restores. Any other response will only result in getting hosed. Let God be the fire inspector of your life. Let Him raise the alarm as to anything that might put at risk the rescue that Jesus Christ effected for you. Leave any embers of iniquity on the ash heap of history. As a Christian, remember that you are now living His story and serving in His company, heroically rescuing those at risk of perishing in the fires of Hell as well as tending to those who are recovering and rebuilding their relationship with God. Only such labors will survive the trials by fire and serve as proof of your reasonable service. God's reward for the fireproof will be a real blast.

CHAPTER 50

ALL YOU CAN EAT—JUST DON'T BE FULL OF YOURSELF

Satire is a form of humor that calls attention to human weaknesses and failings, such as hypocrisy, greed, selfishness, and so on—generally with the intent to encourage personal or social reform. Good satire will present a notion that seems preposterous on its face, yet with just enough realism to make you wonder if it could possibly be true in this wacky world in which we live. Satire is likely to make you laugh at first, but then it will make you think. It has been said that "the rules of satire are such that it must do more than make you laugh. No matter how amusing it is, it doesn't count unless you find yourself wincing a little even as you chuckle."[76] For instance, I am a little ashamed that the following headlines from the Christian satire site, *The Babylon Bee* could be riffs on my life.

"Local Church Offers Introvert Service Where No One Has to Talk to Anyone Else"

"Introvert Hires Personal Representative to Engage in Church Small Talk"

"Introvert Fires Off Smoke Bomb to Escape Church Greeting Time"

---

[76] Credited to: "Forecast," *Galaxy Science Fiction*, June 1968, 113. by Wikipedia contributors, "Satire," *Wikipedia, The Free Encyclopedia,* accessed 2020, https://en.wikipedia.org/w/index.php?title=Satire&oldid=955376925.

What follows is my own effort to write a satirical news story reflecting on the observance of the sacrament of Communion in modern day churches. Hopefully, it is more ridiculous than realistic.

* * * * *

Church Institutes All-You-Can-Eat Communion Buffet

Church in the Way in Showme, Missouri announced that it has instituted a new all-you-can-eat Communion service in an effort to cater to those who hunger and thirst for righteousness. "Those small servings in our traditional service just weren't fulfilling," said Pastor Dawson McClawson. "Last month we had to call 911 when one of our parishioners got his tongue stuck in the tiny Communion cup trying to get at every last drop of juice. Come to think of it though, that cup is the only thing that ever tamed that man's tongue," Pastor McClawson added. Previously, Church in the Way relied on traditional potluck dinners once a month after Sunday morning services to satiate the congregation's appetite for food and fellowship, but with today's busy lifestyles, congregants complained that they just did not have time to prepare the Hamburger Helper and Minute Rice.

Dr. Jerry Cooper, an expert on modern church culture consulted for this article, noted that Church in the Way's efforts are not entirely without precedent. The St. Simon Catholic Church in Fogville, Vermont tried a similar tack with an open bar for Communion wine, but by most accounts the effort was a mass disaster and was never tried again.

Critics of the trend for churches to appeal to fleshly appetites to attract churchgoers consider Church in the Way's overture to be tasteless, much like the unleavened Communion wafers that most people would pass over if given a choice of emblems developed for modern tastes. "Gluttony is after all one of the seven deadly sins," noted Thurston Cassman, founder of the church reform advocacy group, Christians Who Count. Pastor McClawson is undeterred, however, noting that Jesus came eating and drinking and was called a gluttonous winebibber.

"The challenge," says Helen Williams, the church's newly appointed Communion chef, "is to offer a variety of selections without straying too far from traditional Communion cuisine. We have our bread bar with various selections of emblems that have been used to represent the body of Christ in churches over the decades, especially as last minute substitutes when someone forgot to order the official Communion wafers from the church supply house," she stated somewhat sheepishly. Williams continued, "You can create some unique combinations of bread sandwiches. We have many leaven-free varieties for those concerned with sin analogies. We also serve a variety of grape juices, including your traditional Concord as well as white, lite and every grape juice blend that we could create, such as cranape, grange, and grapple, not to mention grapefruit. We will stick with nonalcoholic selections, however, out of respect for Protestant tradition—and since we were denied a liquor license."

After a brief but heartfelt prayer casting the calories out of the Communion elements, Pastor McClawson reminded the congregation that "the Communion buffet can be a reminder of Jesus's death because after all, the Bible says in Mark 14:65 (KJV): 'And some began to spit on him, and to cover his face, and to **buffet** him, and to say unto him, Prophesy: and the servants did strike him with the palms of their hands.' At least that is the way I interpret it," McClawson mispronounced.

Of course, no actual bodily fluids are allowed at this smorgasbord. The Truman County Health Department has required the church to install a sneeze guard on the Communion table in future services, noting that the lack thereof could be why there were many who were weak and sickly among the congregation soon after the inaugural meal. Pastor McClawson has begun a series teaching the congregation proper buffet etiquette, including take all you want, but eat all you take. Last week, twelve baskets of leftovers were delivered to the local food pantry. Congregants are encouraged to make their way patiently and politely through the buffet line. "It's not like it will be your last supper or anything," said Deacon Todd Radcliffe.

McClawson admonished the congregation "to make sure that you come to the table with cups and dishes that are clean both inside and out." "Come with a clean plate, leave with a clean slate" reads the inscription on the Communion table. "We are not finished catering to our culture," McClawson stated. The next project for Church in the Way: raising funds to buy bigger chairs in anticipation of the growing size of their congregation.

* * * * *

Satire offers a little prodding to evaluate ourselves according to how others see us. Partaking of the Communion sacrament offers a gentle reminder to examine ourselves according to how God sees us (1 Corinthians 11:28). Self-examination is likely to make us wince a little and thereby encourage us to make the necessary corrections that come with being crucified with Christ so that we will not be condemned with the world (Galatians 2:20). Are we full our ourselves or full of Jesus Christ? Our daily bread is our service to God, and He provides all-you-can-eat.

CHAPTER 51

THE GHOST OF COMMUNION—PAST, PRESENT, AND FUTURE

As I mentioned earlier, much of what I have included in this book has been modified from church service presentations that I prepared to introduce the sacrament of Communion, also called the Lord's Supper or Eucharist. The Bible presents this ceremonial consumption of unleavened bread and grape juice or wine as an opportunity to examine our relationship with our Creator and to seek to draw closer to Him. Symbolically, we absorb the body and blood of Jesus Christ into our own being and proclaim His death for the sins of everyone, as well as our own death to our sinful desires.[77]

For any of my readers who may be unfamiliar with the backstory, please permit me to do a brief review from the Old Testament of the

---

[77] I know that there are some Christians who believe that Communion bread and wine literally become the elements of the body and blood of Jesus Christ—transubstantiation this is called. I come from a faith tradition in which the elements of Communion are only considered to be symbolic representations of the physical sacrifice that Jesus made to provide for the spiritual sustenance that comes from relationship with our Creator. This theological debate is far beyond the scope of this book and even my understanding, but I would rather not try to explain to people that I invite to church, "Oh by the way, every week we literally drink some blood and eat some flesh, can we look forward to seeing you this Sunday."

Holy Bible. Some "climate change" forced the Jews, the descendants of Abraham through his son Isaac, to leave the land that God had promised to them and to seek sustenance in Egypt. Over the course of several generations, these displaced persons went from honored guests to despised slaves of the Egyptians. Eventually, God sent Moses to them, the man with God's plan to lead the Jews out of bondage and back to their Promised Land.

After God unleashed a series of horrible plagues on the Egyptians to persuade them to let His people go, the grand finale was the death of the firstborn sons of everyone who continued to resist God's plan. However, God declared that the destruction would "pass over" everyone who applied the blood of a lamb to the doorways of their homes and who partook of a specifically prescribed but hastily prepared meal. After this last and most devastating plague, the Jews were free to make their graceful exit from Egypt with their firstborn sons among them. After a harrowing journey of attrition through the wilderness, they returned to the land that had been promised to their ancestors and to their descendants as a permanent inheritance, or at least as their possession for as long as they were obedient to God's commandments. Even to the present day, devout Jews (and some Christians) will commemorate this deliverance from slavery with a ceremonial Passover meal, or Seder.

Let's flash forward a few centuries to when the New Testament tells the story of Jesus Christ commemorating the Passover with His disciples and adding a new dimension of symbolism and instruction to what has come to be known as Jesus's Last Supper with His disciples, His closest followers. Jesus presented himself as the firstborn Son of God and as the Passover Lamb whose blood shed on a cross would allow those who applied it to their lives to escape slavery to sin and to be reborn as sons (and daughters) of God. All of this is communion past.

Communion present is the journey of Christians through the wilderness of this worldly existence to the Promised Land of Heaven. During this earthly sojourn, we seek to become increasingly like Jesus Christ, striving to deny the selfish desires of our own flesh and blood in pursuit of the will of God (2 Corinthians 5:14–15). Jesus assures us that we can live in divine connection with Him, and He we will live with us as if He is a vine and we are branches of that vine bearing fruit that brings God's flavor, and favor, to a lost world. This relationship becomes evident through our obedience to God and through our love for Him and for each other, a love so intense that we are even willing to lay down our own lives for the sake of serving God and others. Such an expectation may sound scary, but this opportunity to sacrifice ourselves comes with the promise that living according to God's purpose for us will fill us with overflowing joy. It also offers the assurance that the Author and Creator of the Universe will consider us to be His personal friends who can have Him on speed dial through prayer (John 15:5–16). Every day will feel so good when you are connected to the True Vine.

The Passover commemorated in the Old Testament and by Jesus and His disciples is described as a feast. No Communion service that I have ever participated in offered enough food and drink to be considered a feast in the modern American sense of a repast where the calories seem to require exponential measurement. Even the strictest diet regimen allows larger portions than those offered in the traditional Communion observance. Indeed, Communion is a great meal for losing weight, primarily by shedding the weight of sin through self-examination and repentance. Nonetheless, feasting in the Bible is more about the presence of God than the presence of food. In fact, the kingdom of God that Christians are helping to build is not so much a place to feast, but rather it is what we feast on—the surfeit sustenance obtained from presenting and modeling the Gospel message to others.[78]

This brings us to communion future, which involves a new heaven and a new earth where God will dwell among His people. There will be no more crying or pain or sorrow or death. We will feast on the presence of God for all of eternity and at long last achieve fulfillment of our promise. It will be like being married to someone who completes us like no romance novel or "reality" show or wildest fantasy could ever begin to portray (Revelation 21:1–5).

Through the Communion sacrament, we partake of the appetizer for an eternal feast of fellowship with our Heavenly Father. The sacramental observance is intended to whet our appetites for serving God, who

---

[78] Peter J. Leithart, *Blessed Are the Hungry: Meditations on the Lord's Supper* (Moscow, ID: Canon Press, 2000), 14.

communes with us through His Holy Ghost, or Holy Spirit, in the past, present, and future (John 14:26). The main course of communion arrives with the end of our natural lives and the acquisition of our new bodies and our new home. And to top it all off, I understand that the divine dessert prepared for us is simply to die for.

CHAPTER 52

OUT ON A LIMB

I took advantage of a fall break to revisit the New England states in all their illustrious, autumnal splendor. It is the deciduous trees that make for such a spectacular, showy season; deciduous means falling off when no longer needed and can refer to things like deer antlers and baby teeth as well as trees that lose their leaves seasonally. The vibrant, green, summer color of most trees is a function of chlorophyll delivered to the leaves through the trunk, branches, and stems. Through the process of photosynthesis, chlorophyll captures light energy from the sun to produce simple sugars from water and carbon dioxide, thus providing the sole sustenance for the tree's growth and development. The chlorophyll is broken down in the process and needs to be consistently replenished during the growing season.

During the autumn when there is less daylight, or when there are unusually dry conditions, chlorophyll production declines and other pigment colors, such as yellow, brown, and orange become more evident. Some trees produce red or purple pigments in late summer when sugars become trapped in the leaves after abscission begins. Abscission occurs when the layer of cells holding the leaf to the tree begins to break down, thus precipitating the leaf's fall to earth to further decay into the soil. Jeremiah 17:7–8 (NLT) quotes God as saying:

> But blessed are those who trust in the LORD
> and have made the LORD their hope and confidence.
> They are like trees planted along a riverbank,

with roots that reach deep into the water.
Such trees are not bothered by the heat
or worried by long months of drought.
Their leaves stay green,
and they never stop producing fruit.

As beautiful as fall foliage may be, it reflects the dying of a generation of leaves that are separating from their source of nourishment and energy. Christians in communion with their Creator make for a vibrant and growing church, or body of Christ. When that connection weakens, Christians begin to display their hidden, sinful colors, and while this may make for a spectacular show for a season, a fall from grace is likely imminent. I do not want to stem appreciation for the beauty of the fall season, so please allow me to leave a more positive light on things. The shedding of old leaves makes way for a new generation of vibrant, green foliage for another growing season.

If I was a tree, what kind of tree would I be? There are advantages and disadvantages for both deciduous plants that tend to shed all their leaves at once, and coniferous, or evergreen, ones that dispose of a few at a time all year long. Perhaps both types can provide illumination as to why God compares those connected with Him to flourishing trees (Psalm 1:1–6). Upon salvation, we make like a deciduous tree and leave all our old, sinful ways behind as we are grafted into God's tree of life (Romans 11:16–24). When it comes to growing in our relationship with Jesus Christ, perhaps we should aspire to be more like the evergreens, consistently shedding the occasional sins that still so easily beset us so that we can avoid a period of dormancy where we bare all to the world (Hebrews 12:1).

Regardless of which type of tree you decide best speaks of thee, notice how God speaks to us through trees. The knowledge of good and evil came from a tree in the Garden of Eden. Through crucifixion on a tree, the Son of God took upon Himself the curse and death penalty that we deserved because of our treasonous behavior (Galatians 3:13). God has allowed us to see His healing plan for restoration through the Tree of Life in Heaven (Revelation 22:2). Communion with God requires examining ourselves so that we can leave our sins hanging on the cross and strengthen our connection to our Creator through the shed blood of Jesus Christ that nourishes and energizes and binds us together. Bare yourself of sins and become the foliage and fruit of the old wooden cross. Join together with other members of the body of Christ and go out on a limb together.

CHAPTER 53

A BETTER PILL TO SWALLOW

People who are not well-versed in the teachings of the Bible may be somewhat discomforted by the notion of consuming flesh and blood, which is the illustration offered by the Communion sacrament. As noted earlier, most Protestant Christian denominations consider the observance of sacraments such as Communion, baptism, and marriage to be strictly ceremonial and symbolic undertakings. Personally, I have never been much of one to stand on ceremony, or to seek solace in symbolism, but the Word of God is filled with both. So, I must ask myself, "why?" A *National Geographic* article by Erik Vance entitled "Mind Over Matter" may offer some insight with this assertion: "science is showing that how you feel isn't just about what you eat, or do, or think. It's about what you believe."[79]

Scientific researchers have long realized that people may unconsciously react to something introduced to them according to their expectations rather than because of any actual direct cause and effect relationship—a phenomenon known as the placebo effect. If a scientist hypothesizes that a variable introduced to people, such as a drug or medical treatment, will have a certain effect, then the researcher must reckon with the prospect that the research subjects may respond as anticipated, not because of the efficacy of the treatment, but because the attention that they receive creates a subconscious expectation within them for a certain change to occur.

---

[79] Erik Vance, "Mind Over Matter," *National Geographic*, December 2016, 30-55.

To counteract this phenomenon, researchers may create an experimental group that receives the drug and a control group that receives a placebo, or a substance like a sugar pill that would not be expected to cause any reaction. If a significant change is seen in the group receiving the treatment relative to the subjects receiving the placebo, then there is a great deal of confidence that the change is in fact due to the treatment and not just to the attention. However, appropriately controlling for the placebo effect requires a blind study in which the subjects do not know if they are receiving the drug or the placebo. Better yet is a double-blind study, which will neutralize the effects of any researcher bias by also preventing researchers from knowing which subjects are receiving the medical treatment or the placebo until after the study is completed.

Vance describes how even the sights, sounds, and smells of a hospital or doctor's office have been found to trigger natural healing processes due to the placebo effect. One gentleman participating in a double-blind trial for a drug developed to treat Parkinson's disease showed a dramatic reduction in symptoms. The man was devastated when he learned that the drug would not be marketed due to its overall ineffectiveness. When the identities of those in the experimental and control groups were at last revealed at the end of the study, the researchers were stunned to learn that this particular subject had been receiving the placebo all along. In fact, some recent research mystifyingly indicates that people may get better even when they know that they are only receiving a placebo treatment.[80] It seems that mere attention to a health problem can unleash a power of expectation that will trigger natural healing processes to take hold. Conversely, an expectation that something might cause an unpleasant reaction has been shown to increase the experience of negative outcomes. This is called the nocebo effect.

Research has suggested some preconditions that enhance the placebo effect. It is stronger when there is a trusted, supportive, authority figure who offers a plausible story as to how a certain, clearly defined experience or action could cause an improvement to a recipient who is an active listener and participant in the experience. Furthermore, the placebo effect

[80] Sumathi Reddy, "A Placebo for Pain Relief—Even When You Know It's Not Real," *The Wall Street Journal*, January 20, 2020, https://www.wsj.com/articles/a-placebo-for-pain-reliefeven-when-you-know-its-not-real-11579525202.

seems to be compounded within a community of fellow believers sharing expectations of outcomes.

Perhaps there is a phenomenon similar to the placebo effect in the spiritual as well as in the physical realm. Therefore, maybe God prescribes certain symbolic actions, even though they are not necessary to secure salvation. Developing a faith in Jesus Christ only requires hearing the words of Jesus Christ (Romans 1:17), yet Christians are also instructed to put away sinfulness and to humbly allow these words to be implanted within them (James 1:21–22). Sinfulness can create a nocebo effect as guilt leads to expectations of bad consequences. In contrast, acting in obedient service to God can create an anticipation of spiritual health and well-being.

So what if sacraments such as baptism and Communion are "merely" symbolic actions. They can still serve to reinforce the faith by which we identify ourselves with the death of Jesus Christ, and it is His death that provides the actual healing from the disease of sin. We have a trusted, supportive, authority figure—the Great Physician—who offers us a plausible story in the Word of God as to how the experience of Jesus Christ on the cross offers us the blessed hope of eternal life with Him. We participate in these symbolic acts within a community of fellow believers who are active listeners and willing participants.

Sacraments such as Communion, baptism, and marriage provide intersection points between the natural and spiritual worlds. They may have no significance in and of themselves, yet they serve to reinforce our belief in and attention to the supernatural forces already at work within us. It is these forces that allow us to prosper and be in physical, mental, and spiritual health (3 John 1:2). Sin provides only a bitter pill to swallow. Jesus took the poison pill for us and provides us with a better pill to swallow. The taste of His medicine has the direct effect of saving us from our sins and the side effect of making us more like Him. Through the observance of Communion, God has prescribed symbolic doses of the body and blood of Jesus to call our attention to the health of our relationship with Him, which can in turn enhance the prognosis for our spiritual life. We have received the cure for what ails us, now let us act accordingly by sharing the cure with people who are spiritually blind, sick, and dying from the human condition.

CHAPTER 54

DON'T MISS A BEAT

Sometimes there is controversy about how often we should partake of the sacrament of Communion in church services. The Bible gives no specific instruction regarding frequency other than "whenever" (1 Corinthians 11:26 in the NIV). Those who express concern about partaking of the Lord's Supper too frequently cite the possibility of the practice becoming a rote and meaningless routine. That is certainly a possibility to diligently guard against, especially if there is an expectation that the sacrament must be observed according to a rigid timetable. However, routines need not be a bad thing. Most of us get up and go to work most every day. For some, going to work is a dreadful drudgery, and for others, gainful employment is eagerly anticipated as another exciting opportunity to serve the Lord in an assigned mission field. Some people begrudgingly practice a daily exercise regimen as a necessary evil, while others embrace it as a refreshing change of pace. Perhaps attitude and perspective make all the difference.

Routine can provide a rhythm to life. Repetition does not necessarily mean that each occurrence must be the same. The sun rises every morning. Some sunrises are more beautiful than others, but surely we should be grateful for each one that we are privileged to see since each daybreak gives us a fresh opportunity to serve the Lord with gladness (Psalm 100:2).

So, perhaps **how often** we should observe the Communion sacrament is a concern that can best be addressed by first considering **why** we should partake. Communion provides us with an opportunity to remember the incredible investment Jesus has made in us, to evaluate the closeness of our relationship with our Savior, and to renew our commitment to serve Him. We partake of Communion because the Lord has invited us to "whenever." Routine can provide a rhythm to our lives. Let's not miss a beat.

CHAPTER 55

DON'T FORGET TO REMEMBER

Relationships require remembrance, or at least so I have been told—I have not sailed on a lot of relationships. Anniversaries, birthdays, favorite things, pet peeves, names—remembering these things reflects an investment of time and attention in another person. I am sure it works best when there is a mutual interest between both parties in a relationship. Relationship with God is no different, and partaking of Communion provides moments of intimacy to remember what our Creator has done for us.

Remembrance requires struggling against the natural tendency to forget. It is strange what we remember, and what we do not—sometimes easily recalling trivial details that mean nothing unless you are a contestant on *Jeopardy!* while struggling to remember much more practical things. Indeed, I am often reminded of my trivial mind.

My psychology class alumni may recall an activity that I use to illustrate the quirkiness of what we remember—and of what we forget. I warn students that I am about to give them the most difficult assignment of the year. In fact, the assignment is so difficult that no one has ever passed it, and I expect all of them to fail. Then I visually present to them a random number and make a big to do about it. I have the students concentrate their attention on the number and have each student repeat it out loud while the number zooms and spirals repeatedly in front of them. After such a big setup, I then tell the students that their assignment for the next day, and for the rest of their lives, is to forget that number.

This activity illustrates how relatively insignificant details can get emblazoned on our memories. It also shows how difficult it can be to make ourselves forget. Although none of my students have been able to demonstrate that they truly forgot the number, I still initiate them all into an unforgettable club consisting exclusively of students who were fated for me to mess with their minds in psychology class. I once had a student tell me that this activity was about the only thing her mother remembered from my classes when she was one of my students decades ago.

There are many reasons why we forget things, or people, that we may wish to remember. Just the busyness of life is one important factor. The information before our conscious attention is constantly being replaced by new information. Distraction is also an enemy of remembering as is a lack of effort to encode new information. I often remind my students that getting what they should learn from my classes to stick between their ears is likely to require some hard work.

There are some techniques that can aid our memory. Mnemonic devices can help by creating retrieval cues. For instance, "HOMES" provides the first letter of each of the Great Lakes, and "ROY G BIV" may help in the recall of the colors of the rainbow or the visible portion of the electromagnetic spectrum. Portions of the Bible are written as acrostics with each verse starting with a letter matching the sequential order of the Hebrew alphabet. Setting information to music, rhyming, or making new information meaningful by connecting it with what we already know can also increase retention. I once remembered four digits of my license plate number, 1462, as "thirty years before Columbus sailed the ocean blue," despite this mnemonic device counterintuitively requiring the storage of a lot more than just four bits of information. I still remember that old license plate number better than my current one since I have not made an effort to encode the new information. I suppose I have just had too much on my plate.

Remembrance is an important theme of the sacrament of Communion (1 Corinthians 11:24–25). What does Jesus want us to remember? He wants us to remember what our lives were like without Him. He wants us to remember that He paid a price to ransom us from bondage to sin. He wants us to remember our relationship with Him. The Prodigal Son left his father to squander his inheritance by wining and dining friends who promptly forgot him when the money ran out. Left to literally pigging out, eating food meant for pigs just to survive, the Prodigal Son came to his senses when he remembered what it was like to live in loving relationship with his father (Luke 15:11–32).

Imagine there's no memory. It's easy if you try. Just live for today and forget the perspective offered by your past. Forget that living is about relationships that you are willing to die for, and there will be nothing worth remembering. The world will be as one—big mess.[81]

Tragically, some people lose their ability to remember due to disease or natural physical decline, and they often become increasingly isolated as they lose the ability to relate to others. The word "remember" itself offers us a reminder of what is required to become and remain a member of a relationship. The natural tendency is to pursue our selfish desires, with relationships as merely a means to that end. Remembering other people in relationships requires sacrificial service. The sacrament of Communion reminds us that Jesus Christ remembered us when He sacrificed His literal body to obtain salvation for our sinfulness, and it reminds us of our brothers and sisters in the family of God. We remember our need for a Savior, and we re-member with the body of Christ.

There is some irony in the relationship between remembering and forgetting. We must know something before we can forget it. We must acknowledge our sins to ask God to forget them. We rely on God to remember us and to forget our sins. There is quite a contrast between our tendency to forget God and His remembrance of us. God says that His ability to remember us is even greater than that of a mother remembering her child nursing at her breast. So how is God so able to remember us? He has written our name on His hand (Isaiah 49:15–16). Jesus remembers us every time He sees the nail scars on His hands. Every time we partake of Communion, we are remembering His sacrificial provision for us.

The bread and wine of Communion are retrieval cues associated with something meaningful in our lives—the grace of God that offers us all His riches rather than the punishment that we so richly deserve. I still remember my high school Bible club adviser's way of saying grace: **God's**

---

[81] With apologies to John Lennon.

Riches **A**t **C**hrist's **E**xpense.[82] See, those mnemonic devices really work. We do not usually have too much trouble remembering to eat and drink to sustain our physical bodies. Communion reminds us to sustain our place in the body of Christ. Our trivial minds encounter many demonic devices to distract us from the only thing that truly matters in the ultimate scheme of things, relationship with our Creator through Jesus Christ. Don't forget to remember.

---

[82] Thank you, Dennis Baum, wherever you are.

CHAPTER 56

THINK THANKS

Showing appreciation for others is an important part of any relationship, and thankfulness is certainly called for in our relationship with our Creator. When Jesus modeled relationship with the Heavenly Father, thankfulness was a common theme in His communication. Relatively few things about Jesus's life and ministry are recounted in all four Gospels, but the last meal shared with His disciples made the cut to be included in Matthew, Mark, Luke, and John.[83] This Last Supper was a commemoration of the Passover, but it also marked the institution of a new and improved celebration of God's provision. A common denominator in each telling is an emphasis on Jesus giving thanks as He offers both the bread and wine that symbolize God's spiritual provision for restoring relationship with humanity. In fact, a common name for the sacrament of Communion, which was instituted from this Last Supper, is Eucharist, a term that can be translated from Greek to me as thankfulness for the goodness of God's grace.

Thankfulness for the Lord's provision is a theme throughout the Bible. What does it mean to be thankful? Sometimes saying thank you is simply good manners, like routinely saying "thank you" when people do trivial things for you that you could just as easily do for yourself. Thankfulness takes on a whole new intensity when someone who is intimately familiar with your needs and wants does something for you that you could not easily do for yourself, if at all.

---

[83] Matthew 26:17–30; Mark 14:12–26; Luke 22:7–39; and John 13:1–17:26

God desires for us to give thanks in everything (1 Thessalonians 5:18). He starts us off easy, encouraging us to give thanks for food and drink; who cannot be thankful for that? Every time I step on the weight scales, I realize how much I have to be thankful for. Those of us who cannot boil water without having 911 on speed dial can especially appreciate our dependence on others for food. I am certainly grateful both to God for His provision of sustenance, and to those who prepare food for me so that the only butchering that I do is to the rare recipe that I try to bring to fruition. If it were not for prepackaged food and microwave ovens, I do not know how I would have survived my many years of living alone.

Giving thanks in everything, however, must mean even in the circumstances that make us miserable. Jesus expressed thankfulness during His last meal with His disciples despite knowing that betrayal, abandonment, torture, and execution were imminent and were even being set in motion by this very event. Prepositions are important, and I would note that God's expectation is not thankfulness **for** everything, but rather thankfulness for the promise of His provision **in**, during, and through every circumstance that comes our way.

After Jesus was crucified, two of His followers who had not yet wrapped their minds around His resurrection were walking along a road having a pity party because Jesus had not performed to their expectations, and all seemed to be lost. Jesus appeared to them incognito, walking with them and listening to their sob story for a while. Then Jesus set them straight by explaining how all the apparently horrible things that happened were necessary parts of God's grand plan to make everything right. When they reached their final destination, they recognized that their mystery companion was in fact Jesus only as He broke bread with them and gave thanks to God for it (Luke 24:13–35).

It was through the act of giving thanks that Jesus revealed His identity and, more importantly, confirmed that God will turn even the worst of circumstances into the greatest good. We just may not recognize the blessings through the journey until we reach our final destination. So, when you, like Jesus, have to partake of the cup of suffering (Matthew 20:22–23), don't whine, but thankfully partake of the cup of wine or juice that represents Jesus's blood that was poured out for the forgiveness of our sins, and partake of the bread of His presence that sustains us come what may. You do not need a think tank to solve your problems, just think thanks.

CHAPTER 57

PRAY TO PLAY

Indeed, followers of Jesus Christ have much to be thankful for; not the least of which is having the Author and Creator of the Universe on speed dial (John 16:23) and a total access pass to His kingdom (Matthew 16:19). Communion with the Creator includes communication, and the communication should go both ways. Prayers can express thankfulness and requests to our Provider. God's responses will often come through reference to the instruction manual that He has already provided, the Holy Bible, or perhaps through a sense of conviction spoken to our spirit by God's Spirit living within us. I have never personally heard the audible voice of God, but I would not rule that possibility out either. Regardless, we can rest assured that God has His ways of letting us know what we need to know, when we need to know it—if we only know how to listen. As has often been said, God always answers prayer—sometimes with a "yes," fortunately with a "no" if our request is not for the best, and very often with a "not yet" if the timing is not quite right.

We are truly dependent on God for every breath and heartbeat and all that flows from them. God needs nothing from us; however, He welcomes us to work with Him. This shows how He values us, not as pets, but rather as partners in building His kingdom. Obviously, in this relationship with God, our desires must be subordinate to His because only He has the knowledge, presence, and power to deliver what we need.

God wants us to know and to trust Him as a Father. When we were little children, we quickly developed the habit of asking our parents for everything because we were almost completely dependent on them. We asked, we received, and off we went on our merry little way without a care or trouble in the world. Ok, maybe some trouble, but only what we caused. Adult responsibilities may make you a little nostalgic for those times. I suspect, however, that you do not really want to go back to that level of dependency. As you grew, so did the dimensions of your relationship with your parents as you began to relate to them in deeper and even more mutually satisfying ways.

We have all seen the spoiled rotten kids who do not get enough dose of "no" from their parents. There is nothing like a "no" from someone we love to make us think about the nature of our relationship. "No" makes us realize that life is not all about us. "No" teaches us that there are consequences, responsibilities, and expectations in a relationship. "No" reminds us that we must give as well as receive. "No" is central to how we can know God's best plan for our lives.

Hearing an occasional "no" is what gives us hope, for no hope is required if we already have everything that we want. Hope is one of the blessed gifts that God gives to His children, but we only need hope for things that we do not yet have. Hope provides patience and perspective (Romans 8:24–25). Do not mistake a "no" for no answer. God always answers with a "yes," a "not yet," a "no," or perhaps a "grow before I answer that one." Do you ever remember hearing a "no" to your request for a toy you just thought you had to have, only to find it wrapped up under the Christmas tree? Perhaps as a toddler you asked for a bicycle and received a tricycle instead. Sometimes we need some three wheelin' before we are ready for some free wheelin'.

Many times, we do not know what we are asking for. Consider the man who encountered the genie who could grant him one wish, anything that the man's heart desired. So, the man asked for enough money to live comfortably for the rest of his life. The genie said, "Granted, you have one day to live." Sometimes we may not be bold enough in our requests. The Bible tells the story of a blind beggar named Bartimaeus who called out to get Jesus's attention as He was passing by (Mark 10:46–52). Jesus asked him, "What do you want me to do for you?" Imagine if Bartimaeus had asked for a seeing-eye dog instead of restoration of his sight. I know that sounds far-fetched, but perhaps our requests can be that short-sighted. God can provide us with

221

so much more than we can ask or imagine through His power working in us (Ephesians 3:20).

Sometimes the answers are much different than what is hoped for. If you think relationship with God means escape from suffering, then I am afraid that I have some bad news. The Apostle Paul was afflicted with issues **because** of his close partnership with God. Three times Paul pleaded with God to remove a problem that he referred to as his "thorn in the flesh." God's answer was, "My grace is enough." So, Paul concluded, if you can't escape it, embrace it. He delighted in his problems because they made him even stronger in his service to his Lord (2 Corinthians 12:7–10).

I am more of a wimp than Paul; I pray that I will not suffer any more than I must. That is part of the reason why I pay so much attention to politics, in addition to doing so being an occupational hazard for a government teacher. I worry about what might happen if certain politicians beat other politicians, or if an election outcome favoring a certain party will mean there may be no tomorrow. I often feel confident that I know which candidates would make the wisest decisions, and which would spell disaster if it wasn't such a long word. However, even if I am right in the short-term, I have an extremely limited understanding of the complexities and possible outcomes apparent from God's infinite perspective. It is like God is playing four-dimensional chess with politicians as pawns in His universe, and the contribution of my opinion is more like rolling the die in a game of "Chutes and Ladders." So, I must pray for everyone in authority to govern in such a way that we can all live peaceful, prosperous, and proper lives in God's sight, and I must let the King of Kings check the powers that be (1 Timothy 2:1–4).[84] My vote is to be anxious about none of the above, but in every circumstance to make my requests known to God with thanks in advance (Philippians 4:6).

Since you can reach out and touch the Author and Creator of the Universe, keep in mind that divine communication is not just for 911

---

[84] I am in no way suggesting that Christians should disengage from politics, which is merely the process of contributing one's perspective in the formation of the public policies, or the government decisions, that we must all live by. Indeed, this is a civic duty for all citizens. A lot of past prayer and personal sacrifice have allowed for Americans to still live in a political system in which Christians, and everyone else, have the opportunity and the responsibility to participate in electing, influencing, and even becoming political leaders. This, however, is a topic for a whole other book.

emergencies, when you get yourself into a real jam. God offers a panoply of numbers reserved to keep the lines of effective communication open with those in relationship with Him. You can get the 411—information as to how to proceed when facing life's decisions. The Operator of the Universe is also standing by to answer 211—to connect you with help from fellow followers of Jesus Christ, 311—to provide access to heavenly resources, 511—to inform of any obstacles in your path, 611—when you need some healing repair, 711—when you are having problems hearing God, and 811—when you are in a hole and want to stop digging.[85] In any language, God's phone tree is always answered by a living person, Jesus Christ, whose sacrifice on a wooden cross allows direct access to the throne room of Almighty God.

When an answer is not evident, or when the suffering is great, welcome the opportunity to develop a deeper understanding of God's plan in which all things work together for the benefit of those who love Him and who are called to help fulfill His purpose for humanity (Romans 8:28). As a child of God, I believe that you can expect far more good than bad by any measure as you grow in your relationship with Him, but no matter how bad things may seem, you always have a prayer for His provision, come what may. Just remember that you must pray to play in God's league.

---

[85] The North American Numbering Plan (NANP)
211 – Community services and information; 311 – Municipal government services; 411 – Directory assistance; 511 – Traffic information; 611 – Phone company repair; 711 – TDD and Relay for the Deaf; 811 – Underground public utility location; 911 – Emergency services.
Mark J. Fletcher, "Beyond 911: Other N-1-1 Codes You Should Know," *Network World*, IDG Communications, October 25, 2016, https://www.networkworld.com/article/3134324/beyond-911-other-n-1-1-codes-you-should-know.html.

CHAPTER 58

MOVE TO TABLE

Auctions can assemble an intriguing cast of characters and provide an interesting opportunity to see what people value. My parents held an auction after living for 52 years in the home that they had built together. My mother's beautiful, like new living room sofa sold for $47.50. An old pickle barrel sitting next to it went for $55. One hundred dollars was the winning bid for my father's 75-year-old toy metal motorcycle, orange of all colors (at least with what paint was left on it). If I had known it was worth that much, I would have been more careful when I played with it as a kid. A couple old desks that we had preserved from previous generations but almost scrapped due to their decrepit condition were not written off by the bidders. No doubt someone will restore them into beautiful pieces. There is probably an encouraging lesson in the observation that people still value old things, even if they are a little worse for wear. If we had tried to paint the toy motorcycle or fix the antique furniture, we would have probably diminished their value. In the hands of an experienced restorer, they will no doubt dramatically increase in value. God purchases us how He finds us and restores us into relationship with Him. Trying to fix ourselves up will just make things worse.

Another observation that I made during this moving sale was how many tables of various sizes, shapes, and purposes we had accumulated. Most of these tables were purposed for holding other items for sale until the table was sold out from under the knickknacks that did not attract a bidder. This speaks to the practicality of tables, in my case mostly as catch-alls for everything else that I accumulate. It grieved me to part with some tables going back to my great-grandparents and to my mother's childhood. I was also reluctant to leave our warped, mildewy ping pong table in the basement. I insisted on keeping the kitchen table where we shared so many meals over the decades along with many other tables that we will eventually incorporate into new living space.

In most homes today, there are likely many kinds of tables that can indicate our personal habits. Some homes have a pool table to provide a break from daily life chores. Mine in the basement is usually racked up with too much junk to rack up any billiard balls. Many homes have workbenches for various projects, often unfinished. Some small, decorative tables may just sit there and look pretty or support something else that does, like a vase or a plant. Folding tables can be closeted away when not needed. How about the coffee table, which is much more likely to support our feet or an attractive yet seldom read book rather than a cup of coffee? For that we have the end tables that place our beverage of choice in easier reach.

Each of these types of tables could also serve to analogize spiritual health habits that may be either supportive of or obstructive to our relationship with God. Recreation is an important part of God's design for His creation, so take your breaks and do not allow other responsibilities to crowd out the joys of life that God offers to restore your physical and mental well-being. Yet be careful not to pocket your faith or miss cues for productive service. Our Christian lifestyles can be a collection of unfinished projects, or perhaps an occasional spectacular display intended to impress others while offering little functionality. Alternatively, our Christian faith can make us problem solvers who rise to the occasion when needed and add beauty, support, and practicality within easy reach to a collapsing world.

Perhaps the table most representative of relationship is the dining table—not necessarily the formal one rarely used, but rather the kitchen table where our lives and the lives of those closest to us are sliced and diced on a regular basis. This is the table where fellowship occurs as we receive our daily bread.[86]

---

[86] This chapter was partly inspired by the following two sources:
Nancy Karpenske, "Bring It to the Table," *Christian Standard*, Christian Standard Media, July 15, 2016, https://christianstandard.com/2016/07/bring-it-to-the-table.
Mark Krause, "What Kind of Table?," *Christian Standard*, Christian Standard Media, April 22, 2016, https://christianstandard.com/2016/04/what-kind-of-table.

Tables are naturally gathering places to fellowship and troubleshoot. In my capacity as a collective bargaining representative for teachers in our school corporation, my colleagues and I "bring to the table" matters that need to be "chewed on" with the administration so that we can better serve our students. Fortunately, unlike at many bargaining tables, "chewing out" by either party in the negotiations is relatively rare given our mutual respect and responsibility for civil, cooperative discourse. In other capacities, when I must lead meetings according to parliamentary procedure, tabling a motion controls discussion. Although tabling a motion American style generally means delaying or even killing consideration of a proposal, in Great Britain and the rest of the English-speaking world, to table means to begin consideration of a matter. Regardless, tables are places where business is done.

A choice of tables determines our spiritual destiny. As First Corinthians 10:21 (NIV) proclaims: "You cannot drink the cup of the Lord and the cup of demons too; you cannot have a part in both the Lord's table and the table of demons." God sets a table for us in the presence of our enemies (Psalm 23:5). At the Lord's Table, Jesus offers Himself to us for sustenance, fellowship, and guidance. At this Table we can fellowship with the family of God and mingle our lives with the Lord's. I hope that I have set the table for you and offered you some food for thought; when faced with life's pressing decisions and responsibilities, move to table.[87]

---

[87] Given the earlier consideration of geographic differences in the meaning of "move to table," be sure to read this last sentence with a British accent so that it best comports with the theme of the chapter.

CHAPTER 59

SECTS APPEAL

Christianity and "going to church" are likely linked in many people's minds, but the word "church" can have different connotations in different contexts. Regardless of your religious experiences, you might be surprised to learn that you may never have been in a church, at least as sociologists define such a thing. In a sociological sense, a church is a life-encompassing religious organization that all members of a society are born into. To be a citizen of the country is to be a member of the church or predominant religion—unless you opt out, you are in. This has been somewhat typical historically and currently in many European and Muslim nations, but not so much in the United States.

So, if you thought you had been darkening the door of a church regularly, or at least on occasion, you might wonder where you have been going if not to church. According to sociologists, most Americans associate with a denomination rather than a church in the classic sense. A denomination is defined as a voluntary religious organization that generally accepts the values and norms of the secular society and government while being accepted itself by most everyone in society. For many people, such mainstreaming seems to translate into "nothing to see here," which may be why many denominations have been losing membership during a time that is increasingly being thought of as a post-Christian age in Western Civilization.

Certainly, many fine Christians are doing the Lord's work as members of organizations that identify as denominational churches, but perhaps another label is warranted for Christians of any stripe who are more interested in acceptance by their Savior than by society. The sociological definition of a sect may suffice to describe such people. A sect is formed when members of an existing religious organization break away from the mainstream because they believe that some valuable beliefs have been lost. A sect does not seek to establish a new religion, but rather to redeem an existing one that, in the name of social acceptability, has compromised fundamental truths.

Although it does not seem at first glance that there is much of a "church" that people are born into in the United States, perhaps there is a tendency for many people to assume that Christianity is their cultural birthright. After all, how many people do you know who will call themselves Christians because their family and friends do, or because they go to "church"? Yet they might struggle to tell you what being a "Christian" means to them?

One summer, I took on a landscaping project in front of my house, working on it a few hours a day when I got time amid many distractions. One day I started a little later than I intended, and just as I was getting my hands dirty, someone from down the way came by for a casual chat. He was carrying a can of beer, and from the smell of his breath even from several feet away, I could guess that it was not his first one. He gave every indication of settling in for a conversation, and I was inwardly resenting the distraction. I had never had occasion to say more than a friendly "hello" to this person in the past, and I did not even know his name. Cue the conviction that I spend too much time on tasks and do not make enough effort to get to know the people around me. I prayed silently that if this was to be a divine appointment to speak into someone's life, then I would rise to the occasion to make the most of it.

Sure enough, before long an opening to discuss spiritual matters arose. Now usually when I have an opportunity to share my Christian faith with others, I tend to be indirect and just lob a few seeds in from a distance in hope that the kernels of Christianity will find some fertile soil in the individual and be nurtured and watered by others so that they eventually grow into a personal relationship with Jesus Christ. This time though, I was more resolved; if this conversation was going to distract me from my intended task, then I was not just going to shoot the breeze about the weather. I figured that I might as well try my hand at some spiritual landscaping, if indeed this gentleman's life was now my appointed ground. So, I eventually dropped my shovel, focused my full attention on the conversation, and became rather direct in asking the man questions about his religious beliefs while responding with my own. I figured that this conversation would either tend to my neighbor's spiritual soil or encourage him to move on so that I could return to my physical toil.

It soon became evident to me that this man had some knowledge of Christianity. He expressed a belief in God and Jesus Christ and seemed to figure that this and some good deeds would assure his eternal future. It was also evident that he did not have a conception of Christianity as a personal relationship with Jesus Christ. I could tell that God was trying to ripen him for a harvest. He described a recent health crisis during which he died for a few minutes and sensed approaching Heaven, only to find the gates locked. He still seemed unwilling to embrace the concept that there was more to being a Christian than just believing that Jesus Christ exists. He soon moved on, but hopefully with some seeds planted that took root before he passed on a few years later.

I think it is unfortunate that so many people today seem to believe that being right with God is their birthright, or that it comes in their mothers' milk, or that it only requires identifying as a member of a "church." However, upon deeper reflection on the sociological definition of a "church" as a life-encompassing organization that we are born into, I am struck by the possibility that this conception may not be so different from how God describes His Church as being comprised of "born again" individuals becoming more like Jesus Christ and thus becoming the body of Christ. According to Colossians 1:18–23 (NLT 1996):

> Christ is the head of the church, which is his body. He is the first of all who will rise from the dead, so he is first in everything. For God in all his fullness was pleased to live in Christ, and by him God reconciled everything to himself. He made peace with everything in heaven and on earth by means of his blood on the cross. This includes you who were once so far away from God. You were his enemies, separated from him by your evil thoughts and actions, yet now he has brought you back as his friends. He has done this through his death on the cross in his own human body. As a result, he has brought you into the very presence of

God, and you are holy and blameless as you stand before
him without a single fault. But you must continue to believe
this truth and stand in it firmly.

It is not our physical birth into a so-called Christian family or nation
that makes us right with God, but we are born into a life-encompassing
Church when we are born again into God's family and become citizens of
God's kingdom by choosing to live in relationship with God through Jesus
Christ. The Bible defines the Church as the Body of Christ, and you cannot
get any closer to someone than to be a part of his body. In fact, Christians
are to be the aroma of Jesus Christ to the world. The scent of Jesus Christ
emanating from our lives will seem like a bad case of body odor to those in
love with the world, but to those who come to recognize that they reek of the
havoc of the world, it will be the alluring perfume that draws them toward
a relationship with their Creator (2 Corinthians 2:14–17).

The effectiveness of the Heaven scent is compounded by Christians
assembling together in unwavering unity, lovingly encouraging each other
to be good and to do good. As Christians we are not called to go with the
flow of our culture, but to demonstrate Christianity in ways that will catch
the attention of those who are perishing (Hebrews 10:23–27). Members of
the Church, the Body of Christ, need to be working together to provide the
sects appeal that attracts people into pure, unadulterated relationship with
God through Jesus Christ.

CHAPTER 60

WHO ARE YOU DRESSING UP AS?

Christians are to be set apart from unbelievers, and yet they are also to be spiritual and cultural influencers of those who are not living in relationship with their Creator (2 Corinthians 6:17). The trick for Believers in Jesus Christ is for them to be in this world but not of it (John 17:14–16). There are often some tough decisions for Christians, and a lot of disagreements among them, as to how to engage the world without becoming contaminated by it. Well-meaning Christians have nominated many prohibitions to be the 11th Commandment, as in thou shalt not do this or that, even though the Bible does not necessarily say so in black and white or red.

Reading between the lines of Scripture for guidance in our daily decisions is necessary, but such interpretations should be informed by God's Holy Spirit living within us. A dose of humility is also called for when we rely on our own scriptural analysis to evaluate the conduct of other Christians. We should each individually seek to obey God while recognizing our own limitations and our lack of ability to will other people to see things as we do. Accusing and arguing with each other is exactly the opposite of what God wants us to do (Philippians 2:12–15).

I suggest rather that we should each examine our own actions and motivations in light of God's explicit and implicit instructions in the Holy Bible, as annotated by God's Holy Spirit living within us. Input from other respected followers of Jesus is worthy of consideration as well. By way of application, consider the controversy among Christians as to the appropriateness of participating in secular celebrations of Halloween. Since the Bible does not say, "Thou shalt not dress up in crass costumes or decorate your homes with wicked witches," what follows is not offered as a condemnation or a defense of anyone's personal celebrations or convictions. Consider it an example of a personal, soul-searching effort to reconcile the clear biblical admonition to be set apart from unbelievers with its instruction to also positively influence the spiritual condition of those who are living apart from their Creator.

Ask someone focused on candy or costumes or ghoulish decorations what the meaning of Halloween is to them—exactly what they are celebrating—and you will probably get a good impression of a zombie face. Or if they detect a little condemnation of their flirting with the dark side so often evident in modern celebrations of Halloween, you might get a little chiding to lighten up; after all, it is just a holiday. Just a holiday, a word that has itself lost its meaning as a celebration of a holy day.

Halloween has gone the way of Christmas and Easter, each of which people may celebrate primarily in ways that seem like sad substitutions for the destiny-defining events that these holidays originally commemorated. Instead, people devote their attention and their money to celebrating mindless traditions, such as a fat man in a silly red suit being pulled around by a herd of reindeer. In comparison to the resurrection of Jesus Christ, the Easter Bunny really lays an egg. Christians are sometimes particularly troubled by how our society celebrates Halloween because it seems to make light of and even take pleasure in elements that are otherwise associated with evil.

When I became student council adviser for our school, I inherited with the position the responsibilities for our school's Halloween celebrations consisting of a dance and selling tricks or treats to place in student lockers. I never felt entirely comfortable in the role, not sure whether I was aiding and abetting evil, or just being a Christ-like servant looking for opportunities to light a candle in the darkness. When I opened lockers for students to deliver bags of candy, or to toilet paper them as the case may be, and then looked the other way when they ran out of lockers and started toilet papering teachers' classrooms, was it harmless fun, malicious mischief, or just wanton wastefulness of perfectly good toilet paper? At the Halloween dance, I was often troubled by the costumes portraying blood and gore or seductiveness, and then I would see a student in a gorilla suit chasing another student in a banana costume around the dance floor and have a good laugh. I take comfort and inspiration in Paul's perspective described in First Corinthians 9:19–23 (MSG):

> Even though I am free of the demands and expectations of everyone, I have voluntarily become a servant to any and all in order to reach a wide range of people: religious, nonreligious, meticulous moralists, loose-living immoralists, the defeated, the demoralized—whoever. I didn't take on their way of life. I kept my bearings in Christ—but I entered their world and tried to experience things from their point of view. I've become just about every sort of servant there is in my attempts to lead those I meet into a God-saved life. I did all this because of the Message. I didn't just want to talk about it; I wanted to be in on it!

Halloween can serve as one more example of how the world has taken a "holy day" and tried to distract from its true significance. Just as with many other holidays, if you look at the traditions that have arisen around Halloween, you can get a glimpse of what the Christian meaning of the day is. Christmas is about gift giving, first and foremost the gift of the Son of God to humanity. A theme of Easter is celebrating the prospects that come with new life, most significantly manifested through the resurrection of Jesus Christ from the dead. Halloween, in its origins, is about death and sacrifice.

Some aspects of modern Halloween celebrations apparently trace back to the European pagan festival of Samhain, the lord of death who sent evil spirits to attack humans, who could only escape by disguising themselves as evil spirits. It was scheduled at the time of year when the veil between the living and the dead was thought to be the most penetrable, allowing the spirits of the dead to come back more easily to the land of the living. The longer nights and onset of dreary winter was an occasion for evil spirits to rejoice and play nasty tricks on people, especially those who had wronged the spirits when they were alive. A treat could be offered to appease the offended soul. Score one for Satan's conception of Halloween.

Early Christians developed a different way of confronting evil. Just as people today gather at the location of a tragedy on its anniversary, so Believers in Jesus Christ would congregate around the tombs of Christian martyrs or gather at the places where they died on the eve of the anniversary of their martyrdom. During an all-night vigil, they would tell stories recounting this person's life of faith to inspire each other to persevere through persecution and the prospect of being the next contestant to pay a price for doing what was right. At daybreak, they would break bread together and celebrate the day of the martyr's death as the birthday of a saint. As there tragically came to be more martyrs than days on the calendar, the Church instituted All Saints' Day as a once-a-year commemoration for all of them. Eventually, this day was placed on the Christian calendar on November 1st to preempt the pagan celebration of Samhain, and to bring light and hope to a dark and dreary season. Thus, October 31st became All Hallows' Eve.

The word "martyr" comes from the Greek word for witness. There is no greater witness than to lay down one's life for believing in Jesus Christ. As Christian martyrdom became blessedly less common, however, the commemoration of All Saints' Day was extended to those who lived a life of great faith—who daily crucified themselves to follow Christ. November 2nd was later designated as All Souls' Day to encourage remembrance of dearly departed loved ones—and to remind us that death does not separate us from the love of God, or from those who loved God and now live with Him.

Early Christians were likely inspired by the heroic deeds of the hallowed hall of famers of faith described in Hebrews 11:33–38 (MSG):

> Through acts of faith, they toppled kingdoms, made justice work, took the promises for themselves. They were protected from lions, fires, and sword thrusts, turned disadvantage to advantage, won battles, routed alien armies. Women received their loved ones back from the dead. There were those who, under torture, refused to give in and go free, preferring something better: resurrection. Others braved abuse and whips, and, yes, chains and dungeons. We have stories of those who were stoned, sawed in two, murdered

in cold blood; stories of vagrants wandering the earth in animal skins, homeless, friendless, powerless—the world didn't deserve them!—making their way as best they could on the cruel edges of the world.

The pagans had one thing right in their celebration of Samhain; there is a connection between the living and the dead. It is not about the dead trying to come back to this life to taunt and trick us, but rather about the faithful dead to whom we can be grateful for inspiring us through their examples and whom we can join in victory over sin and death.

All the blood and gore associated with Halloween in the present day might partly reflect the right image but deliver the wrong message. I am troubled by how the celebration in our society seems to invite people to embrace the forces of evil; therefore, I have often said that I do not personally celebrate Halloween. However, upon deeper reflection, I realize that I do and will continue to commemorate the true significance of the holiday. It is an occasion for us to remind ourselves that there is a battle between good and evil, and it has real casualties and consequences. All the imagery of blood and darkness provides an appropriate background from which to reflect on the fundamental reality that the brutal death of Jesus on the cross rescued us from the dominion of darkness and brought us into His kingdom of light. Once we were separated from and enemies of God because of our evil behavior, but now we have been made holy in God's sight and free from blemish and accusation of wrongdoing, as long as we remain established and firm in our faith (Colossians 1:12–13; 21–23).

The apparent glorification of evil during Halloween may be troubling, but it is merely a symptom of a larger, year-round tendency for the kingdom of darkness to try to distract from the true meaning of life and to persuade us that there is no meaning in what we do in our celebrations and entertainment. I once saw a discussion on a business program about whether religious criticism of Halloween could be a threat to our economy if it catches on since more money is spent on Halloween than any other holiday except Christmas. The consensus of the discussion panel seemed to be that the religious zealots should lighten up since Halloween was just a fun occasion for people to flirt with their dark side.

There is meaning in the action that Jesus Christ took to die on the cross, and in the deaths of those martyrs who followed Him. There is meaning in the actions that we take to deny ourselves worldly pleasures that would distract us from taking up our cross to follow Christ (1 Corinthians 9:24–27). There is meaning in what we commemorate, and in how we celebrate. Perhaps it is natural to be troubled that the kingdom of darkness seems to be most powerful during Halloween, but the darker the background, the brighter burns the hope offered through the cross of Christ and the resurrection of the firstborn from among the dead (Colossians 1:18).

Again, I do not want to get all judgmental about how other people celebrate Halloween, or to criticize people's decisions about how they use their time, money, and energy. As the saying goes, it is better to light a candle than to curse the darkness. I do not want to be a party pooper, but rather I would like to introduce the life to the party. I do not want to come across in a way in which people's reaction is that I should just lighten up. Rather I want to lighten up the holiday as an opportunity to celebrate what is truly meaningful.

There is a silly Irish legend about a man named Jack who trapped the Devil in a tree by carving a cross in the bark. Jack only let the Devil go after the Devil agreed not to take his soul. However, when Jack died, he was too sinful to go to Heaven. The Devil gave Jack a glowing ember from Hell, which he placed in a carved-out turnip. Jack used this "jack-o-lantern" while he endlessly roamed the earth looking for a final resting place.

I do not have any artistic talent, and I would probably contribute my own blood and gore to the holiday if I tried to carve a pumpkin. However, some day I envision on my porch during the Halloween season a single pumpkin, and into that pumpkin will be carved an image of the cross illuminated by a candle. As trick or treaters walk past my house dressed as ghosts and goblins seeking to fill their bags with candy, I would like for those who "don't know jack" about eternal life to get a glimpse of the true story of Halloween. I would like to use Halloween as an opportunity to remind people that those who rise from the dead are not zombies, that there is a trickster who seeks to destroy souls, and that the kingdom of light offers a treat much sweeter than you will ever receive flirting with the darkness (Psalm 1:1–6).

Satan is always trying to trick us, but the treats in store for the followers of Jesus Christ result from His death on the Cross for us, and it was no mean feat by which He gave us something good to eat, doing the will of God. Perhaps I am coming across as the annoying person who always puts the healthy food in your trick or treat bag, but at some point, we become tired of the junk food and empty calories and long for something more nutritious. Add to Halloween what you will, but why neglect the deeper meaning?

Like any holiday, the way that we celebrate Halloween can be an occasion to bring our attention to themes that should be a part of our lives throughout the year. Every day on the calendar is one in which Satan competes with God for our allegiance and service. Hallow means holy and is the same word used in the Lord's prayer where Jesus says to God, "hallowed be thy name" (Matthew 6:9–13) The cross of Christ hallows us and brings us into communion with Him, and with Christians who have gone before us.

Perhaps the next time Halloween rolls around, it can be viewed as an occasion to put the hallow back into Halloween by embracing eternal life as we face the death of our mortal bodies. We can costume ourselves in a robe of righteousness. We can forgive those who wronged us and seek the forgiveness of those whom we have wronged. We can add some of our own exploits to inspire those who follow us. We can testify of the treats of serving God to those who have been tricked into serving Satan. We can fondly remember and draw inspiration from the heroes and heroines who are but a few steps ahead of us on the journey of faith. We can tell each other how those who have gone before us have inspired our lives, and we can look forward to catching up with them some day. We can follow the hollow, or the hallow. So, who are you dressing up as?

CHAPTER 61

NO JUNK IN THE TRUNK

Christmas is probably best known to the world at large as a season for giving and receiving gifts. I wonder how much time people devote to contemplating the original inspiration for the Christmas gift exchange. Even Christians can lose site of the true meaning of the season in all the hustle and bustle. Christmas, and every day for that matter, is an occasion to reflect on how Jesus Christ offers us the gift of forgiveness of our sins in exchange for us giving our lives to Him.

I must confess that I have become something of a scrooge when it comes to the formality of giving gifts. Most adults in the Western world are blessed to have their basic needs met. If I see something that I want that I can afford, I usually just buy it for myself. If I cannot afford to buy something, then chances are it is too expensive to expect someone else to buy it for me. It can be frustrating to come up with gifts that are truly a blessing or that "scratch an itch" for family or friends that they cannot scratch for themselves. Even more frustrating for me is answering that question, "So what do **you** want for Christmas?"

The tradition of gift giving runs deep in my family, however, and it seems like my extended family cannot resist showing up at the Christmas get together with at least a little something to give to each of the other households represented. These gifts generally fall in to one of three categories: calories, clutter, or gift certificates. Really, what else is there that is cost-appropriate to give on such occasions to those who already have their basic needs met? When you start exchanging gift certificates to the same location, you know that you are having trouble thinking outside of the gift box. I suppose there is always the old standby gift of underwear, which should be a bare necessity for everyone, but that can be rather awkward to open at an extended family gathering—whether the unmentionables are the functional or the fun kind.

Even though I certainly do not need any more calories or clutter, I do appreciate the thoughtfulness of my family in giving gifts because, after all, it is the thought that counts as the true gift. The best gifts, and the most challenging to give, are those that show that you have thought enough about others to provide them with things that are meaningful, yet that they likely could not or would not own on their own.

A truly meaningful gift is also one that costs us something—not just a few bucks that we will not miss, but rather a sacrifice of time or other resources that will remind **us** of the gift we gave. These are not the kinds of gifts that you find in the checkout line on Christmas Eve; they require thinking about a person the whole year through. Such inspired gift giving may be stressful, but it will at least be far from a formality.

One of the most beloved and timeless Christmas carols is "Silent Night." Perhaps the song describes Christmas as it should be rather than how it was—or is. Given the crowds and commotion in Bethlehem when Jesus was born, I suspect the hustle and bustle would make the shopping malls on Christmas Eve look tame. I doubt that many people stopped to notice a humble babe in a manger. This description sounds about right—now.

God's gift was wrapped in swaddling clothes in a manger. Like a bunch of fruitless nuts with our sins already baked in the cake, all that we can present in exchange is the unrighteousness regifted to us through a long line of sinners going all the way back to Adam and Eve. The present that we receive is forgiveness for our past, with a future wrapped up in eternal fellowship with our Creator (Romans 5:15–17). If you have ever seen one of the viral videos in which a child is surprised by a parent returning home after a long separation due to military service, then you get just a glimpse of the joy in store for us when our restored relationship culminates in the eternal presence of our Heavenly Father.

My personal goal is to remember the birth, death, and resurrection of Jesus Christ every day of my life, but perhaps God ordained holidays for those who might need occasions to stop, think, refresh, and strengthen their memories of what is important in the year to come. Unfortunately, there is a tendency to make holidays a time of stressful distraction. Christmas becomes a time of going into debt to buy gifts rather than a time to reflect on how Jesus Christ came to earth to sacrifice Himself to pay our debts.

If, after the holiday season, you are still distressed from your efforts to find the perfect gifts, or if you are trying to cope with the not-so-perfect gifts that you received by attempting to burn the calories, find a place for the clutter, or wait through the return line, remember that the thoughtfulness itself is the gift that counts. If you are thinking of regifting some of those things that did not quite meet your needs or tastes, remember that you can never go wrong regifting the hope of salvation that was freely given to you. It is indeed the gift that keeps on giving and that leads to many happy returns.

Jesus's answer to the question of what to give people that they would not otherwise have is, "You give yourself." Stressing the Savior as the reason for the season is thinking outside of the empty box of meaningless gift exchanges, and giving of yourself in sacrificial service is the bow on top. You may feel like a white elephant gift that is useless and more trouble than it is worth, but your Christlike example of service will not end up as just so much more junk in the trunk.

CHAPTER 62

KISS OF DEATH

There is a saying that seems to have originated in the field of military weapons design that has since become a motto in the development of technology in general. Perhaps you have heard the admonition to "keep it simple" or KISS.[88] The phrase proposes that things often work better when they are more simple rather than more complex. Greater complexity means that there is more that can go wrong, and fixing what does go wrong is likely to be more difficult. The KISS method is attributed to a military aircraft designer who challenged those who worked for him to design jet aircraft that could be repaired by an average mechanic with basic tools under combat conditions. In combat conditions, equipment that breaks down and is difficult to repair is much more likely to become worthless than a simple machine with a basic function.

Consider your mobile phone. Are you a smartphone or dumbphone person? Which type of phone must be replaced more often? Maybe smartphones should be called phony phones because, actually making phone calls seems to be one of their least used functions. Ironically, more advanced phones become obsolete quicker, even if it is just because we tend to want more newfangled features as soon as they become available. According to the Pew Research Center, as of 2019, eighty-one percent of

---

[88] Editorial restrictions do not allow me to include the word represented by the second S, even though it is not in the context of an insult. If you are unfamiliar with the complete KISS acronym, that is what search engines are for.

Americans owned a smartphone, but fully ninety-six percent relied on a cellphone of some kind. So, another benefit of the KISS concept is that, the more basic and easier a contraption is to understand, the more people there are who will likely find it to be useful.

The KISS concept asserts that sometimes the simplest solution is the most practical one. The stuff of genius is not always in creating more complexity, but rather in simplifying the complex. First Corinthians 1:18–21 (NLT 1996) explains KISS in a Christian context, straight from the lips of Paul:

> I know very well how foolish the message of the cross sounds to those who are on the road to destruction. But we who are being saved recognize this message as the very power of God. As the Scriptures say, "I will destroy human wisdom and discard their most brilliant ideas." So where does this leave the philosophers, the scholars, and the world's brilliant debaters? God has made them all look foolish and has shown their wisdom to be useless nonsense. Since God in his wisdom saw to it that the world would never find him through human wisdom, he has used our foolish preaching to save all who believe.

In other words, keep it simple. Every year that I have the privilege of accompanying our seniors to our nation's capital, laying a wreath at the Tomb of the Unknown Soldier is a highlight of the trip. The epitaph on the Tomb states: "Here rests in honored glory an American soldier known but to God." In fact, three unknown soldiers are entombed there, one each from World War I, World War II, and the Korean War. A soldier from the Vietnam War was buried there but was later identified and reinterred elsewhere.

The Tomb of the Unknown Soldier has been guarded constantly day and night every day of the year without exception since 1948. During the changing of the guard ceremony, the relief commander orders the relieved sentinel to "Pass on your orders." The sentinel responds, "Post and orders remain as directed." The new sentinel replies, "Orders acknowledged" and then begins his solemn vigil during which his eyes remain fixed straight ahead. Their orders are simple to understand: to maintain "the highest standards and traditions of the United States Army and this nation at this National Shrine," with a special duty "to prevent any desecration or disrespect directed toward the Tomb." Yet the preparation for this solemn duty is intense, with months of training and many hours preparing the uniform for each "walk" to guard the Tomb. Uniform details must be within $1/64^{th}$ of an inch of the standard. Several hours are spent on the shoeshine alone.

In our sacred walk with Jesus Christ, our direction has remained unchanged since the mission began. Our vision is straightforward and clear. In the Bible, you can find different iterations, but the basic orders never change: act justly, love mercy, and walk humbly with God (Micah 6:8); love the Lord your God with all of your heart, soul, strength, and mind, and love your neighbor as yourself (Luke 10:27); or go into all of the world and preach the gospel to everyone (Mark 16:15).

When you enlist as a follower of Jesus Christ, your orders are not always easy to carry out, and the preparation is meant to be intense and ongoing. Yet the orders are simple for all to understand. Perhaps Christians can modify KISS to mean "keep it simple service," or even "keep it simple sacrifice." We have a keep it simple Savior. So, today I pass on your orders. Your post and orders remain as directed: to maintain the highest standards of Jesus Christ, to proclaim the death of Jesus Christ until He comes again, and to guide others to the empty tomb of a Savior whom we can know and who wants to know us and to keep us from the kiss of death.

CHAPTER 63
GO TO THE HEAD
OF THE CROSS

Service to our Creator is a collaborative effort with other Christians. Communion with God requires communion with each other. As we individually seek to allow Jesus to replace our being with His, we merge with others to form the Body, or the Church of Jesus Christ. Just as each of us has one body with many parts that function as a whole, so the Body of Christ consists of each Christian playing a specialized role toward maintaining and growing the whole body (Romans 12:4–5). Deciding to commune with God through Jesus Christ is an essential first step; integrating into the community of fellow Believers is an important subsequent step that may require more sustained attention and effort.

Competition can be a problem in a community structured for cooperation, and the competitive spirit is often one of the last parts of our old sinful self to die. In the natural world, competition is par for the course, occurring whenever a goal is sought by but cannot be shared by more than one person or group at a time, like winning a game for instance. Competition is a zero-sum game. What one person gains is not available to others. For someone to win, someone else must lose. There is a time and place for some healthy competition in human interaction, but not so much when it comes to building the kingdom of God.

Some teachers use a grading system that I reject as fundamentally unfair. With this approach, a teacher decides before a course begins that a certain number of A's, B's, C's, D's, and F's will be given no matter what the students achieve. Usually, the distribution of grades looks like a bell-shaped curve, with most grades in the middle, and the other grades symmetrically tapering off to either side of the average grade so that there are relatively few A's or F's. Student grades are determined by how well they do relative to others rather than by how hard they try or how much they individually learn as measured according to an absolute standard. God does not evaluate Christians relative to the performance of others. At first blush, God's grading standard might seem even more stringent. He compares our human performance to the absolute standard of perfection. Since no one will ever measure up to His requirements for righteousness, God implemented a curve, a curve in the shape of a cross.

I once had a graduate school professor who told of offering classes with one million points possible during a semester. Students might only need to earn a thousand points to get an A, but the message was that there is always room for improvement—always more to learn than is realistically possible for one to learn. That is the way it is on God's grading scale. You automatically get a passing grade upon accepting Jesus Christ as Savior; whether you matriculate to Heaven with a GPA (God-Pleasing Accomplishment) of a D- or an A+ will be entirely determined by your performance on divine assignments and tests.

Your grade is earned according to your effort rather than according to how your performance compares to that of others. Even before the disciples digested their Last Supper with their Savior, they were bickering as to which one of them would be the greatest in the kingdom of Heaven. Jesus was quick to instruct them that status in God's society is determined by service to others (Luke 22:24–30).

Unlike competition, cooperative service yields a win-win outcome. Every time you take time to help someone else, you better their situation while earning some good marks in God's gradebook.[89] Just do not expect God to release the names on His honor roll until after school is out (Matthew 6:1–4). We need not compete because there will never be a shortage of

---

[89] Remember that, while service may earn rewards, salvation from sins requires more points than we could possibly earn. Fortunately, we only need "to put our name on the paper" because Jesus took the test for us.

opportunities to serve the Lord and each other. No matter how much you serve, you will never exhaust the need, you will never take opportunity from others, and you will never exceed the supply of rewards that you can store up for yourself in Heaven (Matthew 6:19–21).

Passing grades in school earn you an opportunity to walk across a stage wearing a funny looking cap and gown to receive a piece of paper. As I have stated before, the reward that I crave, what keeps me focused on serving Jesus Christ, is the stage of existence where I will hear my Savior say to me, "well done my good and faithful servant, enter into the joys of the Lord" (Matthew 25:21) What a commencement ceremony that will be!

Comparing yourself to other people can tempt you to think too much, or maybe even too little of yourself and thus divert your focus away from serving others. If you feel the need to compare yourself to someone, compare yourself to the greatest Teacher of all time, Jesus. Doing so is more likely to prod you to do better rather than to puff you up. Remember that you do not achieve greatness by besting others but by serving them so that they can become their best.

We will also be graded on our groupwork. Every time we sacrifice our own desires to make life easier for others, even if it is just bearing a splinter of their cross, we become a part of the sacrifice of Jesus Christ for all of humanity, and we contribute to building a community of fellow Believers with whom we will share eternity (Matthew 10:42). Making God's commandments and teachings the apple of our eye and helping others to follow them makes us star pupils in God's eyes (Proverbs 7:2). We are each ultimately responsible for the quality of our own work for God, and our efforts should give us the satisfaction of a life well lived. If we think that we are too important to help others, then we make fools of ourselves (Galatians 6:1–6).[90] Making the grade of the path to eternity easier for each other is no doubt a way to go to the head of the cross and to make the honor roll of Heaven.

---

[90] One of my personal favorite Scriptures is Galatians 6:6, which essentially says to share all good things with your teachers.

CHAPTER 64

LIFE'S A BEACHHEAD—
SHORE UP THE OFFENSE

During World War II, Adolph Hitler and his Nazi regime seemed to be on an unstoppable tear, conquering much of Europe and beyond. Then came June 6, 1944—the date of one of the most significant military events in the history of the world. This was D-Day, or the beginning of the Allied effort led by the United States to open up a western front against Germany and the Axis Powers in order to liberate France and the rest of Europe from the scourge of Nazism.[91] In the largest amphibious operation of all time, the Allies landed five divisions on the beaches of Normandy, France.[92]

Erwin Rommel, the commander of the German military forces, knew that an invasion was coming, but He did not expect it imminently since the weather was so bad. Indeed, the weather was too bad to storm the beaches, except for one fortuitous break on June 6th. Rommel was convinced that, once the invasion came, it would have to be crushed on the beaches so that the Allies did not gain a foothold from which to push back against the

---

[91] Not to be confused with the D-Day celebrated by many of my students when they find out that they will at least pass and be liberated from the scourge of a social studies class.

[92] This chapter is partly inspired by:

"D-Day," in *Meditations on the Lord's Supper* (Becoming Closer Adult Bible Fellowship, n.d.), 42, http://www.becomingcloser.org/Downloads%20PDF/Communion%20 Mediations.pdf.

German occupation. Although the Germans mounted a fierce and deadly resistance, the Allies were able to secure a tenuous beachhead.

Once the Allies established the beachhead, they needed a breakout into German occupied territory. Eventually they overcame the German defenses and raced across France, chasing the Germans back to their border and beyond with momentum limited mostly by the ability to supply the advancing army. The Germans would continue to mount a ferocious defense and even another desperate but deadly counteroffensive that became the Battle of the Bulge, but the consensus of historians seems to be that, once the beachhead was established on the Western Front, the defeat of the Germans was just a matter of time.

Just as Adolph Hitler led a Nazi conquest of so much of the world decades ago, so Satan, the prince of this world, launched a "sinvasion" of humanity. He has since occupied God's good earth, holding people as prisoners in the war between good and evil. Around two thousand years ago, when conditions were most favorable, Jesus Christ left Heaven as the Son of God to infiltrate behind enemy lines to establish a beachhead in Bethlehem from which to begin the breakout of those imprisoned by sin. From day one, Satan desperately fought to thwart God's plan to restore relationship with humanity. First, Satan tried to stop the incarnation in its infancy by provoking King Herod to slaughter all the babies that might become the King of Kings. Later, he tried to tempt Jesus to betray God's plan, and when nothing else worked, he got humanity to turn on and crucify its Savior. Fortunately for us, this was all a part of God's strategy to lose the battle on the cross to win the war on the grave consequences of sin.

Regardless of all of Satan's counteroffensives, Deliverance Day has occurred, and a beachhead has been established in every individual who has accepted Jesus Christ as Savior. Presently, Christians are enlisted on the frontline of the fight against good and evil that Aleksandr Solzhenitsyn described as running through the heart of every person. Satan is still mounting fierce resistance, but the breakout is underway and is limited only by our energy, knowledge, and obedience to God's battle plan. Satan will eventually be consigned to his dungeon as the King of Kings returns in person to mop up all the resistance until every knee bows and every tongue confesses that Jesus Christ is Lord (Philippians 2:9–11). Until that day, we defend against Satan's temptations and advance in fighting the good fight of faith to lay hold of eternal life in relationship with God (1 Timothy 6:11–12).

The counterinvasion began with an infant in a manger over two thousand years ago. That infant came to establish an infantry, of which you and I are recruits if we have been liberated from our sins by enlisting Jesus Christ as our Savior. We may be in the midst of daily battles, but Psalm 23:5 says that He prepares a table for us in the presence of our enemies. So, we feast, and we fight in fellowship with God the Father and with fellow Believers in Jesus Christ, the Son of God. In fact, Jesus proudly calls us His brothers and sisters now that we have been adopted into the family of God (Hebrews 2:11). Just as in the popular book and TV series inspired by D-Day and the ensuing fight to liberate Europe, we are a band of brothers—and sisters—in the fight to liberate fallen people occupied by a soul-destroying enemy.[93] The beachhead is established, the breakout is underway, the enemy is headed for his bunker, and V-E day, victory in eternity, could be any day now. God wants you to enlist in the mission to restore humanity to communion with Him. Become a part of the greatest generation in the battle between good and evil and help to hasten that final victory in the war that will truly end all wars (Micah 4:1–4).

---

[93] Stephen E. Ambrose, *Band of Brothers* (New York: Simon & Schuster, 2012).

CHAPTER 65

LIFE IS LIKE A BOX
OF CHOCOLATES

The events culminating in the Berlin Airlift in 1948 created one of the tensest moments of the entire Cold War, as well as one of the finest moments in American history.[94] To set the stage, at the end of World War II, the United States and the Soviet Union were racing each other to occupy Germany as they pushed the Nazis from both the west and the east back toward the German capital of Berlin. The United States devastated Berlin from the air with one of the most intense bombardments ever to occur, while the Soviets brutalized the city from the ground in ways beyond description. However, the Germans found the American bombs raining down from the sky to be even more terrifying than the face-to-face atrocities committed by the Soviets. When Germany surrendered, the democratic Allies and the communist Soviet Union divided the defeated nation and the city of Berlin amongst themselves until some type of reunification plan could be negotiated. Thus began a tense, often dramatic competition for the hearts and minds of the demoralized Germans.

As you might imagine, the spilled blood resulting from years of mortal combat had created a lot of bad blood between Americans and Germans. On top of that, German citizens had been indoctrinated for years to believe that

---

[94] For this summary of the Berlin Airlift, I primarily relied on:
Andrei Cherny, *The Candy Bombers: The Untold Story of the Berlin Airlift and America's Finest Hour* (London: Penguin Group, 2008).

Americans were practically evil incarnate and responsible for much of their hardship and suffering. Quite frankly, the Americans were not any more favorably disposed toward the Germans in the aftermath of the Holocaust and the devastation of Europe by Nazi aggression.

The Allies viewed the occupation of Germany as first and foremost an effort to put the Germans in their place so that they would never again be a military threat. Secondarily, the Allies wanted to get the Germans back on their feet economically and politically, primarily to prevent the decimated nation from becoming an international burden or a communist stooge of the Soviet Union. Whereas the Allies sought to instill democracy and free markets as the path to peace, the Soviets preferred communist domination as the way to keep the Germans under control and in their place.

Worried that the Allied efforts to create an independent Germany would catch on and spread into other areas under their control, the Soviets decided to turn up the heat in the Cold War. They cut off all ground transportation of supplies to West Berlin, which was completely surrounded by East German territory that was thoroughly dominated by the Soviet Union. As you might expect, the initial thought of many Americans was to use force to get supplies through to avoid ceding more territory to Soviet hegemony. However, the Soviets outnumbered U.S. soldiers sixty-two to one in the region. There were more Soviet troops near Berlin than the United States had in the entire world. So, you can understand why America and its allies, already exhausted by war, decided to consider other options. Since the Allies had little to bargain with, negotiations were going nowhere fast, and food and other essential supplies were disappearing. With Berliners saying that they preferred domination with security over freedom with starvation, abandoning the city to the Soviets seemed to many to be the only viable option.

Until a decision could be made about what to do, almost on a whim, emergency supplies were flown in on the few available aircraft. No one—American, Soviet, or German—believed that the basic survival needs of over two million people living in a bombed-out city could be supplied by air for any length of time. Yet, while the people in charge dithered over decisions, a few resourceful Americans began organizing an increasingly successful airlift operation that endured through some of the worst fogs and winter weather conditions ever recorded in Germany. Eventually, the Airlift was landing a plane in Berlin every three minutes and was able to deliver well over two million tons of supplies in total.

The irony that the same American bombers that were, just a few years before, raining death and destruction on the city were now delivering its very sustenance seemed lost on the Berliners, however. They distrusted the American will to stand behind their former sworn enemies and to offer a viable alternative to what the Soviets were promising—and threatening. In fact, the Germans were convinced that they were just pawns in a growing conflict between two new superpowers.

Berliners waited for the inevitable abandonment by the Americans and listened to the enticements of the Soviets to trust them to provide for the needs of the residents of the beleaguered city. It would only cost them any hope of freedom. The Soviets had many strategies for winning the allegiance of a desperate people. Even though the Americans were risking life and limb to deliver supplies through a Soviet blockade, the Soviets blamed the Americans for the German deprivation and tried to persuade them that the Americans were planning to abandon them. They tempted the Berliners with food and fuel, if they would only participate in the communist economy, and they threatened violence as a consequence for cooperating with the Allied plans for self-government.

In this desperate situation, one minor, chance encounter may have changed the course of history. One day, an American airlift pilot, Gail Halverson, decided to buck his orders to stay close to his airplane while he awaited clearance for a return flight after his plane was unloaded. Instead, he used his short downtime to walk the two miles to the end of the runway to take pictures of planes coming in for a landing. There he noticed a couple dozen German kids also gathered to watch the planes fly in. A simple "how are you" led to a little conversation with the children in their broken English. Realizing that it was almost time for his return flight, he turned away from the kids to hurry back to his plane. He felt a couple sticks of Wrigley's Doublemint gum in his pocket. His inclination was to give the gum to the kids, but on second thought, he wondered how it could be divided among so many. Nonetheless, he tore the sticks in two, and four kids got their first ever taste of chewing gum. The other children passed the tinfoil wrappers around, tearing off small slivers and savoring the smell. For Gail Halverson, at that moment, the faceless evil of Nazi Germany was supplanted by the faces of human beings who were ecstatic over just a small taste of a good life.

Somewhat impulsively, Halverson promised the children that the next day he would drop some candy from his plane as he flew overhead. "How will we know it is your plane," they asked. "Mine will be the plane that wiggles its wings," he answered. "Vhat is a Viggle," asked one little girl. He spread out his arms and put a little wiggle in his walk. To condense a fascinating story, the next day Operation Little Vittles began and grew to rally thousands of Americans to gather millions of pounds of candy and to make tens of thousands of small parachutes. American pilots, who had formerly delivered death and destruction on the Germans with great satisfaction, now eagerly anticipated dropping small candy-laden parachutes across the city. Germans, who had once lived in mortal dread of the sound of American bombers overhead, now heard the sound of hope for a better future.

For those of us whose sweet tooth has never been deprived, we might wonder what difference candy could make. Chewing gum was unheard of in much of Europe at the time. In fact, one European airline handed out sticks of gum labeled "to prevent unpleasant pressure in your ears during start and landing." A passenger flagged down a stewardess saying, "Help me get this stuff out of my ears. It doesn't help anyway." Even before the blockade, a five cent Hershey chocolate bar would cost twenty percent of a German's monthly wage and would more likely be used for currency than consumption. After the blockade began, candy was nonexistent in the besieged city. Delivering sweets from the sky served to give extra meaning to the mind-numbingly monotonous and seemingly incessant missions for the pilots, and it humanized formerly mortal enemies. Germans were reminded of the sweetness of human kindness and began to trust that the Americans had their best interests at heart. They steeled themselves for the sacrifices that would be required to be a free people.

Despite the overwhelmingly unfavorable odds, the Berlin Airlift outlasted the winter and the will of the Soviets, who after fifteen months gave up the blockade and their aspirations to spread communism to the rest of Germany. In fact, after this united stand of the Allies and the West Germans against the blockade, the communist revolutions sweeping Europe would not gain another inch of territory on the continent.

The Bible tells us to not "repay evil for evil," but rather to respond by doing good to those who do harm to us and to work hard to receive blessings from God. The Lord watches over those who do what is right but turns away from those who do evil. We are to maintain a clear conscience and work hard at living at peace with others while always being ready to explain our Christian hope with gentleness and respect. Thus, any criticism of us will be neutralized by our exemplary Christian lives. Suffer we must as a part of the human condition in this life, but it is better to suffer for doing what is right rather than for doing what is wrong. Indeed, we may still suffer at the hands or words of others, just as our role model Jesus Christ suffered, but by so doing, we will join Him in bringing others into relationship with their Creator to receive the reward that He has in store for them, and for us (1 Peter 3:9–18).

Perhaps the story of the Candy Bombers can serve as a spiritual illustration. I do not have to stretch my imagination too far to imagine the Soviet Communists, led by Joseph Stalin, in the role of Satan, and the Americans as Christians who have experienced forgiveness of sins and who wish to share this freedom with others. Okay, maybe that is a little wishful typecasting. As for the Berliners, well I will compare them to lost souls caught between two superpowers with two different visions for their future.

The lesson then for those of us already living freely in communion with Jesus Christ could be that our mission is the Great Commission, to penetrate enemy territory, bringing sustenance and hope to win the hearts and minds of a captive people. Satan will try to convince those in bondage to sin that God is the source of their suffering rather than the One who suffered for their deliverance through Jesus's brutal execution. We will be portrayed as the enemy and must avoid playing to type as judgmental, holier-than-thou Christians. We must recognize that sinners, no matter what depravity they are caught up in, are not the enemy, and we must deliver the message of John 3:17, that Jesus did not come to condemn the world but to save it. The last flight of the Berlin Airlift—the 277,264th—landed on September 23, 1949 with a reference to Psalm 21:11 painted on the nose of the plane: "If they plan evil against you, if they desire mischief, they will not succeed."[95]

---

[95] Richard Reeves, *Daring Young Men: The Heroism and Triumph of The Berlin Airlift—June 1948—May 1949* (New York: Simon & Schuster, 2010), 271.

I wish that I could promise sinners an easy existence if they would just embrace freedom in Jesus Christ, but the truth is that, in both the physical and spiritual realms of this life, freedom and security cannot be guaranteed to exist together. Freedom in Christ means taking up His cross and giving up everything that makes us secure in this physical life in order to secure a place in the next. What we can offer to sinners are words of kindness, which Proverbs 16:24 describes as sweet to the soul and healthy for the body, and we can offer the Word of God, which Psalm 119:103 describes as sweet to taste.

Candy from the sky did not eliminate the suffering of the Berliners, but it did change their attitude and offer them hope for things to come. A proverb from an extra-biblical source describes life as "like a box of chocolates, you never know what you're gonna get."[96] Jesus knew exactly what He was going to get when He laid down His life, the least appetizing of the assortment— like the lemon-lime, coconut, mint crème concoction that everyone wants to spit out upon first taste—and yet Jesus offers us His all-consuming love anyway.

---

[96] *Forrest Gump*, directed by Robert Zemeckis (Paramount Pictures, 1994), Film.

CHAPTER 66

TAKE ME TO YOUR LEADER

I suspect that I am not the only one who is often discouraged by the choices of candidates for public office. Sometimes one might think that, if a candidate changed his legal name to "None of the Above," then he would win in a landslide. However, I am often reminded of a tendency for cohabitants of our present age to have an exaggerated sense of the significance and uniqueness of our own time and place in history. The study of history can remind us of how sordid politics has always been. I cannot help but to be somewhat amused when I encounter an historical account that seems ripped from today's headlines. As Mark Twain is credited with musing, history may not repeat itself, but it certainly rhymes.

Although some may consider each generation to be more enlightened than the last, the historical record indicates that the human condition is consistently and predictably deplorable. There is nothing new under the sun (Ecclesiastes 1:9), and our time and place are not beyond the pale when it comes to evil. I am encouraged when I realize that Jesus was no stranger to discouraging circumstances, and that the darkest of times often precede the dawn of great triumphs.

Consider the night of Jesus's Last Supper with His disciples. After years of prepping His closest followers to carry on after His physical presence on earth came to an end, Jesus's time was running out. Before the night was over, Jesus would be betrayed, abandoned, and denied by these very people in whom He had invested so much time and energy. He would find them asleep at the switch and by all appearances far from ready for primetime.

Perhaps most troubling was their lack of understanding of His purpose on this eve of a major turning point in God's grand plan to once and for all establish a path to relationship with humanity.

Imagine someone taking an exit poll of the disciples as they left the Last Supper with their Leader in the Upper Room and headed out to the Garden of Gethsemane. There Jesus would long for the prayerful support of His followers as He poured out to God His anguish over His imminent betrayal, torture, and execution.[97] Perhaps the poll results would be reported as follows.

"Excuse me sir, do you have a minute? What is your name?"

"I'm Judas Iscariot, I don't have time to talk. I have something I have to do."

"Well ok. How about you sir, what is your name and what did you think about this evening?"

"My name is Matthew, former IRS agent. I was just wondering why Judas left so quickly. He took the money with him. I am sure he is up to no good. I wasn't a tax collector for nothing you know. I can spot a crook a mile away. He probably told Jesus that he was going to donate the money to charity, but my deduction is that he will keep the money for himself. I don't know why our Master didn't have his number and try to stop him."

"Thank you, and you sir, what is your name and what are your opinions about Jesus and His claims to be the Messiah?"

"I am Simon the Zealot. I am deeply disappointed. As you can tell from my name, I am zealous for a fight. I thought for sure that when He asked if anyone had a sword, we were finally going to rise up and give those Romans the boot back to where they came from. Instead, He kept talking about Heaven and apparently about how He would die soon. And people say I'm morbid."

"And you sir?"

"Yeah, my name is Philip. I am really confused. I asked Jesus to reveal God the Father to us and suggested that would be an offer we can't refuse.

---

97 This illustration is partly inspired by John 13–16 and:
Douglas Feaver, *This Do in Remembrance of Me* (Greenville, SC: Ambassador International, 2008), 40–42.

Instead, Jesus said that, when we were talking to Him, we were talking to God the Father. I didn't even get a chance to ask a follow up question."

"I doubt you know me. I'm Thomas. I really love this guy. I mean, I would even die for him. It's just that, well, I need some more evidence to genuinely believe all of the claims that he has made about himself."

"How about this gentleman here, what do you remember most about this evening?"

"I'm Andrew, and I was really bothered when He said that our friends, from the church no less, would turn against us and possibly even kill us thinking that they were doing God a favor."

"Sir, your name and what did you think?"

"I'm Judas, just J-U-D-A-S; don't confuse me with that rascally Iscariot fellow. I wondered why He just wanted to tell us all these things and not tell them to other people also. From what I could gather He wants us to do the telling."

"Tell me about it, brother. You know, if you just went by Jude, you could avoid all that confusion with that black sheep Judas. Anyway, they call me James the Lesser so as not to confuse me with that older and better-known James, who is John's brother. Like my brother, Jude, I expected Jesus to lead us in great military feats. Instead, He washed our feet. I mean, who does that except for some kind of servant? I suppose that He is trying to tell us that being a servant doesn't stink. So much for that promotion to James the Greater that I was hoping for."

"Excuse me. I'm Peter, and I've got to say that I was more than a little hurt. Here I am strapped with our only sword, and, let him who has ears hear, I am willing to cut to the chase if anyone gets in His way. But He predicted that I would deny Him three times before this night is over."

"And finally, you sir. I understand that you were very close to Jesus."

"Well, I'm John, and I thought there were so many wonderful things that He said that I need to write them down so that no one forgets them. I just hope that I don't run out of paper, because now I understand that we have a new commandment to follow—that we need to love each other. I wonder if that includes even that Judas Iscariot fellow."

"And there you have it. On the very night before a three-day sequence of events that will usher in the culmination of God's plan for restoring communion with His creation, one hundred percent of our respondents do not seem so sure as to why they have been following this Jesus for the past three years, or what they should expect next."

Disappointment with leadership is nothing new. I think that we can be forgiven for being somewhat disillusioned with and uncertain about our candidates at times; after all, they are flawed human beings just like those of us who vote for them. It could be our expectations that are amiss. However, just remember that Jesus Christ is our perfect leader, and we are His elect (Romans 8:33). Our mission has been clearly revealed: to take up our cross, to follow Jesus Christ, and by so doing, to lead others to Him (Luke 9:23).

I do not know what God's plans are for the future of the United States, but I do know what His plans are for us (Jeremiah 29:11). Christians are aliens and exiles from the world, and even at war against an enemy who seeks to steal, kill, and destroy everyone's relationship with God. Christians are instructed to live upright lives and to do good to bring glory to God while being impervious to all the mudslinging. That may inspire those who have not yet cast their lot with Jesus Christ to be receptive to God's campaign for their souls (1 Peter 2:11–12).

Although Christians should by all means participate fully in the democratic process, we must also think outside the ballot box. I suspect that, even though followers of Jesus Christ are aliens in this strange land, the madness of the times will inspire more people to ask us to take them to our Leader. Then we can introduce them to something new under the Son, the Son of God.

CHAPTER 67

STRETCH ARMSTRONG

There is an old saying that what is old is new, and that can include disappointments over the way things are going in the world around us. Many Christians wonder if the United States has fundamentally changed and is past the point of no return to founding principles of individual liberty, responsibility, and equality. Maybe we can take some odd comfort in the realizations that our founding principles have always been aspirational, and that the current state of the Union is merely a function of the human condition's perpetual state of disunion with the Creator.

Administering the cure for the human condition is the ultimate reason for being a Christian on God's good earth. Indeed, there is a danger of complacency when Christians are feeling comfortable with the cultural direction of the country, or with the political leadership. I do not expect that, if the candidates who seem best to me just win their races for political office, then the Devil will take a powder and allow me to take a victory lap in my running of the race of service to God (Hebrews 12:1). Rather, I expect that the forces of darkness will just work all the harder, perhaps making subtle but substantial advancements of evil under the cover of Christian complacency. There is no coasting in the kingdom of God as we strive to do our part to help build it one soul at a time.

As I mentioned earlier, each year I have the pleasure of accompanying students to the Tomb of the Unknown Soldier in Arlington National Cemetery. Through every natural and manmade trial and tribulation faced by our nation, the Tomb Guard has kept constant vigil every hour of every day since 1948. Each guard must be meticulous in appearance, often spending as much as eight hours just shining shoes for a half-hour walk guarding the Tomb. As one sentinel is relieved by another, he states, "post and orders, remain as directed."

As soldiers of the most high God, our post remains this earth, and our orders remain to know God and to make Him known to lost human souls who are merely pawns of evil spiritual forces. Our standard equipment, or armor, for standing firm in the face of fierce opposition from the forces of darkness is described in Ephesians 6:10–17. Salvation from our sins serves as a helmet that protects our thinking and attention from being diverted from our reason for being or from our mission. We also have a belt of God's absolute truth buckled around our waists so that we do not buckle to whims of wickedness. Logic, reason, and science are very fashionable with this belt. Those without a standard for truth have lost their pants, so to speak, exposing their moral nakedness and lack of legs to stand on. Christians have also been issued a shield of faith to block all the incoming darts of doubts about our beliefs or abilities that are fired at us by our enemy. Anything that makes it past this shield can be blocked by the breastplate of right living that protects us from suffering the consequences of bad behaviors. Our spiritual shoes should fit perfectly and shine brilliantly as we carry forth the sword of God's Good News of peace and good will toward humanity. This double-edged sword will cut to pieces the Devil's deception that binds lost souls in sins that separate them from God (2 Timothy 3:16).

I cannot help but think of Christians so blessed to live in the United States of America when I read about God's chosen people of a different time and place. God brought the Jewish people into a promised land with an incredible abundance of food and natural resources. He instructed His people to credit Him for the abundant provision, and He warned them that it would be in the good times that they would be most inclined to forget about Him, about the bondage that He delivered them from, and about His commandments that would make prosperity possible for posterity (Deuteronomy 8:7–14). Unfortunately, God's warning went unheeded, and what follows in Scripture is a recounting of centuries of a cycle where God's people would do whatever seemed right to them (Judges 17:6), get themselves into deep trouble, and then call upon God to send someone to rescue them.

This is the scene into which God raised up men like Samson to rally His people to righteousness and deliverance from their enemies. Samson was called by God to be set apart for special service, even before he was born. The Bible describes him as imbued with superhuman strength, at least of body if not of spirit. Unfortunately, Samson succumbed rather than succeeded. He made several bad decisions to fulfill his physical desires, not the least of which was marrying the wrong person—someone who seemed right to him but who was far from a match made in Heaven, at least for the purposes that Samson intended (Judges 14:1–3).

The summary of Samson's sad story is that he lost sight of his purpose, lost his strength, and lost his eyesight to boot.[98] Like Samson, Christians have been endowed with supernatural strength to help bring deliverance to those held captive to sin. Also, like Samson, our eyes can tend to wander after the world, and we can become part of the problem rather than the solution.

Christians need to be careful to avoid the ditches on either side of the straight and narrow path in pursuit of God's plan. The Pharisees were the most respected religious leaders of Jesus's day. They prided themselves on their rigorous efforts to follow to the letter every one of God's laws and many more of their own making, and they were quick to let everybody know that they were holier than thou. Christians sometimes need to repent of a pharisaical spirit that preaches the letter of the law that is beyond what they can deliver themselves, while at the same time ignoring the spirit of the law, which is intended to bring hope of a better life to everyone. In other words, Christians should take more care to offer compassion rather than condemnation. Jesus did not condemn sinners seeking to repent; He only condemned those who thought that they had nothing to repent of.

Christians must also be careful not to overcompensate and end up in the ditch on the other side of the path to Heaven. This can happen when Christians take down the guardrails for human behavior while seeking to lead others into right relationship with God. The Holy Bible, God's instruction manual for humanity, provides the absolute standard for determining right and wrong. Indeed, it is the most effective anchor for cultures adrift in a sea of moral relativism. Not only are Christians often reluctant to point out to

---

[98] See Judges 13-15 for the complete Samson story.

others the pitfalls of sin, but they are also often averse to holding themselves to such standards. Many churches have apparently normalized divorce, sexual immorality, and general irresponsibility. I do not say this to condemn Christians who have failed to meet God's standards in these areas; indeed, all Christians should recognize their susceptibility to and inevitability of falling short of God's expectations for righteousness. As the saying goes, Christians aren't perfect; they are just forgiven—if they realize that they need to be.

My concern is for Christians who see no point in trying to live according to biblical standards, or in offering guidance to others to do so. Both Scripture and social science offer abundant evidence of the benefits associated with living according to the measures that the Bible prescribes, as well as clear indicators of the negative consequences to be expected from practicing biblically proscribed behaviors. Ignoring, excusing, or enabling failures to heed biblical instruction due to misguided compassion can amount to neglect of duty by those whom God may be counting on to offer constructive correction to others who are on a path to destruction.

Jesus truly offered love, compassion, and forgiveness to all comers, yet He did not shy away from telling people coming to Him in dire straits that they should instead walk the straight and narrow path to relationship with their Creator—to go and sin no more (John 8:1–11). Christians must seek God's guidance as to how to offer the proper balance of compassion and accountability necessary to nurture the kingship of Jesus Christ in other people's lives. By words and by actions, Christians should lend credibility to God's Word as the absolute truth for all people, in all places, at all times.

Christians should recognize and renounce any spirit of condemnation, but they must also offer a biblical perspective to those who believe that they get to decide for themselves what is right and acceptable in the eyes of God. That is the very spirit of rebellion against God that got the parting started in the first place, the Garden of Eden, and a bad time has been had by all ever since. Humanity's communion with the Creator ended, and the fallen human condition began when Satan convinced Adam and Eve to rely on their own judgment as to right or wrong rather than on God's instructions (Genesis 3:5). Immediately, the parents of us all stood naked and afraid before God, with the shame of human limitations readily apparent (Genesis 3:7). The mission for Christians in the current age of God's grace and mercy is to introduce with Christlike compassion both God's desire for relationship and His standard of righteousness to whosoever will listen—before it is time for them to stand before God in judgment.

How do we as Christians present the truth of God's Word with compassion rather than condemnation? The precondition is to have our own house in order—to give our best effort to exemplify the qualities of lives well-lived in obedient relationship with God. Then, with gentleness and respect, be ready to credit Jesus Christ for the positive attributes that will attract the attention of those without such hope. Such a lifestyle not only assures a clear conscience, but it will also serve to silence our critics, or at least to make their criticisms fall on deaf ears (1 Peter 3:15–16). As St. Francis of Assisi put it, "Preach the Gospel at all times. When necessary, use words."

Christians cannot lead people to a saving knowledge of Jesus Christ if they have only one eye on the Word of God and the other eye on the world. Rather, Christians are to be "cross-eyed," in the sense of being focused on giving up the pleasures of sin for a season and instead taking upon themselves the cross of Christ by sacrificially serving God and others (Luke 14:27). In Philippians 3:15–21 (MSG), Paul offers the following advice to those pursuing God's call to relationship with Him:

> So let's keep focused on that goal, those of us who want everything God has for us. If any of you have something else in mind, something less than total commitment, God will clear your blurred vision—you'll see it yet! Now that we're on the right track, let's stay on it.
>
> Stick with me, friends. Keep track of those you see running this same course, headed for this same goal. There are many out there taking other paths, choosing other goals, and trying to get you to go along with them. I've warned you of them many times; sadly, I'm having to do it again. All they want is easy street. They hate Christ's Cross. But easy street is a dead-end street. Those who live there make their bellies their gods; belches are their praise; all they can think of is their appetites.

But there's far more to life for us. We're citizens of high heaven! We're waiting the arrival of the Savior, the Master, Jesus Christ, who will transform our earthy bodies into glorious bodies like his own. He'll make us beautiful and whole with the same powerful skill by which he is putting everything as it should be, under and around him.

Unfortunately for the Children of Israel, all their deliverers were flawed human beings offering at best temporary restoration of relationship with God. Unfortunately for us, and for the U.S., the frailties of those of us whom God has chosen to make Him known are as evident as in any previous generation. Fortunately for Christians, we are only responsible to do our level best to be followers of Jesus Christ and communicators of the salvation that He has already delivered once and for all. God is responsible for taking us to the next level.

Like Samson, Christians have been endowed with supernatural strength, although of a spiritual sort. Unlike Samson, we must keep our eyes on the prize of our calling if we are to fulfill the purpose for which we have been placed on this earth. Hebrews 12:2 (MSG) says: "Keep your eyes on Jesus, who both began and finished this race we're in. Study how he did it. Because he never lost sight of where he was headed—that exhilarating finish in and with God—he could put up with anything along the way: cross, shame, whatever. And now he's there, in the place of honor, right alongside God."

Back in my day as a child, there was a classic toy called Stretch Armstrong, which was essentially a doll that might strike a boy's fancy. It was a latex rubber and corn syrup filled action figure of a muscular man wearing only what would appear to be a black Speedo. He could be stretched from around a foot in size to over four feet, after which he would shrink back to original size. I do not recall ever having one. Maybe my childhood was more deprived than I remember. I understand that Stretch Armstrong was recently resurrected as a toy for the modern era, so maybe it is not too late for me to go for a Stretch.

For Samson's swan song, he really brought the house down. Samson stretched out his arms between two support pillars of a large temple filled with thousands of his enemies. With the last ounce of his renewed strength, he pushed the columns apart, collapsing the building and thus avenging the loss of his sight and freedom by bringing down destruction and death upon his jeering tormenters, and himself. He accomplished more in his death than he did in his life.

Jesus Christ stretched out His arms on a cross and brought salvation and new life to His enemies who surrender to Him—that would be us (Romans 5:10). The harsh reality is that most people will reject as foolishness the message that we bring, but our orders remain to preach Christ crucified and risen from the tomb so that as many people as possible can have relationship with God. His outstretched arms are strong enough to hold whosoever will fall into them.

CHAPTER 68

SURF'S UP

Making the last notch on my continental travel belt required a trek to the farthest away of them all, Australia. So, I embarked upon the most ambitious journey of my lifetime, an odyssey of over 28,000 miles to and from and around the land down under via planes, trains, and automobiles, not to mention some walkabout. One of the most profound moments of the trip for me was touring the Great Ocean Road along the southern coast of Australia. This is widely considered to be one of the most scenic ocean drives in the world, and it is spectacularly beautiful looking out over the rough and tumble Southern, or Antarctic Ocean. One of the noteworthy sites along the route is the Loch Ard Gorge.

The *Loch Ard* was an 18th century clipper ship. My journey of 25 hours flight time to get to Australia may have seemed long, but in the early morning hours of June 1, 1878, the *Loch Ard* was nearing the end of a three-month voyage from England to Australia with 54 passengers and crew. The final destination, Melbourne, was tantalizingly close when the *Loch Ard* struck a reef and broke apart just off the coast. Nineteen-year-old Tom Pearce, a ship's apprentice, was able to hold on to debris and wash ashore in this gorge. He heard the cries of one other person in the surf and was able to swim back out to get nineteen-year-old Eva Carmichael to shore. All fifty-two other souls perished in the ocean. Tom and Eva sheltered in a cave until Tom was able to climb up the cliff face and get help from some shepherds. Eva lost her parents, three sisters, and two brothers that night.

Loch Ard Gorge, Australia (Photo by author)

While I was blissfully gorging my eyes on the panoramic view, I began thinking about differences in perspective. From where I was standing, listening to all the "oohs" and "aahs" of the tourists, this was the Great Ocean Road. The other side of the shoreline is called the Shipwreck Coast. Well over 600 ships and an untold number of lives have been lost along this coastline over the years. No doubt Eva could never appreciate the rugged beauty of the place where her family perished.

During its final hours afloat, the *Loch Ard* was sailing through a thick fog in the early morning darkness, so close to the shore that the cliffs blocked the site of a nearby lighthouse positioned to warn ships away from the reefs. How many people that we interact with daily are just offshore of salvation, blissfully sailing through life, anticipating arrival at some destination, yet oblivious to the peril around them?

For those of us who have been rescued from the sea of our sins, we can see the beauty of the contrast between where we were, and where we are, safe on the shore. This marvelous vantage point of a saved soul is only possible because of the unimaginable sufferings of Jesus Christ, who is the Captain of our Salvation (Hebrews 2:10 in the KJV). In this present life, we will remain cliffside, with the tumultuous tides of our past behind us, and a view of the Promised Land on the near horizon before us. We must remain ever vigilant in looking out for God's guidance lest we be swept back into the sea. Disobedience to God can shipwreck our faith, or the faith of others following us, on the shoals of sin (1 Timothy 1:18–19).

Another beautiful attraction along the Great Ocean Road is a series of sea stacks. These particular rock formations carved out of the coastline are popularly known as the Twelve Apostles in reference to the first Christians who introduced the Gospel message to new lands. They were shaped through centuries of wind and water erosion enhanced by extreme weather conditions along the coast. The sea stacks have gradually been worn away by the wind and waves; however, these same forces are constantly creating new formations along the shoreline. Christians get shaped by the tempests of life, especially when staking out turf between the sea of sin and the shore of salvation. For the time being, this is where we are stationed as lifeguards, rescuing people drowning in sin and helping them to gain a firm footing for an eternal future in relationship with God in the Promised Land of Heaven. As one generation of apostles passes away from the rough and tumble of rescuing the perishing, another generation is being formed to mark the edge of eternity.

What's Left of the Twelve Apostles Rock Stacks in Victoria, Australia (Photo by author)

Christians are safe on the shore with a great view of the Promised Land, but for now our course is cruising the coastline of God's kingdom, hugging the shoreline between sin and salvation. We experience the buffeting of an occasional storm, but our future is secure, both for this life and for the one to come. We can marvel at the view formed by the contrast between where we are and where we were. However, the primary reason for our sojourn along the great ocean road is for us to watch and listen for those calling for help from the surf of sin so that we can throw them the lifeline of salvation through Jesus Christ and then shepherd them safely on shore. Someday God will call us into even closer communion with Him, and we will take a sharp turn toward the Promised Land. But for now, the surf's up.

CHAPTER 69
FRUIT LOOPS

Late one night, as another sixteen-hour workday was ending, I was brushing my teeth and apparently reflecting subconsciously on the day's efforts to educate the students entrusted to me. Although I was wishing for a few more hours off the clock before my 5:30 a.m. alarm went off, I was feeling the satisfaction of a hard day's work and was looking forward to the next day's opportunities. Teaching, it seems, has become my occupation in the fullest sense of the word—not only my vocation, but also my avocation, my recreation, and even my procreation as I seek to leave a mark on the future. So, it was rinse, spit, and reflect on a sudden, sinking feeling that my instructional labors, momentarily satisfying though they are, may not have as much lasting value as I would like to think. Perhaps it was just a flash of fatigue, or maybe the reflection in the vanity mirror was an image of a mid-life crisis in the making.

My concern that my life's work to combat societal decay through education might amount to trying to squeeze the toothpaste back into the tube was alleviated when a couple Scripture verses popped into my mind, one from the Old Testament and one from the New. I do not recall ever thinking about these two verses at the same time before, but all the sudden a connection seemed to become crystal clear.

The first Scripture that I thought of was Genesis 1:28–29 (NIV), which describes how God blessed Adam and Eve in the Garden of Eden and said to them, "'Be fruitful and increase in number; fill the earth and subdue it. Rule over the fish in the sea and the birds in the sky and over every living creature that moves on the ground.' Then God said, 'I give you every seed-bearing plant on the face of the whole earth and every tree that has fruit with seed in it. They will be yours for food.'"

As a single man whose biological clock is increasingly raising alarms about the merciless progression of life, I have occasionally felt guilty about being so distracted from fulfilling this Old Testament commission to reproduce. But then I thought of what Jesus said in Matthew 28:19–20 (NIV): "Therefore go and make disciples of all nations, baptizing them in the name of the Father and of the Son and of the Holy Spirit, and teaching them to obey everything I have commanded you. And surely I am with you always, to the very end of the age."

With the juxtaposition of these two Scripture passages, I felt that God was giving me a little reminder that, with a New Testament, Christians have a new commission. Our modern-day mission is not so much to populate earth as it is to populate Heaven. Having children and raising them in the nurture and admonition of the Lord is a wonderful way to populate Heaven, especially since those children can become fellow laborers in the mission field for harvesting lost souls. And of course, if we bring children into the world, preparing them for Heaven must be priority number one. Otherwise, instead of creating helpers for the harvest, we are just creating more work for the harvesters. Whether we have our own children or not, in the present age, our reproductive efforts are to be not so much about increasing the size of our own family as they are to be about growing the family of God.

The Old Testament commission was corrupted in the Garden of Eden by the curse resulting from Adam and Eve's disobedience to God. Life went from caretaking the Garden without a care in the world, to toil and trouble requiring painful labor through sticky situations to produce both fruit of the soil and fruit of the loins. After the fall into sin, the occupation for all of humanity became merely a function for marking time until the body returned to the dust from which it came (Genesis 3:18–19).

Because of this curse, our physical bodies are like a dying plant whose only hope to leave a lasting presence on earth is to produce seed for another generation. The curse, however, was ended by the cross. The death, burial, and resurrection of Jesus Christ became the "dustbuster," or the prototype of a new pattern and a new hope for perpetuating our seed—no sweat! Just as a seed essentially dies as it leaves its plant of origin and then sprouts into a new plant, so we leave our perishable old lives originating from the dust of the earth and sprout into new, imperishable lives in Christ that are suitable to inhabit the environment of Heaven (1 Corinthians 15:36–50).

The effort of all organisms to reproduce "after their own kind" is likely the strongest of all compulsions, even more so than the instinct for individual survival (Genesis 1:11-28). This is evidenced by the willingness of parents in many species to sacrifice themselves to save their offspring. Even bacteria and viruses seem programmed primarily to perpetuate the species, although their reproductive measures may seem counterproductive since they may debilitate or kill their host organisms and thus themselves. Yet disease symptoms such as sneezing, coughing, and even less pleasant and more deadly evacuations of contaminated bodily fluids and particles are generally reproductive strategies of infectious organisms seeking to "go viral."

I used to feel very strongly, and sometimes still do feel, the desire to father children to make a splash in the gene pool that will at least ripple if not make waves long after I am gone. However, I am reminded that Jesus left His disciples, including all of us who would follow Him in perpetuity, with a new example and a new commission. As children of God, reproducing after our kind has an entirely new meaning. It is not about what we accomplish in our daily busyness or careers, and it is not about how many offspring we leave behind on earth. It is about how many people we help to bring into relationship with their Heavenly Father, thus putting offspring in our steps to Heaven.

We are to plunder Hell and populate Heaven. It does not matter if we are preparing the soil, planting the seed, watering the growing crops, or pulling the weeds—we are sharing in the harvest (1 Corinthians 9:10). I am under the impression that in Heaven, earthly family ties are superseded by the common inheritance of all brothers and sisters in Jesus Christ. If we feel any special closeness to any certain individuals in Heaven, I wonder if it will be to those whom we helped to bring into the kingdom, whether through the fruit of our loins or through the fruit of our labor. Make some fruit loops and reproduce after your own kind.

CHAPTER 70
FRUIT PRESERVES

Whether in career, interpersonal relationships, or any aspect of earthly existence, the calling for any of us who are growing in relationship with our Heavenly Father through Jesus Christ is to build God's kingdom by sharing with others our hope for eternity. The seed that was planted within us grows and matures and bears fruit, which is in itself seed to be planted for the next generation. Some of that seed may sprout into the salvation of souls that are nipped in the bud before blossoming into fruitful relationships with God. One reason why many new Christian converts may not stick the landing in eternal relationship with their Creator is because they are unprepared for the challenges of living "like Christ." They may expect that the hand of God will wave a magic wand to make all their difficulties disappear. Some may expect the Christian life to be like a beautiful bed of roses, and maybe it is. But any good rose garden has its thorns, and perhaps some manure as well.

Over the years of preparing our school's senior class trip to Washington, D.C. and Gettysburg, I have come to realize that, for a good time to be had by all, the students must have realistic expectations for the trip. Students anticipating a party excursion with all fun all the time end up disillusioned and disappointed. They soon develop a bad attitude that spreads to others. Since they are hundreds of miles away from home, they are not going anywhere, but their disillusionment diminishes the enjoyment of the trip for everyone else. To minimize this eventuality, I started making a point of emphasizing to students in advance that, although the trip offers priceless opportunities for fun and memories, it requires discipline to eat and sleep well, willingness to listen and learn, and patience for those with whom they will share the experience. I compare the trip to a short but very intense boot camp due to the many physical and mental demands of trying to pack as many experiences as possible into a six-day and five-night escape from the confines of normal school days. Afterward, the seniors are exhausted but generally report a great sense of satisfaction in the memories made. I am convinced that the preliminary attitude adjustment makes the trip a more positive experience for everyone, which is not to say that there is never any testiness before it is all over. Just imagine, four teenagers sharing one hotel room with only two beds and one bathroom for five nights.

Central to the Gospel is the message that we share in the sacrifice of Jesus Christ—that we are crucified with Christ and that daily we take up our cross to follow Him (Matthew 16:24–26). Fortunately, Jesus offers us glorious riches now and forevermore, but not without sharing some of his gut-wrenching suffering on the journey. King David said that he would not offer to the Lord something that cost him nothing (2 Samuel 24:24). Sharing in the sufferings of Jesus is an investment that strengthens our resolve to endure to the end. In the investment world, there is a saying that you should avoid trusting a financial intermediary to invest your money unless that person also has some "skin in the game." In other words, do not let financial advisers talk you into putting your money where only their mouth is. If they are true believers in the investment, then their money should be at risk as well.[99]

When we are encouraging others to invest their faith where we have placed our faith, they need to see that our trust and our hope in Jesus Christ, the intermediary between God and people, will endure through the bad times as well as the good ones. Whether we are relative newcomers, or grizzled veterans in Christian service, we must work to prepare others, and ourselves, to weather the difficulties and distractions that are inevitable while growing up in the family of God. Saved or unsaved, the hard times will come. We have an enemy who will try to discourage us and distract us from

[99] Economics teacher disclaimer: Of course, there are exceptions and many additional factors to consider when deciding where to invest money, yet Heaven offers the only investment where past performance guarantees future results.

275

the only hope there is in this world. Only we can determine if we will yield fruit or yield to pressure—whether tough times will get us going or gone.

So, do not be surprised or disillusioned when life's inevitable difficulties and persecutions arise. In fact, embrace the trials of life with pure joy, for such testing of your faith produces perseverance, and perseverance will allow you to mature completely into whom God wants you to be without lacking anything, especially wisdom (James 1:2–5). When you find yourself in a jam, do not let it jar your faith and turn it into jelly, just think of it as fruit preserves.

CHAPTER 71
THE DEVIL IN 3D

There once was a comedian named Flip Wilson who was known for his catchphrase: "the Devil made me do it." In popular culture, the Devil and demons seem primarily to populate horror shows or harmless humor. While writing this manuscript, an effort that has certainly required the most extensive use of a word processing program in my lifetime, I could not help but think of demon possession straight from the Gates of Hades every time some strange formatting that I thought I had fixed once and for all suddenly manifested itself again on my screen, not to mention upon every appearance of unsolicited popup advertisements that persist despite my best efforts to exorcise the malware from my computer. The absolute bane of my "e-xistence" is popups advertising programs to stop popup ads. Responding to such an ad could be an able analogy for selling one's soul to the Devil.

Modern imagery of the Devil often pointedly entails some fiendish figure sporting a red suit with caricatured features such as horns, pointy ears, goatee, malevolent smile, and a pitchfork, and perhaps this suits the Devil just fine since not taking him too seriously may work to his advantage. I have heard it said that there can be two equally grievous errors when it comes to dealing with the dirty details of our lives: giving the Devil too much credit for our own mistakes or failing to give due diligence to thwarting the Devil's very real efforts to steal, kill, and destroy our relationship with our Creator (John 10:10). The Bible clearly posits that there is an enemy of our souls who competes for the allegiance that we owe only to our Creator; however, his work can be very subtle and deceptive and may even mimic God's designs for our lives (2 Corinthians 11:14).

Personally, I find one of the most humbling and unsettling Scriptures in the Bible to be Matthew 7:14, which indicates that there is a rather narrow path to a righteous relationship with God, and relatively few who find it. Furthermore, Matthew 7:21–23 states that many people who think that they are right with God, and who put on a good show for others, will not make the final cut to play on God's team. I would be remiss in my efforts in this book if I did not give some consideration to what can cause people to miss out on the fullest possible relationship with God. Be careful not to rely solely on a profession of faith without progression in the Faith.

In Matthew 13:1–23, Jesus tells the story that has come to be known as the "Parable of the Sower." As the story goes, a farmer plants seeds in a few different environments, but only a portion of the seeds mature into new plants that bear fruit for harvesting. Some of the seeds fall along the path and become food for the birds before sprouting. Many people hear the Gospel message but do not fully understand or retain it. The Devil snatches the truth away from them, and they remain under his deceptive spell.

Some of the sower's seeds fall on rocky ground and actually sprout quickly in shallow soil, but without much root, the tender plants shrivel in the heat of the sun. Similarly, many people make an enthusiastic commitment to follow Jesus Christ, but their expectations are not rooted in reality. They fail to realize that the promise to those serving Christ is not that they will have a perfect life, but rather that they will have provision through life's inevitable hardships. When the trials and tribulations of life in a fallen world continue, they become discouraged and give up.

Some of the seeds fall among thorns and are choked out by weeds, just like many Christians become distracted by the pursuit of other priorities, such as material possessions or entertainment. Squirrely Christians may also chase after the latest nutty doctrines that fall far from the truth that grows from the Tree of Life in God's kingdom.

However, a portion of the sower's seeds falls on rich soil, sprouts into lush plants, and bears an abundance of fruit to become food for the present and seed for future generations. These seeds represent those who receive Jesus Christ as Savior, serve Him through thick and thin soil, and spread the Good News to others.

I understand (although not from personal experience mind you) that FarmersOnly.com is a good place to pick a soulmate. Try FatherOnly.god to find your "soil mate" so that you can be one of the seeds that not only survives but thrives and changes lives. Do not live a life for the birds. Tend to your soil so that you are one of those who grows in relationship with God and who makes it through the narrow gate into eternal life with your Heavenly Father. Set your expectations and your priorities in line with God's promises and plan for your life. As you sow seed into the lives of others, do not be one of those who puts hand to plow and then looks backward, creating crooked rows and furrowed brows (Luke 9:62). Look through the lens of God's Word to see the Devil in 3D, seeking to deceive, discourage, and distract you; then push forward on the straight and narrow path to lead others into another dimension of relationship with God (Philippians 3:13–14).

CHAPTER 72

DON'T LET ANYBODY SINK YOUR DISCIPLESHIP

Unfortunately, many people who profess to have had a conversion experience and thus to be "born again Christians" may give an appearance of being stillborn—never developing into mature Christians who reproduce after Jesus's kind. As I hope that I have made clear before, I do not believe that Christians are ever in a position to judge someone else's relationship with God. Romans 10:9–13 clearly states the minimum requirements to be a part of the family of God. You are assured of salvation and right relationship with your Heavenly Father as long as you believe and confess that Jesus Christ is God in human form, that He died and rose from the dead for your sins, and that He is your Lord whose commandments you will do your best to obey. Of course, even the best of us, and certainly the rest of us, who are children of God will inevitably fail to obey our Heavenly Father from time to time; nonetheless, I assert that everyone progressing in their Christian faith is likely to be going against the flow of the prevailing cultural currents that carry people away from God.

There once was practice in which doctors would deliver a gentle slap to the bottom of newborns when they made their entrance into the world. This may seem like a rude introduction to life outside of the womb, but the purpose was to clear any breathing obstructions so that an infant could breathe on its own in its new environment. Similarly, newborn Christians delivered from the tomb of sin and making their grand entry into God's kingdom may need a helping hand in the form of instruction in righteousness to clear any obstructions to the breath of God flowing through their new being. Older Christians such as I may need some occasional CPR (Christian Priority Resuscitation) when our heart stops beating for God.

Discipleship is the process of maturing as followers of Jesus Christ. Disciples model and guide others to Christlikeness and right relationship with the Creator through their words and deeds. Sometimes, those of us who seek to introduce Christianity to others seem consumed with delivering as many new births into the kingdom of God as possible while neglecting efforts to nurture new Christians in lifelong relationships with their Heavenly Father. When someone makes a commitment to serve Jesus Christ, it is not just the initial contact with Jesus that is important, but also the follow through that will serve to minimize faults and win game, set, and match.

After salvation should come sanctification, which is becoming a Christian in the truest sense of becoming more like Christ. My purpose for writing this book of Christian life reflections and experiences is not just to introduce people to the possibility of a new life in Jesus Christ, or merely to toy with salvation, but also to help build their faith and determination to take His story to infinity and beyond. If you have accepted Jesus Christ as your Savior, then please allow me to offer some practical considerations as to how to stick the landing in an eternal relationship with your Creator.

Senioritis is one of the scourges of my profession as a high school teacher. I did not have the luxury of slacking off as high school graduation approached. I was in a neck and neck race to the finish to clench the valedictorian spot. I lost, but not because I did not finish strong. I just got off to a slightly slower start than my competitor and never could quite catch her. Nonetheless, I am grateful for the extra, mostly self-imposed pressure that helped to shape my character and work habits to the present day. My admonition to my high school seniors is that it is not how you start, but it is how you finish that most reflects your character and determines your future success.

The stakes are even higher for matriculation to Heaven, and dropouts and slackers may experience limitations that last even longer than a lifetime. A divine diploma qualifying you for higher education in the knowledge of God, a career of service to Him, and entry into His kingdom is received at the stage of salvation (Colossians 1:10), but awards day comes later (2 Timothy 4:7–8). Jesus has offered a vote of confidence that you are most certain to succeed with His help if you commit your talents, abilities, and efforts to serving Him (Proverbs 16:3 and Philippians 4:13). A lifetime achievement award awaits you as a measure of how closely your life ends up reflecting the righteous life of Jesus Christ (1 John 3:2–3). When your Faith is flagging and you need a second wind or motivation to mount a strong finish to your spiritual race, remember the price that Jesus Christ paid for your salvation (Hebrews 12:1–3). Your Father will be beaming with pride from the Throne of Heaven.

Another character trait that I have found to be invaluable in many aspects of life, although often in short supply in modern society, is the ability to delay gratification, or to endure short-term sacrifice to experience long-term benefits. For instance, exercise and responsible eating contribute to a longer and healthier life. Body-numbing, repetitive practice and discipline develop physical skill sets. Mind-numbing study and discipline enhance educational and occupational success. Waiting until you have the economic resources to satisfy your wants rather than borrowing money and paying interest, or even better yet, investing money now rather than spending it, allows for a substantially higher standard of living over the course of a lifetime. Abstaining from sexual activity until marrying an exclusive sexual partner for life as prescribed in Scripture is highly correlated with satisfying and successful relationships in which both the partners and their posterity prosper. Sacrificially spending time with your children increases the chances that they will be there for you in later years. Prioritizing God's work over your own builds up treasures in Heaven that will endure for eternity (Matthew 6:19–21).

Like just about everything else in life, our faith in Jesus Christ requires attention and maintenance to keep it from breaking down. Anything that we aspire to be good at is likely to require discipline and effort. I remember someone describing himself as a practicing Christian who needs more practice. No pain, no gain is also a spiritual truism. I believe there is a Christian-inspired t-shirt that sums up salvation through Jesus Christ as, "His Pain, Our Gain." This is certainly true, but crucifying our own selfish desires and sharing the pain is very much a part of the package deal that will allow us to say, "been there, done that, got (as in understand) the t-shirt."

What follows is a list of a few practical steps to build and maintain a faith in Jesus Christ and a relationship with your Creator that will endure into eternity (Matthew 24:13). It is not intended to be exhaustive, or exhausting for that matter, but discipleship is demanding. Discipleship and discipline are rooted together. If you ever find yourself flaccid in your Faith or struggling with sins that you just cannot seem to shake, consider giving more attention to the following, even if doing so means more short-term pain for long-term gain. Check out the appendix of this book for additional resources that may be useful in securing a successful Christian life.

Study the Holy Bible Regularly

The Holy Bible is like an owner's manual providing operating, care, and repair instructions for the most complex creation ever to exist, a human life. Some have proposed that Bible could be an acronym for **B**asic **I**nstructions **B**efore **L**eaving **E**arth. Do not just read the Bible—study and reflect on it. There are many credible versions that are written in modern language and that are relatively easy to understand, at least for most scriptural passages. Some of my personal favorites include the New Living Translation, the New International Version, The Message, and the Living Bible. There is also the good old standby King James Version that I was weaned on, but it reads kind of like Shakespeare on steroids and takes some getting used to.

Do not be frustrated if you do not understand everything that you read in God's Word. I certainly do not after decades of study, and I would suggest that anyone who claims to fully understand the mind of God does not even understand the limitations of his or her own mind (Romans 11:33–34). Do not let perfect understanding be an enemy of good and growing understanding. Also, be careful to consider Scriptures in context of the entire Bible. The Bible is God's roadmap to eternity for humanity, and it is intended to be interpreted and applied in its totality.

Pray

God does not just text us, BTW; He carries on intimate conversations with us if we only know how to listen. Remember that you have the Author and Creator of the Universe on speed dial for responsible requests and even for the desires of your heart (1 John 5:14–15). Do not forget to communicate expressions of gratitude and worship. Speak to Him, but also listen. Audible statements from God seem rather rare, but His Holy Spirit living within us has our number and has ways to speak to our conscience to provide us with a sense of what to do in every situation.

Fellowship

Spend time with other like-minded believers and followers of Jesus Christ (Hebrews 10:25). Connect to a church that holds true to the fundamentals of the Christian faith. Most churches make a statement of their beliefs readily available so that you can vet them with the Bible and other trustworthy spiritual sources. Remember that Church is not just a time and place for Christians to gather, but it is much more a community of Believers who comprise the Body of Jesus Christ that is formed to minister to lost and hurting people. Churches provide connections with others who can offer support in both the good times and the bad; remember that it is often during the good times that we are most inclined to forget God and to go out on our own, thus becoming a useless appendage in God's design.

One of the most important aspects of what churches should offer for us is accountability. People in prolonged isolation go insane, and isolated Christians are also likely to go off the spiritual reservation. Attending church services has been falling out of fashion for many in the modern day, but churches provide an essential opportunity to plug in and amplify the voice of God in our lives. Listening to a pastor preach may seem as boring as listening to a social studies teacher teach. However, as I tell my students, listening is a skill to be developed, and you kind of get out of such experiences what you bring to them. Unlike my poor students, who are generally stuck with me, Christians can seek the classrooms and communicators that most accurately, interestingly, and effectively teach the core curriculum of Jesus Christ to them.[100] If you cannot find any such environment, then it is possible that the problem lies more within than with others—perhaps reflecting more of a lack of interest than a lack of interesting spiritual stimulation.

Nowadays, there is an incredible variety of churches to fit about every personality type, yet these churches are to be united under the person of

---

[100] Remember that the core curriculum for communion with your Creator consists of what you need to hear, not necessarily what you want to hear.

Jesus Christ despite some doctrinal differences. Do not expect any church to be the perfect fit for your tastes. Each one is a blend of Believers, and you can add to the flavor. I happen to attend a church where most members are socially outgoing, and many are often emotionally expressive in their worship. I am somewhat of a socio-emotional misfit. In social settings, I am like a fish in a frying pan, out of its element and about to create an awkward smell that lingers long after it is served. I am not a big fan of making small talk in casual conversation, lest everything that I say be placed under a microscope.[101] And as for emotion, well, going online on my computer is my most common display of e-motion. Nonetheless, it does me good to be around good people who are different than me.

Consider that belonging to and actively engaging in a church is every bit as much about what you can offer to others as it is about what you can get for the time spent. Tithing by giving at least ten percent of your income to a church allows it to carry on its vital activities and demonstrates that you recognize and are grateful to God for being the provider of everything that you have, including the very breaths and heartbeats that allow you to earn a living.

Do not be turned off by imperfect people and hypocrites who claim to be Christians. Every church likely has room for one more flawed individual to join, so you will be welcome. If a church is not constructing room for improvement, then perhaps it is best to look for one that is.

Studying the Bible, praying, and connecting with other Christians are all tried and true contributors to consistently and successfully following Jesus Christ. Second Timothy 2:22–3:5 offers further guidance for shunning Satan and pursing right relationship with others and with God, all the while experiencing the faith, love, and peace that comes with such priorities. Avoid foolish arguments, quarrels, and resentments. Be kind and both a teacher and teachable when it comes to learning to be Christlike. Do not be selfish, self-indulgent, greedy, prideful, arrogant, reckless, ungrateful, unloving, unforgiving, malicious, full of oneself, disobedient, or disrespectful of authority (ok, deep breath). The bottom line is this: be lovers of God, not lovers of pleasure, and be around people of like mind.

---

[101] And yet strangely, I relish rational, deep discussions of weighty spiritual and secular matters with anyone and everyone willing to engage in them.

One point that I lay on rather heavy in my economics classes is that each of us makes a living in this world by contributing to the production of a good or service that people are willing to pay us for. Even if you never start a business, you are still in the business of you, developing a product that you will market to an employer who is the consumer in this equation. The more knowledge, skills, dependability, and positive attitude that you offer, the more you will be worth to your employer. Even with a higher price tag, you'll be it when it comes to hiring the best employee. You are the entrepreneur of your own existence![102] Your value to God is determined by the price that He paid for you, the life of Jesus Christ, but we determine the return on His investment in us through how consumed we are in our efforts to serve Him until He returns.

One business that I try not to get into is other people's business, and that includes evaluating their personal choices based on my beliefs or even my interpretations of the Scripture. I will seek to humbly share my personal understanding of biblical and Holy Spirit instruction as well as my convictions with anyone interested, but I will leave it to individuals to ultimately discern God's will for them and their relationship status with Him (Philippians 2:12–13).[103] I do not understand the choices that many people make in regard to lifestyle or what they seek to entertain themselves with, whether it be in relationships, music, movies, video games, or the like, but I am sure that there are also people who do not embrace my personal standards for such things. Nonetheless, I would advise any Christians who are struggling with developing their lives into the image of Christ to evaluate their exposures to worldly culture in light of the old admonition of "garbage in, garbage out." Growing in relationship with Jesus Christ can require us to turn away from some things that obstruct our walk with God.

There are many incredible Christians who have different personal standards than I do when it comes to engagement in secular culture; some are stricter, and some are less so. Indeed, cross-cultural connections between sinners and saints (recovering sinners) is necessary to some degree

---

[102] If I had an entrepreneurial spirit, I would trademark and market this statement as a slogan.

[103] I assert that such allowances for personal discretion are limited to matters where the Bible has not clearly spoken.

for our physical survival and for having a connection with those with whom we are to share our Faith (again see First Corinthians 9:19–23). There is an old saying that may offer some good advice: "Don't be so heavenly minded that you are of no earthly good." However, this humble cultural observer proposes that secularization and increasing media saturation are exponentially increasing cultural change in the values of society, and even among Christians—sometimes for good, but probably more often for ill (1 Corinthians 5:9–13).

In the present age of Western Civilization, there seems to be a lot of soul-searching as people and institutions examine the values and actions that have shaped the distribution of wealth and power within and among nations. Such personal and cultural self-examination can be a constructive force, but unfortunately, there seems to be little agreement as to the standard by which to evaluate ourselves and others. There also seems to be little mercy extended to those who fail to measure up. As I write, "cancel culture" has become a growing phenomenon fed by social media. People are being vilified and persecuted based upon past words and actions and are losing jobs and opportunities even if they are repentant and reformed. Some of these past or present misdeeds are indeed reprehensible, yet forgivable. Other "unwoke" offenses condemned by the culture cops are in fact principled positions that merely provoke modern sensibilities, and such contemporary standards often defy common and Christian sensibilities.

Christians who have their sins cancelled should be in the business of forgiving and not cancelling others. Furthermore, Christians are to be in the business of nonjudgmentally raising God's standards for human behavior, which may or may not comport with modern norms. Followers of Jesus Christ may be cancelled for defending biblical definitions of sinful behavior. The cost of being a Christian can include forfeiting status and inviting persecution, but such sacrifice is what secures us an invite into the most happening place of all time, the kingdom of Heaven (Matthew 5:10). Be prepared to lay down any personal ambitions for worldly popularity and success, and do not value any acclaim of the world enough to compromise your core beliefs. You will gain far more than you lose by sticking with the One who cancels your sins (1 John 2:15–17).

Here is the rub: are you rubbing off on the world, or is the world rubbing off on you. As long as I am offering some instructive "soothe-sayings" intended to increase your future comforts and success, here is a somewhat customized version of a popular moral maxim: what occupies and entertains you will shape your thoughts, your thoughts will establish your values, your values will drive your actions and develop your habits, your actions and habits will create your character, and your character will determine your destiny. I might also add, what shapes you will affect how you shape others around you.

On occasions when I have changed my actions or my exposures to certain things out of conviction that they were hindering my walk with God or normalizing self-destructive and socially irresponsible behaviors, I found the sacrifice to be inconsequential to my life satisfaction within a short period of time and ultimately well-compensated for from the riches of God's kingdom (Mark 10:28–31). To make things even easier, God offers constructive alternatives to forgone passions and pleasures that bother our conscience. These more fulfilling occupiers of our time and attention include inspirational Christian entertainment mediums (music, movies, etc.) with life-affirming messages that can really grow on you if you give them a chance. There are also opportunities for family gatherings with Christian brothers and sisters, and most importantly, productive work assignments from our Creator that improve lives and leave a mark that will last for eternity (Ecclesiastes 3:9–14). Who knows? You may even end up writing a book someday.

Christians, of all people, should be the cultural influencers, not the cultural followers. The battle is the Lord's, not yours, but you are one of the hands on deck. As you sail on, be one in relationship with God and fellow followers of Jesus, be to others an example of righteous living, be threefold in serving God in body, mind, and spirit, and be forever humble and grateful before God.[104] Do not let the Devil, or anyone, sink your discipleship.

---

[104] An homage to the classic board game Battleship and a hint as to where I tend to place my battleship.

PART THREE
WHAT WILL BE ~ HAPPILY EVER AFTER

And I heard a loud voice from the throne saying, "Look! God's dwelling place is now among the people, and he will dwell with them. They will be his people, and God himself will be with them and be their God. 'He will wipe every tear from their eyes. There will be no more death or mourning or crying or pain, for the old order of things has passed away."

He who was seated on the throne said, "I am making everything new!" Then he said, "Write this down, for these words are trustworthy and true."

He said to me: "It is done. I am the Alpha and the Omega, the Beginning and the End. To the thirsty I will give water without cost from the spring of the water of life. Those who are victorious will inherit all this, and I will be their God and they will be my children. ~ Revelation 21:3-7 (NIV)[105]

---

[105] I am anticipating the best for all my dear readers who have stuck with me thus far, but I would be remiss if I selectively edited out God's parting shot to those who reject communion with Him. The unhappily ever after is described in Revelation 21:8 (NIV): "But the cowardly, the unbelieving, the vile, the murderers, the sexually immoral, those who practice magic arts, the idolaters and all liars—they will be consigned to the fiery lake of burning sulfur. This is the second death."

CHAPTER 73

ANCHORS AHEAD

Consider a ship dropping anchor. A shipshape anchor generally has some hooks that dig into the bottom of a body of water to prevent the ship from drifting from where it is intended to be. Anchors provide stability and safety for the vessels to which they are attached. Based on my experience as a mariner, which admittedly is limited to a rowboat that I had on a fishing pond as a kid, when it is time to move on, it is "anchors aweigh" from the bottom. Our human tendency is to anchor ourselves to what we know from our past experiences. However, the Bible offers hope as a firm and secure anchor for our souls (Hebrews 6:19) and proclaims that hope comes from faith in the future that God has promised to us (Hebrews 11:1).

Perhaps instead of a boat anchor, a grappling hook would be more to the point for illustrative purposes. We plant our feet and toss the grappling hook outward and upward. Once the hook makes contact, we take hold of the rope and give it a couple tugs to make sure that it is secure, and then, with the helping hand of God, we pull ourselves out of the muck and mire of our past and toward the goal of an eternal relationship with God (Philippians 3:12–14). Many passages in the Bible have a lot to say about what the future holds. Perhaps their purpose is not just to build some chronology of future happenings. In contrast to the hopelessness of what holds us back, these foretold events provide a solid and sure destination to anchor ourselves to as we navigate our way through our present to new heights in relationship with God. So, we look to the future as a source of strength and a guiding light as we grapple with our present circumstances. Why thrust our anchor forward? Because our future is more secure than our past. Our anchor does indeed hold, not to hold us back, but to seize our future.[106]

The song "Anchors Aweigh"—the anthem of the United States Navy in which both of my grandfathers served during World War II—may offer some sound spiritual application:

> Blue of the mighty deep
> Gold of God's great sun
> Let these our colors be
> Till all of time be done, done, done, done.
> On seven seas we learn
> Navy's stern call
> Faith, courage, service true,
> With honor, over honor, overall

Anchors ahead, and "until we meet once more, here's wishing you a happy voyage home."[107]

---

[106] Dan Schmidt, *Taken by Communion: How the Lord's Supper Nourishes the Soul* (Grand Rapids: Baker Publishing Group, 2003), 122.

[107] Alfred Hart Miles and Charles A. Zimmermann, "Anchors Aweigh," 1906.

CHAPTER 74

IT'S A WONDERFUL
LIFE FOR A CHANGE

I am a sentimental soul, to a fault no doubt. I value old things more than new, especially if I associate those old things with fond memories of people and past events in my life. A case in point would be the old desk at which I have written part of this manuscript, including these very lines. It is cheaply made of scuffed, warped pressed wood, and due to its time of banishment in my parents' basement, it emanates whiffs of mold and mildew when I open the drawers. Nonetheless, it is serviceable and reminiscent of my high school days pecking out English papers on a typewriter.

As you can probably tell from the many references thus far in this book to Philippians 3:13–14, these Scripture verses have special meaning to me since, throughout most of my life, I have wrestled with perfectionistic tendencies to give compulsive attention to my past and present endeavors while neglecting to give proper regard to moving forward. In other words, I let my behind mess with my ahead. A few years ago, however, these verses instructing us to forget the things that are behind us and to push forward in pursuit of God's perfect plan took on a whole new meaning in my life.

You see, I had this pleasant problem of having had such a wonderful life that I did not look forward to transitioning into anything new or different. Although I owned and maintained a house of my own for a quarter century, home to me was still the house that the stork brought me to. Throughout almost fifty years of my life, home was the house that I grew up in, and the house to which I had the privilege of regularly returning to visit my parents and to bask in the environment in which I grew up.

Then one summer, that era of my life came to a close. As my parents grew older and more burdened by the upkeep of the old homestead, we prayed for God's perfect plan to unfold in transitioning us to what was best for us as a family going forward. The first summer that there was a prospective buyer, I prayed that, if it was within God's perfect will and plan, then there would be another year for me to prepare for the parting, and there was. The next summer I prayed that there might be yet another extension if possible, but I felt that God spoke to my spirit that this was the best time to transition to something new and different. Looking back, I marvel at how God prepared me so gently and with such perfect timing for a new normal for my parents and me.

This was not the first time in my life that God prepared me for an inevitable transition. The homestead of my youth was carved out of my grandparents' property, which offered dozens of acres of ponds and fields and woods in which to boat, fish, play, and roam, not to mention to mow and mow and mow as I welcomed opportunities to help my grandparents with the upkeep. The busyness afforded to me by this idyllic environment no doubt spared me from a lot of temptation and trouble during my formative years. I long dreaded the occasion when my grandparents would have to leave for greener but more distant pastures. I was off to college when the property finally became too much upkeep for them to handle. Finding a buyer for the place in a somewhat depressed local economy became a pressing necessity. Amazingly, I was not only prepared but relieved and excited to help talk some neighbors into buying the property. In my experience, God allows us maximal enjoyment for each season of our lives, but He prepares us for moving on when the time is right.

A fondness for the past is not all bad. It pays tribute to and shows appreciation for the blessings the Lord has given us. The challenge is letting go when God is ready to move us to a new phase of our lives. As much as I dreaded saying goodbye to the house that had always been my home, it was not too hard to remind myself that the house itself is just bricks and mortar. The more difficult adjustment was accepting the end of an era of my life that I will never go back to. It was the memories of the wonderful events that transpired where I grew up with the people that I have always been closest to in life that tended to make me more than a little melancholic in contemplation of the move, but those memories would move with me. How blessed I am that the most depressing thing in my life is that I cannot keep everything just as it is.

I confess that I also tend to be content with the communion that I have been able to enjoy with God thus far in my habitation of this planet. After all, I have never known any different environment. It is easy for me to lose sight of the new home that God is moving me toward as I enjoy the physical and intellectual pleasures and stimulation that God has granted to me in the here and now, and it is hard for me to wrap my limited mind around and fully appreciate the wonders of Heaven and what happens there. Yet in my spirit, I know that the life to come will be at a time and place where everything will be made new, where there will be no more sadness or death, and most importantly, where I will dwell in the immediate presence of my Heavenly Father for all of eternity. I am not one to name drop, but did I mention that my Heavenly Father is the King over all of creation (Revelation 21:3–5). If you have not yet joined His family, He still has an open adoption policy.

As my parents and I get older, I am more and more reminded of just how fleeting our earthly existence is. We do not know what tomorrow holds, or how many tomorrows our future holds. In the scope of human history, let alone eternity, our lives are like mists that appear briefly and then disappear (James 4:14). I have been happy and healthy through every stage of life thus far, and there is so much more that I would like to experience before I "shuffle off this mortal coil."

I have often wondered why God puts us through the changes of life, and even more confounding, why we must experience the ravages of aging and the passing of loved ones. I have concluded that it is to keep us from holding on too tightly to this present life and to keep us looking forward to what is to come. With all due respect to Shakespeare's Hamlet, the question is not "to be or not to be," but rather to be here or to be in the hereafter. If we are blessed with a long life, then our minds and bodies will inevitably slow down, allowing our age to catch up with us as more loved ones pass on to their eternal reward. The world will eventually wear out its welcome for us, and the wellness and reunions of Heaven will beckon.

The theme of the Holy Bible, the Word of God, is restoring humanity's communion with its Creator. Our earthy existence is just a means to the end of knowing God and helping others to know Him. I was tremendously blessed in that my transition from the home of my origin allows me to be even closer to my parents and to make more memories in a new setting, even if only for a season. It is the sacrifice that Jesus made on the cross that makes a new and better home possible for us, and it is that memory that I am most thankful for (John 14:2–4).

Upon the closing of the sale of a home, although the seller may still have the rights to a few weeks of occupancy while arranging to move out, the rights of ownership have already transferred to the buyer. The seller is essentially a guest in what once was home. If you have accepted Jesus Christ as your Savior, then Jesus has closed on the purchase of your life with the payment of His own life. Your life now belongs to Him, and although you likely have a few remaining years of occupancy of your earthly existence, the move is being arranged. Think with your ahead and not your behind.

I am comforted by my Landlord's assurance that every transition that I will ever face in this life will serve to move me toward the home of my destiny, in communion with the ones that I love, and in the presence of my Creator for all of eternity. One day, my mind and body will know what my spirit already knows. It's a wonderful life for a change.

CHAPTER 75

IT'S MY FATHER'S
WORLD AFTER ALL

A few years ago, I took a spring break trip to Florida. The trip was never intended to be a stereotypical fun-in-the-sun spring break excursion. For one thing, my mother came along—not that I would have acted any differently on my own, mind you. From the beginning, we were on a mission; however, our mission changed even before we arrived. We can make our plans, for our reasons, but sometimes God appropriates our plans for His reasons. There are many tourist destinations in Florida that seek to offer escape from the real world, but on this trip, I was reminded of the need to be prepared to interact with people with up close and personal problems, and especially those desperate individuals who are lacking a sense of purpose that makes enduring the complications of life worthwhile. Our prosperous culture provides many pleasures to distract such people from the very real pain that they are feeling, but the pain is still there, it is deep, and it inevitably comes to the surface.

The original purpose of our trip to the Sunshine State was to visit an uncle, my mother's brother, for what would likely be the last time due to his declining health. But God did not wait that long to call my uncle home. He died less than two weeks before our arrival. Our main reason for the trip was no more, but our tickets and hotel room reservations were nonrefundable. So, we proceeded with our plans, presuming that God still had a purpose for this trip.

I am inspired to think about preparedness when I read about how Peter and the other disciples wimped out on Jesus when the going to the cross got tough. There are times when I feel like I could bear any burden, pay any price, or make any sacrifice for my Savior. Other times, I have myself pegged as someone who would fold like a cheap tent at the slightest flap. I am occasionally reminded of the importance of praying that my times of testing will come during my times of strength rather than weakness. I want to live like God's boy scout, always prepared for whatever comes my way.

During our Florida visit, several last-minute schedule adjustments placed my mother and me at an aunt's house at a certain time, although not the time that we originally planned. As we were visiting, we heard a commotion outside the house. It sounded like banging and screaming. We could not quite tell how close it was, and we first assumed it was probably just some kids playing nearby. When the noise returned a few moments later, we decided to investigate. I began to sense that perhaps something was in fact wrong, and I had the opportunity to prepare myself mentally for the possibility of responding to an emergency.

Once outside, we saw a panicked, young neighbor girl indicating that something was wrong in a shed next door. My aunt was the first to reach the shed and returned distraught and yelling for us to call 911. I helped my mother find the phone and then went outside to see if I could help with whatever emergency was at hand. As I got to the shed, I saw a young man of about twenty hanging from the ceiling by a cable around his neck. He was gasping for breath and drooling. I grabbed him and tried to lift him up to alleviate the pressure from the cord that was obstructing his breathing. I also tried to reach up and loosen the cable around his neck, but it was beyond my reach. Fortunately, his sister, distressed as she was, found a knife, climbed up on a chair, and cut the cable allowing me to ease the young man to the floor as gently as I could.

I have been trained in CPR, but I have always been grateful that I have never been called upon to use it since I do not have great confidence in my ability to raise the dead, so to speak. At this moment, however, I felt great calm and preparedness to respond to this emergency as the training kicked in. I checked to make sure that he was breathing and had a pulse. His breathing was labored and his pulse racing, so I was relieved of the need to put my CPR skills, such as they were, to a life-or-death test.

I tried to make him as comfortable as possible, and once I was sure that his physical needs were tended to as best I could, I turned my attention to his spiritual condition. I prayed over him and told him that Jesus loved him. The young man was unconscious, and I learned later that he was a recent Haitian immigrant who spoke French Creole and probably had limited understanding of English. Nonetheless, I have hope that the Lord had me there to speak those words to him for a reason.

Emergency personnel were on the scene relatively quickly, and I was able to turn the young man over to their more capable care. He had taken the battery out of a car, and as best as we could discern from his sister's emotionally distressed communication in broken English, she was concerned that he had also ingested battery acid. Fortunately, this turned out not to be the case, yet according to the updates that I received, his condition was serious enough for them to air flight him to the nearest hospital with a trauma unit where he spent the next several days in a coma on life support, and much longer in recovery.

While sitting around in an area marked off with "crime scene" tape waiting for the police to finish their investigation, I had opportunity to think about divine appointments. If circumstances had been just a little bit different, we would not have been present to render aid, such as it was. I also had the opportunity to think about second chances. I understand that this young man eventually fully recovered. I believe that God intervened in this situation to give him an opportunity to live. My prayer for this young man remains that this second chance will be one where he comes to know and to live for Jesus Christ as his Lord and Savior.

I also thought about the importance of communion with a father figure. I later heard that one of this young man's apparent reasons for attempting suicide was that his father was dying, and he thought his own death was preferable to the prospect of watching his father suffer and then having to live without his father's presence in his life. I have known other people to respond to paternal relationship deficiencies with substance addictions or sexual encounters.

The disciple Peter could relate to human frailties and the sense of loss. In a moment of weakness, he was not able to suffer with and suffer for his Lord and Savior (Luke 22:54–62). However, that was not the end of Peter's story. For his second act, he became a real rock star in the kingdom of Heaven (Matthew 16:15–20). Christians who can remember their lives B.C. (before Christ) can relate. Separation from your Heavenly Father can seem like slow motion suicide until you reach a point where you recognize that the pleasures of this world are merely temporary distractions from an emptiness that only communion with God can fill. When you reach the end of the rope of sin that is hanging you, try a "not going to let sin keep its hold on me" attitude. Do not hang on for fear of life, but firmly grasp the lifeline that God has extended through Jesus Christ to lift people into His kingdom.

Many years ago, The Walt Disney Company had a Super Bowl advertising campaign called "What's Next." The commercial spots went something like this. One of the prominent players would be asked, "you've just won the Super Bowl, what are you going to do now?" The player would respond, "I'm going to Disney World."

Can you imagine the following conversation with Peter? "Peter, you just agreed to give up your life to serve Jesus Christ, what are you going to do now?" I can hear Simon Peter say, "I am going to spend eternity in my Father's World." How about you? Can you hear the question directed to you: "you have fought the good fight, you have finished the race, and you have kept the faith—what are you going to do now?" Can you say, as Paul did, "I am going to Heaven to receive my crown of righteousness and to live in eternal glory with my Heavenly Father" (2 Timothy 4:7–8)? Forget the mouse ears. Set your sights on a world where laughter wipes away the tears, and hope vanquishes all the fear. There's so much that we'll share that it's time we're aware, it's our Father's world after all.[108]

---

[108] With apologies to:
Robert B. and Richard M. Sherman, "It's a Small World (After All)," 1964.
And apologies to you if this brings out any earworms.

CHAPTER 76

EARNING THE
HIGHEST MARKS

A key component of educating is evaluating. Passing judgment on other people's performance is far from my favorite part of being a teacher, but it is an occupational hazard. I have tried to train myself to refrain from being a critical person when it is not a part of my job description. One personal phenomenon that has helped me to reduce nonessential critiquing of other people is my own reflexive reaction to evaluate critics by the same standards that I hear them apply to others (Romans 2:1). Although I do not react in such a way deliberately and tend to keep my thoughts to myself, I nonetheless consequently assume that, whenever I make evaluative statements about someone, then I am inviting those who hear me to apply the same scrutiny to me—and my life certainly offers much food for critical thought.

There are certainly occasions when responsibly offering critical feedback is warranted and even compassionate (Proverbs 27:6), but I am painfully aware of the self-serving satisfaction that can come from speaking ill of others. Here are a couple tests for evaluating our evaluative comments. The first consideration is whether we are willing to make critical comments directly to an individual rather than to criticize that person to others. The latter is not the way to have someone's back. The second test is whether our personal motivation is to help the subject of the criticism, or to hurt the person, or to gain satisfaction from someone else's weaknesses. I am reminded of what was sometimes suggested to me upon the occasion of receiving a good spanking; delivering a necessary criticism should probably hurt a critic operating out of love and concern more than it stings the recipient. Speaking into someone else's life should also invite some potentially uncomfortable self-scrutiny by the same standards that we apply to others (Proverbs 18:20–21).

I strive to be better at making my critiques constructive and tempered with compliments. I have been on the receiving end of both direct and secondhand critical commentary regarding my personal and professional merits, and I am fully aware from these personal experiences how many positive remarks it can take to offset a single criticism that we receive, or to recover from a failure to meet expectations. In other words, it is difficult to digest negative feedback, which can lead us to "throw it up" to others.

I would like to be someone who receives criticism in ways that lengthen my stride in my walk with God. I would also like to minimize my need for a lot of strokes in the form of positive comments from other people. I seek to be internally motivated to heartily give my very best efforts in all that I do in my life-consuming mission to call attention to the incredible qualities of my Creator (Colossians 3:23–24). When it comes to compliments, it behooves Christians to be like camels and sources of water, able to go long distances between them. Yet it is also good to go the extra mile in bearing the burden of offering compliments to get others over the hump. Dealing with criticism, whether deserved or not, or just pressing forward despite a lack of encouragement, is a lot easier when one is secure in the unconditional love of family, friends, and most of all, of Father God.

As a public educator, I am routinely evaluated—formally by administrators and informally by students, parents, colleagues, and perhaps harshest of all, myself. I am flattered on the infrequent occasions when a student says, "you're my favorite teacher." My response has occasionally been, "Well, thank you that means so much. My mother won't even say that I am her favorite, and I am her only child." After I pontificate about politics and someone suggests that I should run for President of the United States, I often respond, "Thank you, but I couldn't even get elected president of my own fan club, and I am the only member."

I have yet to receive the perfect, formal professional evaluation, nor do I live in expectation of ever receiving one since I will always have a classroom for improvement. Over the course of my career, I have been blessed with kind and merciful evaluators who offer more favorable comments than criticisms. By necessity, much of the feedback on evaluations is boilerplate. After all, there are only so many ways to say, "good job" or "needs improvement." Occasionally, an evaluator will say something that really leaves a memorable mark on an evaluation. I remember an administrator telling me at the end of my first year of teaching, "Well, I am glad that I hired you." Nuff said. The comment from another boss that sticks with me the most was essentially that he hoped that I stuck around until he retired so that we could "go out together" (referring to retirement and not to dinner, I presume). I interpreted this remark to mean that he would rather do his job with me than without me working for him, and that seemed like high praise indeed. When another administrator told me how much his own kids enjoyed my classes, I could not imagine payment of a higher compliment (and I didn't even have to pay his kids to say that). The common denominator for each of these comments was the personal touch that I have never forgotten.

Christians have an assignment that supersedes any earthly responsibilities, as well as an Evaluator who is kind and merciful and who came to earth in the person of Jesus Christ to show us how to do our job. Yet God has the highest of expectations for us. In the education business, there are what we call formative assessments that are used to improve student performance, and summative assessments that seek to determine actual achievement. God offers us His Word and Holy Spirit to provide feedback for our on-the-job training as well as reminders of the rewards awaiting us. He even lets us copy from the mind of Christ and share the Answer with others so that we can cheat death out of as many souls as possible (1 Corinthians 2:8–16).

Those who have a foundation of faith in Jesus Christ are assured a secure future, but there will come a final exam where all our efforts to build on that foundation will be put to the test. The Devil is always at the door huffing and puffing, and our industriousness, along with our resistance to temptation, will determine if our efforts to help build the kingdom of God will contribute to providing a haven for lost souls, or just assure our own salvation and entry into Heaven by the hair on our chinny chin chins. Since this "three little pigs" reference is not particularly kosher, I will refer to you to a source that is more fabulous than fable—First Corinthians 3:10–15. When the Devil finally meets his match, a trial by fire will determine the quality of our workmanship and materials, whether we are building with precious and durable stones or flammable wood or straw—whether what consumed us in this lifetime will be consumed or consecrated. Only our words and actions that help to restore or strengthen others in their relationship with God will survive the trial by fire.

Jesus told a parable of a rich man who gave money in different amounts to three servants to manage while he was on a long trip. The two who received the most money invested it, whereas the third man, who received the least, hid the money for fear that he might lose it and have nothing to return to his boss, whom he considered to be a "hard" master. When the boss returned and said, "show me the money," the two good and faithful employees were able to return double the original amount. The third worker was able to return the original investment but had nothing of additional value to offer. When it came to taking some risk to earn some return, he folded. Perhaps he fell for that old line that the best way to double your money is to fold it. The two ambitious employees, who used what was given to them to generate a greater good, were promoted and invited to celebrate in the presence of their boss, while the bitter employee was fired due to his lack of interest in his employer's company. He ended up in a dark, sad place with "gnashing of teeth"—perhaps because he didn't put his money where his mouth was (Matthew 25:14–30). God has invested Himself in us through Jesus Christ, and Christians should first and foremost be in the business of maturing and offering return on investment by helping to bring other souls to Him before His return on evaluation day.

As a teacher and observer of people, I tend to make assessments of others based on effort as much or more than on achievement. Among the most admirable students that I have ever taught were not just the students with the highest grades, but also those who were self-starters and who worked hard without the positive formative influences that many of us had. I believe that God will also evaluate us more based on what we do with what we have than according to how our achievements measure up to others (Luke 12:48).

We will all receive a lot of feedback in our lives—good and bad, fair and unfair—but our ultimate performance is for an audience of One. I propose to you that the key to surviving and thriving through all that life serves you, hot or cold, is to forget all that is behind you and to press forward toward the high calling of communion with your Creator by serving Him and others to the fullest extent possible. When all is said and done, the only evaluation that really matters is the one that you receive on your eternity entrance exam. The highest mark that you can earn in your Creator's classroom is to hear Him call out, "Well done my good and faithful servant, enter into the joys of your Lord" (Matthew 25:21).

CHAPTER 77

SUMMIT ALL UP

One summer, my quest to visit all fifty states took me to Alaska. It seemed like every tourist that I met on this trip had a "must see" or "must do" list. Alaska, however, is a rather untamed environment that does not always accommodate tourists who pay a small fortune to see its wonders. As a geography teacher, I certainly had a must see list. Thanks to what I believe to have been God's special blessing, I cannot think of a thing that I did not get to check off my wish list during my week-long visit: glaciers, fjords, mountains, national parks, humpback whales, and many other species of wildlife. I even saw a grizzly bear in the wild and lived to tell about it.

Most impressive was a beautiful, sunlit view of Mt. McKinley, the tallest mountain peak in North America. Even though, on a good day, Mt. McKinley is visible from over 150 miles away, not everyone who visits Alaska gets to see it. It has some of the most extreme weather conditions of any mountain and is obscured by clouds on average two out of every three days. I overheard someone at the airport comment that he had been in Alaska for fourteen days and still had not seen Mt. McKinley. He probably thought it was obscured three out of every two days.

I saw Mt. McKinley on my first day driving through the interior of Alaska. It would have been nice to see the mountain again the next day when I was much more up close and personal with it during a fifteen-hour ride on an old school bus along a gravel road through the interior of Denali National Park. Instead, I experienced a fog bank, 36° wind chill, blowing rain, and I could swear a few snowflakes in July. Yet I was gratefully content with the memory of my beautiful view of Mt. McKinley from many miles away the day before. Some people, however, are willing to literally risk life and limb to climb to the summit. That is definitely not on my bucket list. The sacrifices required are beyond the pale of my sense of adventure.

I can think of three reasons to climb a mountain. First would be to get to the other side. Second would be to see what you can see, and third would be just because it is there. Throughout human history, most mountain climbing has probably been for one of the first two reasons—some function of practicality or necessity. In the modern-day, people often have the luxury of scaling a mountain for a sense of personal achievement. There is even a Highpointers Club consisting of members who seek to visit the highest elevation in as many states and continents as possible. It is a club that always has peak membership. I have sufficient highpoints in my life that I do not need to join the club, but I love to hike and will certainly step up to the challenge of elevation change when the opportunity presents. In my lifetime, I have summited several mountains around the world by foot, or more frequently by some form of mechanical conveyance, but I have never sought to develop any technical mountain climbing skills beyond just placing one foot in front of the other.

Regardless of how you elevate yourself, climbing every mountain requires motivation of some sort. I grew up in the shadow of the highest elevation in Indiana, an unnamed "peak" that I call Hoosier Hill, but I probably have molehills in my yard that stand out more. Many times in my life I drove past the highway marker pointing to this landmark, but I never mounted an effort to visit until after years as a geography teacher feeling guilty for not making the minimal effort required to see what there was to see. One day, I finally determined that I would venture off my beaten path to document the site for my students. Obviously, I lived to tell about the experience, but then the greatest risks of reaching the 1257 feet above sea level that passes for the highest elevation in Indiana are getting over the barbed wire fence separating farm field from woods, or getting shot for trespassing since the spot is on private land.

Kevin Dean Smith

Mt. McKinley (Denali) vs. Hoosier Highpoint (Photos by author)

More ambitious was climbing Mount Washington in the White Mountains of New Hampshire, perhaps the most strenuous hike that I ever attempted. I think it took more out of me than even my hike to the bottom of the Grand Canyon and back, but maybe that was just because I had many more miles on me by the time of the climb. When the path and my legs both gave out on me with no indication of how many more rocks there were to scramble over before reaching the top, I came as close as I ever did in my life to giving up on a bucket list goal. Yet I had already bought the bumper sticker that said, "I climbed Mt. Washington," so I mustered the fortitude to press on. When I at long last reached the top, my head was in the clouds—quite literally and not just from my achievement. My peak experience amounted to being deposited in a fog bank and nearly blown away by the deafening, fifty-plus mile per hour sustained winds on the spot that holds the record for the highest measured wind gust ever recorded by a human being on the face of the earth.[109]

My sense of accomplishment more than compensated for what I missed experiencing with my senses of sight and sound. The other tourists who topped Mt. Washington after arriving by a cushy cog railway or a cozy car would have probably suggested that I was also missing some common sense. Nonetheless, neither the lack of a view from the top, nor the necessity of sheltering from rain and lightning on the longer and more strenuous descent right back to where I started from, nor even the subsequent days of blisters and muscle soreness caused me to regret climbing Mount Washington—just because it was there.

---

[109] 231 miles per hour on April 12, 1934.

Mount Washington "Views" (Photos by author)

People who summit Mt. McKinley will tell you that it is an experience that rivals climbing Mt. Everest. Mt. Everest may peak 9,000 feet higher above sea level, but Mt. McKinley actually has a more dramatic relief, or rise, from its surrounding terrain. Standing at the base of the mountain, you would have to look up over three miles to get a peek of the peak. If you also consider that the northern latitude makes the temperature colder and the oxygen thinner, then you can understand why many who summit Mt. McKinley consider the climb second to no other. Pushing my bicycle up a 300-foot hill is strenuous enough for me nowadays, thank you very much.

Under ideal conditions, reaching the peak of Mt. McKinley takes two weeks. Throw in a ferocious storm or two, and a climber better be provisioned for at least three weeks to maximize the chance of summiting successfully. Part of the wait is to allow for adjusting oneself to exertion at high altitudes where the oxygen is much thinner. One day might be spent carrying provisions up to the next camp, then returning to base camp to rest before dragging yourself back up again the next day. I have heard mountain climbers say that they cut off most of the handle of their toothbrushes to eliminate every fraction of an ounce of excess weight. And to preserve the pristine mountain, climbers must carry everything back down, and I mean everything, even human waste. Given all the obstacles, it is not surprising that almost half of those who set out to reach the summit fall short.

The Bible tells of several occasions where people climbed mountains to be close to God. In our "walk" with God, spiritual highs are often described as mountaintop experiences. I may have no desire to climb Mt. McKinley, but I do have a yearning to summit in my walk with God as often as possible. This requires a high level of spiritual conditioning, exertion, and sacrifice. No doubt the higher you want to climb, the more you must deny yourself other desires. When I did a word search for "mountain" in the Bible, I was struck by how many times Jesus went up a mountain to be close to His Father and to prepare Himself for the ultimate sacrifice.

Spiritually speaking, mountains are multipurpose metaphors. They can represent obstacles that we must overcome, or vantagepoints from which we can see where we have been or where we are headed, or peak experiences in our relationship with God. We can climb to mountaintops of spiritual accomplishments, or move to mountaintops to better see God's plan, or move mountains with even just a little bit of faith (Mark 11:23).

The state flower of Alaska is the forget-me-not. An essential part of communion with God is remembering Jesus Christ's sacrifice and renewing our determination to move beyond a mere viewpoint of the summit to actually following Jesus to the peak of relationship with our Heavenly Father. To reach a highpoint, we will no doubt need to discard worldly pleasures that consume our energy and that divert our desire to reach higher ground. So, to reach peak relationship with God, we must provision ourselves with the Word of God and discipline ourselves to pray for the strength to press on, even when the air is getting thin. One of the greatest dangers for mountain climbers is when the blood stops circulating, for that is when frostbite occurs. Pieces of the body cease to function and may require amputation. The blood of Jesus Christ must circulate through our body and through the members of the body of Christ so that none are cut off.

Climbing Mt. McKinley solo is greatly discouraged since there would be no one to help look for hidden dangers or to seek help if things go wrong, as they often do during the climb. The chances of reaching the summit and returning alive are much greater for those climbing in a group. So, ascend to new heights in relationship with God accompanied by climbing companions who can help when someone falls, and who can share the exhilaration when all succeed.

The Native Americans refer to Mt. McKinley as Denali, which means "the Great One." I know that many who fail to reach the summit of Denali express devastating regret, but failure to reach the summit of relationship with "the Greatest One" would be the missed opportunity of a lifetime. No one can live at the summit of Mt. McKinley, and I doubt that it is possible to live at the summit of relationship with God, at least not in this lifetime. Sometimes it is necessary to come down to earth from the rarefied air for a breather and to reprovision to summit again. God in His graciousness and goodness allows us many pleasures during our earthly existence. At times, He summons us to a vantage point above the fray of our daily lives, which are filled with both fun and frustration. This view from above can enhance our enjoyment of life's simple pleasures and allow us to see the greater purpose for the elevation changes on our journey to eternity.

It is worth noting that more mountain climbers may perish while descending from a summit than while striving to reach it. The peak exertion to reach the pinnacle of their climb makes them fatigued, and the exhilaration of the experience makes them careless. Some mountain climbers say that reaching the summit does not count unless you live to tell about it, or better yet to summit again, or to summit with other people—perhaps the next time on an even higher peak. Someday, our peek from one of those peaks will be of the Promised Land, and our descent will be into our Heavenly Father's kingdom to live forevermore in communion with Him. Until then, just do your level best.

CONCLUSION

Back to the Beginning

Whether you are reading this book upon a graduation milestone—or at any other moment of life—each year, each day, each breath is yet a new opportunity to pursue the destiny for which God uniquely and especially created you. I know that anytime we wrap up a stage of life, such as an educational experience, we can tend to look upon such occasions as the end of something that consumed our existence for a period of time. However, ceremonies to mark such transitions are called commencements rather than culminations for a reason. They mark a graduation into something new and more advanced after a period of preparation. Whether a senior in school, or a senior citizen, or anything in between, life is a constant learning and growing process that is moving forward until matriculation into eternity.

I propose that the most important commencement of our entire existence is that of entering into communion, or relationship, with our Creator by embracing Jesus Christ as Savior and Lord of our lives, for this is the point at which our past, our present, and our future intersect to determine our eternal destiny. From this point of salvation, the rest of our natural lives is about replacing our old, sinful, selfish desires with the character and compassion of Jesus Christ so that we can fit into the family of God and can help to introduce others into the family as well. We must become less; He must become more (John 3:30).

One last piece of practical advice that I bequeath to you is to make sure that you leave a will to direct your loved ones as to how to dispose of your accumulated life's work according to your wishes. Such thoughts are probably far removed from my younger readers, but some schools have a precocious practice whereby graduating seniors "will" certain things that they were known for to underclassmen. When you make that trip across the final stage of life, your will to serve yourself or to serve your Creator will have determined your eternal destiny, and your legacy for those behind you. When you change your will to serve God, He will change His will so that you can be an heir to all that He has. His will was executed when Jesus was crucified for our sins, thus proving His great love and making it possible for all of us to enjoy an infinite inheritance together forever (1 Peter 1:3–5). Now that is what I call willpower!

Over the course of this book, I have sought to identify two priorities for every one of us, no matter what stage of life we happen to be performing in at the moment. The foremost priority is to pursue the relationship with our God for which we were created, and the second is to introduce Him to others through our words and actions. I have heard the fundamental purpose of our allotted revolutions around the sun summarized as, "to know God and to make Him known." Anything else is going around in circles with no particular end in sight other than eventual physical death and eternal separation from God. The path before us may be narrow, but it is clearly marked as described in Psalm 119:9–11 (NIV): "How can a young person stay on the path of purity? By living according to your word. I seek you with all my heart; do not let me stray from your commands. I have hidden your word in my heart that I might not sin against you."

If my thesis is correct, that we are created to live in communion with our Creator and to introduce others into relationship with Him, then what a horrible tragedy it would be to miss out on a personal relationship with the Author and Creator of the Universe, who has made it His mission to bring us into His family and to become our personal friend in this life and beyond. If I am wrong, I do not expect to miss out on much of anything at all.

Any sacrifice in serving our Savior only requires the loss of that which we must one day leave behind anyway, or of that which would eventually kill us. In exchange, we gain the ultimate fulfillment of eternal life in the presence of our Creator and Heavenly Father. As it says in Romans 12:1–2 (NIV): "Therefore, I urge you, brothers and sisters, in view of God's mercy, to offer your bodies as a living sacrifice, holy and pleasing to God—this is your true and proper worship. Do not conform to the pattern of this world, but be transformed by the renewing of your mind. Then you will be able to test and approve what God's will is—his good, pleasing and perfect will."

I hope that this humble effort to share some of my life observations and experiences with you will help to induce your new birth into the family of God, or to strengthen your relationship with Jesus Christ, or to reinforce your efforts to serve God by delivering others into His kingdom, or perhaps all of the above. It has been my great privilege to offer you assistance on the ultimate "homework" assignment that we all share, making our way home to our loving Heavenly Father. When it comes to our temporary work assignment of serving Jesus Christ on this earth, the sky is the limit, and as for death—well death is just eternity leave.

AFTERWORD

And Words And Words

Thank you for your time and attention to this humble effort to share what I believe God encouraged me to write for whosoever might be willing to read it. I would very much welcome hearing any thoughts or reactions that you, my dear reader, might have, especially if my writing endeavor raised any questions or concerns, or reinforced your faith, or contributed to a decision to accept Jesus Christ as your Savior and to pursue a personal relationship with your Creator. Please do not hesitate to contact me at letthecommunioncommence@outlookcom if I can in anyway support you through the remaining stages of your pursuit of God's plan and purpose for your life.

APPENDIX

Potentially Useful Suggestions for Further Reading

Christian Apologetics (In Defense of the Faith)

Collins, Francis. *The Language of God: A Scientist Presents Evidence for Belief.* London: Simon & Schuster, 2008.

Geisler, Norman L., and Frank Turek. *I Don't Have Enough Faith to Be an Atheist.* Wheaton, IL: Crossway Books, 2004.

Keller, Timothy. *The Reason for God: Belief in an Age of Skepticism.* New York: Penguin, 2008.

McDowell, Josh, and Sean McDowell. *Evidence That Demands a Verdict: Life-changing Truth for a Skeptical World.* Nashville: Thomas Nelson, 2017.

Strobel, Lee. *The Case for Christ.* Grand Rapids, MI: Zondervan, 2017.

Wallace, J. Warner. *Cold-Case Christianity: A Homicide Detective Investigates the Claims of the Gospels.* Colorado Springs, CO: David C Cook, 2013.

Support for New Believers in Jesus Christ

Anders, Max E. *New Christian's Handbook: Everything Believers Need to Know.* Nashville: Thomas Nelson, 2011.

Beech, Carl. *The Manual for New Christians - You 2.0: Getting You Started with God, the Bible and Faith*. Farnham, Surrey: CWR, 2017.

Hughes, Selwyn. *Every Day with Jesus for New Christians: First Steps in the Christian Faith*. Farnham, Surrey: CWR, 2019.

Schmalenberger, Jerry L. *Preparation for Discipleship: A Handbook for New Christians*. Lima, OH: CSS Publishing, 1998.

Steele, Charlotte J. *Essentials of Christianity and Spiritual Growth: A Guide for New Christians and Christians Who Need to Be Renewed*. WestBow Press, 2014.

SCRIPTURE REFERENCES

God's Word Index

P

R

ABOUT THE AUTHOR'S
NOT WORTHY ACCOMPLISHMENTS

After graduating from Union City Community High School in Union City, Indiana, Kevin Smith earned a Bachelor of Arts with a major in Social Studies Education from Oral Roberts University in Tulsa, Oklahoma and a Master of Arts in Secondary Education from Ball State University in Muncie, Indiana as well as dozens of additional graduate credit hours in social sciences from an assortment of other universities. Since 1991, Kevin has taught social science courses for the Rising Sun-Ohio County Community School Corporation in Rising Sun, Indiana in conjunction with teaching dual credit college courses for many years through Oakland City University in Oakland City, Indiana and currently through Ivy Tech Community College in Lawrenceburg, Indiana.